The Case for Sovereignty

The Case for Sovereignty

Why the World Should Welcome
American Independence

Jeremy A. Rabkin

The AEI Press

Publisher for the American Enterprise Institute

WASHINGTON, D.C.

Available in the United States from the AEI Press, c/o Client Distribution Services, 193 Edwards Drive, Jackson, TN 38301. To order, call toll free: 1-800-343-4499. Distributed outside the United States by arrangement with Eurospan, 3 Henrietta Street, London WC2E 8LU, England.

Library of Congress Cataloging-in-Publication Data

Rabkin, Jeremy A.
 The case for sovereignty : why the world should welcome American
 independence / Jeremy A. Rabkin.
  p. cm.
 Includes bibliographical references and index.
 ISBN 0-8447-4183-3 (cloth)
 1. Sovereignty. 2. International relations. 3. United States—Foreign
relations. I. Title.

JZ4034.R33 2004
320.1'5'0973—dc22

2004041057

10 09 08 07 06 05 04   2 3 4 5

Printed in the United States of America

Contents

Acknowledgments

At the urging of Chris DeMuth, I wrote a short book on the subject of sovereignty that the American Enterprise Institute published in 1998 (*Why Sovereignty Matters*). When AEI sold all the printed copies of that book, Chris asked me if I would be willing to prepare a revised edition. I told him I was already working on a much more ambitious book, taking a broader view of the subject. He urged me to work up a shorter, more policy-oriented version of that project for AEI. I am not sure I would have finished this book when I did, however, if not for the subsequent promptings of John Bolton. As many foreign governments have learned, when John Bolton says that something should be done, it is very likely to be done.

I am also grateful to Jack Goldsmith, John Yoo, Lee Casey, David Rivkin, John McGinnis, John Fonte, and Claude Barfield, who read drafts of various chapters for this book, offered advice and encouragement, and saved me from a number of mistakes. All remaining mistakes must be attributed to the author; I hope they are few and minor. But the argument of the book, like many other things in this world, may still stand on common sense.

—JEREMY A. RABKIN
April 1, 2004

Preface

In October 2003, the European Commission sponsored an extensive opinion survey in the fifteen member nations of the European Union (EU).[1] The survey confirmed that citizens in almost all of these European states were very concerned about the threat of terrorist attacks on their own countries.

When asked which countries posed a threat to peace, respondents in most EU states did not focus on those countries known to be harboring terrorists, such as Pakistan or Saudi Arabia. Respondents did not even focus on states known to be openly promoting terrorism, such as Iran or Syria. Rather, respondents in most EU states thought the two countries posing the greatest threat to world peace were the two that had suffered most from terrorist attacks and had been most active in fighting back against terrorism: the United States and Israel.

In the view that now seems to prevail among Europeans, resistance to terrorism will only provoke more terrorism. The correct response, most believe, is to build international institutions that can deploy peaceful means to contain the threat. This strategy does not seem plausible to most Americans, nor to most Israelis, nor to most people in Russia, India, or China. People in many other parts of the world may also have grave doubts that the United Nations can provide security. Certainly, people in the Balkans and in many parts of Africa know from bitter experience that the United Nations cannot protect them from murderous assault.

Still, the idea remains highly seductive to Europeans. The same survey found that months after the overthrow of Saddam Hussein and the discovery of mass graves for Saddam's victims all over Iraq, the majority of Europeans remained convinced that the Anglo-American war against

Saddam was "illegitimate" because it was not sanctioned by the United Nations. From this perspective, the continued existence of independent nations—nations still able to fight their own battles against terror threats or ignore the United Nations when necessary—is the greatest threat to peace. The two most frightening nations are, in fact, readily confused by many Europeans. In spring 2003, the president of France was the most prominent opponent of the forty nations in the Anglo-American coalition against Saddam. Mobs in Paris shouted, "Vive Chirac! Stop the Jews!" To confirm the French government's endorsement of the slogan, Foreign Minister de Villepin declared that the war was the work of a "Zionist lobby in Washington"—that is, as he explained, of American officials with Jewish-sounding names.[2] In the French account, the president and vice president of the United States, the Congress of the United States, the secretary of defense, the secretary of state, and the national security advisor were all mere bystanders to American policy. The policy was actually determined by a small group of Jewish conspirators.

Few Americans will find this account very compelling. But differences in outlook between Europe and America are nothing new. They did not start with the war in Iraq, nor with the September 11 terror attacks, nor with the advent of George W. Bush's administration. European leaders have often condemned American policies from much the same perspective as that of Foreign Minister de Villepin. In August 1943, for example, the freely chosen leader of France insisted that peace could be negotiated in Europe if only Britain were "not led by the fanatical Churchill and the United States by the Jews."[3]

The United States, Britain, and other English-speaking democracies rejected that perspective at the time. Even today, French schemes for pacifying the world through special understandings between France and Germany raise doubts in the English-speaking world. But the French vision during the Second World War did attract many Europeans. They hoped for peace or an early end to war, and no price seemed too high to pay for peace.[4] The peace offered by Germany in 1940 particularly appealed to many Europeans because it drew on ancient European political traditions. The Germans promised a new Reich, reviving the promises of the Holy Roman Empire of medieval Europe, under which German emperors were supposed to bring harmony and peace to all the peoples of Europe. The idea that distinct peoples could be organized in independent nations was a modern idea, a legacy of the Enlightenment. Many Europeans were quite prepared to give up on such modern, liberal ideas in deference to the nostalgic visions preached in Germany in the 1930s.

Today, many Europeans are even more eager to give up national independence to the European Union. They are prepared to transfer messianic hopes to the United Nations or to almost any international structure promising escape from the burdens of self-defense. The United States, which has invested much larger resources in national defense than other countries, has far less reason to believe that the burdens of defense can be safely offloaded onto the latest international constructions.

Yet military strength is not the main reason the United States has rejected the European vision. Even as a newly independent republic, the United States rejected the precursors of contemporary European thinking. America was founded on quite contrary principles, and the vision that captivates so many Europeans today—as different versions of it captivated so many of their ancestors—is directly at odds with American ideas of constitutional government.

In the prevailing European view, constitutions are of largely ritual significance. Anyone who can look at the United States government and see only the secret machinations of Jews must regard its constitutional structures as mere window dressing. What matters, in the European view, is not whether power is defined by a constitutional structure of offices, with accountability to other officers and an ultimate accountability to voters. What matters is whether wielders of power have the right spirit or the true faith. Those in power must be faithful to humanity or peace or some other fine ideal, or they might as well be sinister schemers.

Europeans have difficulty taking constitutions seriously. Every state in the European Union now acknowledges that its constitution can be overridden by mere bureaucratic directives from the European Commission in Brussels; there is nothing like a fixed constitution to constrain the commission itself. The arrangement is unthinkable in America but taken for granted in Europe. Many things unthinkable to Americans have been embraced by Europeans before.

On the other hand, Europeans recoil from many things Americans regard as inevitable. In a free society, there are bound to be winners and losers in economic competition. Winners in one decade may subsequently suffer sharp reverses. Losers may pick themselves up and triumph over their previous setbacks. But in a society where government control is carefully limited by law, there are bound to be unexpected results, as different firms and individuals try different economic strategies. In most European countries, markets are distrusted. There is far less patience with the idea of unpredictable results. What if wealth is acquired by the wrong people?

If governments cannot achieve adequate control, then, contemporary Europeans believe, higher authorities must be given new powers of control. Throughout the 1990s, while the United States experienced a sustained economic boom, France and Germany faced high levels of unemployment and low levels of economic growth, even with the vast regulatory powers accorded to the bureaucratic authorities of the European Union. The European Union's response to these adverse conditions was to urge wider systems of control. Developing countries must be prevented from "social-dumping" of their cheap goods in the regulated markets of Europe, it was said. European industry required more protection. Also, the earth's environment and its sustainable development required more extensive global controls.

Europeans see no reason all nations should not agree upon international regulatory standards. The United Nations has proclaimed a universal right to "rising standards of living." Who prevents the implementation of this inspiring aim of international law? Europeans are scandalized that the United States has not ratified the treaty on Economic and Social Rights, which the UN calls a "covenant." The failure to ratify this and so many other pious international conventions provokes fury. How does the United States dare to set itself apart from other nations, when all others have affirmed universal ideals?

The problem, according to some European analysts, is not that Americans are manipulated by Jews, but that their minds are numbed by Christian "fundamentalism." In the course of an extended protest against the war in Iraq, Jürgen Habermas, Germany's most celebrated philosopher, took time to express his scorn for President Bush's religious faith. In Europe, Habermas sniffed, it would be "hard to imagine a president who begins his daily business with public prayer and associates his momentous political decisions with a divine mission."[5] An earlier generation of German thinkers, no doubt, reacted with equal disgust to reports that President Roosevelt had implored "almighty God" to bless the American troops embarking for the beaches of Normandy—and offered this prayer not only in public but on the radio. It seems to have escaped the notice of thinkers like Habermas that, even after securing Germany's unconditional surrender, the American army did not try to impose Christianity on pagan adherents of the Nazi movement. It seems inconceivable to Europeans that a faith that inspires and sustains Americans is, nevertheless, not part of our political structure.

But that is only another measure of how far apart American and European views have now become. Even the medieval church, which claimed wider political authority than modern churches, still insisted it was something distinct from government and accordingly acknowledged that government was, in principle, something distinct from religion. The faith that inspires contemporary Europeans is far more ambitious. There can be universal peace and harmony—and "rising standards of living for everyone"—if only people will embrace international authority and believe in its saving power.

Habermas coined the term "global domestic policy" to indicate the necessary reach of the new faith. It will establish a structure of international law and authority that will not merely inspire government, but will control and direct all governments in their governing duties. Those who think differently will naturally inspire resentment.

The United States began by asserting its right to independence—its right to be different. Governments have a right to be different, in the view of the American Founders, because human beings have a right to be different. The American constitutional tradition rests on the premise that "to secure these rights, governments are instituted among men"—that is, distinct governments, separate governments, sovereign governments.

It easy to understand why the American Founders thought about rights in this way. An international authority able to secure universal peace would require the means of enforcing peace. It would require the authority to resolve every dispute that might otherwise lead to war, and then insist that its resolution could never be challenged. If it could do that, it could reasonably claim to resolve disputes provoking civil unrest within each nation. It could reasonably claim to resolve all conflicting claims about the distribution of resources, within and between nations, and all claims about conflicting rights or crosscutting grievances, within and between nations.

Who could challenge or constrain a world authority with such immense power? Even if it were constrained by a formal constitution, who could possibly ensure that the world authority remained within its proper bounds? How could it be anything like a democracy? Would a hundred small nations outvote the half-dozen largest nations? Or would a billion Chinese, a billion Indians, and a half-billion Southeast Asians be allowed to form a permanent majority, dictating law and justice to the rest of the world?

European governments do not take the vision quite this seriously. Even in medieval times, European rulers continually flouted the ostensibly supreme authority of emperors or popes. But visions of assured universal harmony have always stirred sullen resentment and rage against those who did not openly bow to them.

Believers in a post-sovereign world order have few weapons to deploy on behalf of their vision. They are, in the main, great believers in words. They say independent states will provoke more terrorism, and insist that there can be no peace without the universal authority of the United Nations. On the more activist fringes of the European left, advocates even celebrate terrorism as the vanguard of a new, truly universal world system. But mostly Europeans preach patient faith in international institutions, and pour out their frustrated hopes in denunciations of those who fail to subscribe to the new faith.[6]

Their one hope is to demoralize people in independent nations, to make them question their right to govern themselves and live under their own constitutions. And, in fact, the European Union has been quite successful in bullying smaller states in Europe into compliance with European "ideals"— that is, for the most part, with highly detailed bureaucratic directives worked out by French and German bureaucrats at the European Commission.

The main point of this book is to remind readers that the United States has no reason to be defensive about retaining its independence. Our own constitutional system depends on the preservation of American independence. It is not a bad thing for the world for independent countries to remain independent. It is not a bad thing even for small countries—or perhaps especially for small countries.

Empires throughout history have claimed to speak for humanity. In modern times, millions of Europeans placed messianic hopes in murderous dictators claiming to speak for humanity from Berlin or from Moscow. In asserting our independence, Americans should remember that they act from principles that have always offered much more to the world than the sullen resentments or hysterical hopes of Europe. Europeans are eager to forget their past experience. Americans still have every reason to hold to our own constitutional and political traditions, which have preserved the United States as a free nation and done much to maintain opportunities for free government in the wider world.

1

Sovereignty in Principle

All nations claim to favor peace—in principle. Nations differ a good deal on how to secure peace. Debate about the threat posed by Saddam Hussein's government in Iraq displayed these differences in sharp relief.

In November 2002, the Security Council of the United Nations demanded that Saddam's government verify its compliance with previous resolutions requiring Iraq to relinquish weapons of mass destruction. The Security Council had been insisting on Iraq's disarmament since 1991, when, with the council's approval, an American-led coalition had driven Iraqi forces from Kuwait, reversing Iraq's attempted conquest of its oil-rich neighbor. The truce terms in 1991, also approved by the Security Council, had allowed Saddam to remain in power, on condition that he relinquish his weapons of mass destruction and all facilities for making them. For over a decade thereafter, the council repeated this demand in successive resolutions, and Saddam continued to resist or evade mandated inspections to verify his compliance. By spring 2003, there was general agreement that Saddam had still failed to comply with UN demands for documenting Iraqi disarmament. But there was no agreement on what should be done.

Ultimately, the American and British governments launched an invasion of Iraq without authorization from the Security Council. This "unilateral" resort to war provoked intense criticism at the United Nations and in national capitals around the world. As it turned out, Anglo-American forces were able to defeat Saddam's armies and occupy all of Iraq in a three-week war that caused minimal casualties. Discoveries of mass graves throughout the country offered vivid reminders that Saddam's reign had been far more lethal to Iraqis than the brief military campaign. By putting an end to Saddam's murderous rule, the invasion undoubtedly saved countless Iraqi lives. Yet critics, particularly in Europe, remained indignant.

The invading forces failed to discover stockpiles of chemical or biological weapons, even after searching for a year. UN inspectors had found weapons of this kind in Iraq in the mid-1990s and Saddam's government had failed to account for their whereabouts, even during the last round of UN inspections at the end of 2002. The weapons may have been too well hidden to find. They may have been smuggled to another country. The least likely explanation for the failure to find these weapons in 2003 was that Saddam's government had secretly destroyed them at an earlier time—but then failed to reveal this fact or even to maintain records to document it to inspectors when necessary. Critics still seized on the failure to find WMD's in Iraq in 2003 as proof that war had been unnecessary.

Before the war, critics had warned that mass casualties might be incurred as Saddam resorted to using his chemical and biological weapons. When this terrible prospect failed to materialize, that fact in itself became further proof that war was premature—as if it were somehow unfair to attack Iraq until its most terrible potential had been fully mobilized. But critics, particularly in Europe, focused most of their fury not on strategic issues but on moral or legal claims.[1]

The war was denounced as a threat to the fundamental principles of international law and international order. Suspicions and resentments toward American policy had been accumulating over a number of years on a wide range of issues, but the Iraq debate crystallized the difference in attitudes. At the least, the debate dramatized how far Europe had drifted from American opinion on fundamental questions of international law and security.

Still reeling from the terror attacks of September 11, most Americans saw the logic of overthrowing a government that was known to be intriguing with international terror networks and seeking weapons of mass destruction. Saddam's government, after all, had already shown its willingness to embark on unprovoked aggression against its neighbors and to use chemical and biological weapons on its own people. But critics insisted that military action against Saddam could only be "legitimate" if authorized by the UN Security Council. Many governments (notably Germany, France, Russia, and China) insisted on this claim.

The claim presumed a status for the United Nations that was quite clearly at odds with actual international practice. Since the UN's founding in 1945, the world has seen hundreds of armed conflicts. Nearly two-thirds of UN members have engaged in armed conflict at one time or another in the ensuing five decades. In only three cases were these wars authorized by the Security Council. Was UN approval an essential requirement for a "legitimate" war against Saddam's government in 2003? If so, "international legitimacy" could no longer be discerned from the actual practice of states. Instead, "legitimacy" would be determined solely by reference to a vision for the future, which happened to correspond, at that moment, to the hopes of many people in Western Europe. Was that really how the world could be expected to work?

Critics did not argue that Iraq had a sovereign right to develop whatever weapons it might prefer. On the contrary, most agreed that Saddam's regime should be forced to give up weapons of mass destruction and to have this disarmament verified by international inspectors. Seventeen resolutions of the Security Council had demanded as much since the end of the first Gulf War in 1991.

Meanwhile, the Security Council authorized numerous other actions that might be seen as intrusions on traditional notions of Iraqi sovereignty. The council prohibited the sale of Iraqi oil except under UN supervision. It then imposed strict controls on what could be purchased with revenues from those sales. To prevent Saddam from retaliating against rebellious provinces, the UN also prohibited the Iraqi air force from operating over the northern and southern thirds of the country. In the northern part of Iraq, the UN sponsored an autonomous political entity beyond the control of the central government. Specialized UN bodies even claimed to be monitoring Iraqi compliance with international human rights standards.[2] Several resolutions of the Security Council demanded better treatment of Iraqi nationals within Iraq. Most critics did not question these interventions; they simply emphasized that no state could enforce them without the permission of the Security Council.

So the Security Council could make highly intrusive demands on a sovereign state without its consent. It could even make demands with no obvious or direct connection with international security. But the council was not obliged to enforce its own demands, even those most closely connected with the actual security concerns of other states. If the critics of "unilateral action" were correct, the council, by its inaction, could still block action by states more concerned about the security threat and better positioned to act against it. The United Nations would make war unnecessary. And if it could not do that, it could at least make it illegal—even for those seeking to enforce officially recognized international obligations.

The United States was not prepared to accept this version of international order. To judge from their actual conduct, most governments agreed with the American view, at least tacitly. But continual protest over the war, months after the collapse of Saddam's government, highlighted the fact that many nations remained attracted to an alternate vision of how the world is supposed to be governed. Some scholars called the vision "post-sovereign governance."[3]

Any sensible American response to this vision, over the long term, requires more clarity about what a world without sovereignty would entail—and why the United States must reject it.

Investing in Global Governance

On its face, the post-sovereign vision for the world might seem quite impractical. Dictators would be left to acquire the most devastating weapons, even after proving their malevolent intentions in past aggressions. Forces able to stop them would have to await formal international approval—even if that meant waiting until the dictator acquired nuclear armament, making any ultimate check to future aggression vastly more dangerous. Of course, preemptive action can be dangerous in itself, not least because others may view it as a mere pretext for different schemes of aggression. By spring 2003, however, after more than a year of debate at the United Nations and other forums, more than forty countries had endorsed military action against Iraq. The Anglo-American action was hardly a bolt from the blue. No one seriously imagined that the coalition mobilized against Iraq could next be turned, without warning, on Portugal or Paraguay. Critics still insisted that, without the formal authorization of the Security Council, the war against Iraq lacked "legitimacy." The formal machinery of the United Nations, stalemated and sidelined during decades of cold war and even during the NATO campaign against Serbia in 1999, had now become essential to "legitimacy."

At the beginning of the Second World War, only Britain and its loyal dominions—with the temporary support of France—went to war against Nazi Germany. Was the Second World War lacking in "legitimacy" because it was not endorsed by the League of Nations? Because it was not, for over two years, endorsed by any countries not themselves the immediate victims of a German attack? Why should it matter so much in 2003 whether the war against Saddam's murderous regime received the endorsement of Cameroon, Guinea, Chile, and other states that happened to be sitting on the Security Council at the time? Most states on the council had no way of contributing to the war on their own. Nor, for that matter, did they have any inclination (or capacity) to rally to Saddam's defense and threaten the American-led coalition with a wider war to resist the anti-Saddam coalition.

For some countries, insisting on the "essential role" of the Security Council did promise immediate advantages, however. Above all, it promised a check on American power at seemingly little cost. In practice, even France and Germany, among the loudest and most persistent champions of the requirement for Security Council approval, did not have the military capacity to contribute much to the war. What they could offer or withhold was not the hard coin of military assistance but the soft currency of "legitimacy"—so it was much in their interest to insist that this form of "legitimacy" was now the sole legal tender in international affairs.

Meanwhile, there turned out to be serious differences between France and Germany, on one side, and most of their EU partners, on the other. Most EU states were much less ready to enlist in the Franco-German program of "balancing American hegemony." As it turned out, most prospective new members of the EU in Eastern Europe were similarly reluctant to follow the Franco-German lead in this dispute. Most of these governments were rather more concerned about holding on to their historic ties with the United States to "balance" against Franco-German domination within Europe. Public opinion in most European countries remained highly skeptical of American war aims, however. For France and Germany to insist on the role of the United Nations was to invoke something that sounded reassuringly principled and abstract, and altogether removed from power-balancing and diplomatic calculations in their own neighborhood.

There was, however, the problem that this new currency might not be accepted by everyone. Seventeen resolutions of the United Nations Security Council had been rather easily evaded by Saddam's regime itself over the previous decade, without much concern on the part of the general UN membership. In spring 2003, just as the dispute over Saddam's defiance of previous resolutions came to a head, Iraq was still scheduled to chair a UN conference on disarmament a few months later. Meanwhile, UN members had chosen Syria—the tyrannical Baathist regime most closely linked with Saddam's murderous ideology—to sit on the Security Council. If it was in the interest of France and Germany to inflate the importance of UN-conferred "legitimacy," it was also in the interest of much more hostile and dangerous regimes to do so—all the more so because demands with nothing more than "legitimacy" behind them were so easy to resist.

Even Europeans understood this, when they chose to. Only a few years before, European governments decided that something must be done about the civil war in the Serbian province of Kosovo. They supported a NATO air campaign against Serbia—without the approval of the Security Council. France and Germany both contributed to the bombing operations against Serbian cities. How serious was this new doctrine of "legitimacy," if, in practice, it came down to the proposition that no action could be "legitimate" unless sanctioned, in one forum or another, by France? Or by France and Germany?

Perhaps it was not surprising, then, that the United States and Britain—and quite a few other countries—determined in the end to go ahead without Security Council approval. Yet even when the toppling of Saddam's government had become a fait accompli, France and Germany and other states insisted they could not contribute to the postwar reconstruction of Iraq without UN authorization. Former allies of the United States were willing to pay a considerable diplomatic price—most obviously in worsening relations with the United States and damage to Atlantic partnerships in other areas—rather than write off past diplomatic investments in the idea of the UN as guardian of "international legitimacy."

The scale of past investment in the larger program had, in fact, been quite considerable. In the 1990s, the vision was called "global governance." States would not have to yield their own forces to a world state, but international institutions would somehow ensure that states used their power in ways that served the common interests of the international community. A particularly ambitious monument to this outlook was launched at a UN conference in Rome in 1998—the International Criminal Court (ICC).

The ICC was a remarkable innovation in international affairs. The International Court of Justice, founded with the United Nations in 1945 and sometimes called the "World Court," was only empowered to pronounce on disputes between states—and then only when both parties agreed to submit their dispute to arbitration by the court. The design of the World Court followed long-established practice in arbitrating international disputes. Under the new International Criminal Court, by contrast, cases would no longer be initiated by the governments of independent states but by a permanent, independent prosecutor. The so-called "Statute" of the ICC empowered the prosecutor to indict military commanders and civilian officials, who might ultimately be sentenced to prison terms if convicted by the court.

The ICC Statute defined in very broad and encompassing terms the relevant crimes: "war crimes" and "crimes against humanity," as well as "genocide" and "aggression" (although the question of how to define "aggression" was postponed to future determination). By ratifying the statute, a state committed itself to hand over any person within its territory who might be indicted by the ICC. Even nationals of nonratifying states might be subject to extradition and trial if their victims belonged to states that sought such prosecution by the ICC.[4]

Naturally, the United States expressed great reservations about the project at the time it was launched. In principle, the structure of the ICC seemed to authorize international bureaucrats in The Hague (where the court was based) to second-guess decisions of the American military. The ICC could, for example, prosecute American commanders or civilian officials for bombing targets that the independent prosecutor determined to be unlawful simply because bombs caused excessive damage to civilian property, even if actual civilian casualties remained minimal.[5] The Bush administration eventually announced that it would not cooperate with the new court. The announcement provoked intense criticism from European governments, which had become the most insistent champions of the project.

But China and Russia also refused to ratify, as did Japan and India and, indeed, a majority of UN member states. Even among those states that did ratify, there was much doubt whether the ICC could actually compel them to cooperate when national governments judged it more advantageous to let a particular indicted individual slip through their fingers. Despite conventions on the extradition of terrorists, for example, European governments repeatedly allowed terrorists to slip from their grasp in the 1980s. They believed that holding or extraditing them might imperil more urgent national policy objectives (such as maintaining good relations with terrorist states or deflecting terror attacks onto other targets).[6]

The ICC had no means of compelling cooperation by punishing non-compliance. Nor did it have any way to protect a compliant state from retaliation by the home state of a person extradited to the ICC. And, of course, the ICC had no direct ability to stop massive crimes while they were occurring. The ICC rested on the premise that the administration of justice could be entirely disconnected from the power to enforce or defend it. Prior to the 1990s, this idea would have provoked great skepticism. In the history of the world, no open-ended prosecuting authority of this kind had ever been established—certainly not on this scale—so removed from the broader powers of any actual government to enforce the court's rulings.

Advocates, however, hailed the ICC as a great milestone for "international justice." To have any prospects of success, it would need to rely on moral pressure—in effect, rallying public opinion to support the court's demands, even if national governments might otherwise be inclined not to cooperate or not to cooperate fully. Much faith was placed in this vision by its promoters. After all, the ICC was, as its advocates rightly insisted, the culmination of decades of effort, at the UN and elsewhere, to formulate standards for human rights—for the proper treatment of ethnic and religious minorities, of political dissidents and artists, of women and children and convicted criminals, and so on, and so on. These standards were supposed to bind all governments in their dealings with their own citizens.

If one subscribed to this faith, one might believe these standards were widely respected because almost all governments had signed on to them. The world agreed—at least in principle. So the world endorses regulatory schemes that not only seek to stabilize routine transactions between states but also claim to reach into states and lay down rules for the treatment or conduct of citizens within each state. It no longer matters whether national legislatures, even in countries where legislatures are accountable to voters, actually approve of these actions. If one takes human rights standards seriously as international law, one must believe that states can be recruited into service as enforcement arms for the international community, regardless of local, democractic opinions. One must believe that the international community could, in its turn, establish standards of conduct and corresponding protections for every person in the world.

And not just persons. The 1990s also witnessed the proliferation and elaboration of international standards to protect plants and animals, forests and rivers, the earth's atmosphere, and even the earth's climate. The most ambitious of these ventures, the Kyoto Protocol on Climate Change, was launched in 1997. It presumed that all nations would eventually agree to limit the use of fossil fuels (oil, coal, natural gas), in accord with consumption quotas whose precise details would be established by a freestanding international bureaucracy. The scheme would offer financial incentives for various countries to cooperate and might appeal to states that had bargained for more favorable quotas for themselves. But the Kyoto Protocol provided no means of enforcement. Moral suasion was assumed to be a sufficient force for compliance.

Again, the United States, which stood to bear a heavier financial burden from compliance than any other state, refused to go along.[7] The Clinton administration signed the agreement but made no effort to press for ratification by the Senate. The subsequent Bush administration then disavowed any intention to ratify or implement the treaty. Again, European governments protested, and much European opinion blamed the United States for selfishly resisting such an urgent international program. And again, critics failed to notice that the United States was hardly alone in its recalcitrance: China, India, and other nations of the developing world—soon to account for half the world's fossil-fuel use—had been even more emphatic in rejecting limits on their fuel consumption.

The principal aim of the Kyoto Protocol was to reduce the buildup of carbon dioxide in the earth's atmosphere. This could not be achieved without constraining the fuel use of developing nations. In practice, reducing carbon dioxide buildup could not be achieved for many decades unless less-developed nations could be induced to accept far lower levels of fuel consumption—in other words, far lower living standards—than those enjoyed by people in affluent nations. Nonetheless, environmentalists berated the United States for not displaying more "leadership." Somehow American leadership, together with faith in global institutions, was expected to work miracles in securing ultimate international cooperation on the requisite scale. This would not be done by compulsion or force because global governance was not about compulsion or force. It would come about if enough people believed.

By 2003, then, there was quite a bit at stake for believers in the ideals of global governance. After the scale of the September 11 terror attacks, it was hard to deny that international terrorism was a very serious problem. It was hard to deny the awful danger if weapons of mass destruction were allowed to fall into the hands of such terrorists. And it was hard to deny that Saddam Hussein's Iraq was one of the most likely governments to facilitate such a transfer. If one acknowledged that international cooperation was not going to deal with the threat posed by Saddam Hussein, however, one had to acknowledge that international cooperation was not enough, in the end, to deal with the most serious issues.

But if that were acknowledged, a lot of other projects looked equally questionable. So advocates of global governance insisted that the UN could handle the Iraq problem eventually. True, international inspections and controls had failed to assure Saddam's disarmament since the UN first demanded it in 1991. True, the UN had not agreed on an adequate new program to assure Saddam's disarmament in the eighteen months after the September 11 attacks gave new urgency to the venture. But the United States could not act on its own, critics insisted. It could not even act with a broad coalition of like-minded states. It had to work through international institutions, because there could be no security for anyone without international institutions—which, in the long term, promised so much for justice, human rights, peace, progress, the environment, and sustainable development.

After September 11, Americans were not prepared to wait for the long term. Other states, with less capacity to respond, also felt less urgency about doing so. Perhaps the threat of terrorists with weapons of mass destruction was exaggerated. Perhaps, at any rate, it could be diverted. Most European states had also tried to sit out the war against Nazi Germany in hopes that someone else would do the fighting and allow them to remain aloof from such futile endeavors as war. Sweden, which successfully maintained its neutrality when its neighbors fell to Nazi aggression, continued to assert its neutrality all through the Cold War, relying on others to deter Soviet threats to its own territory.

History affords countless examples of the phenomenon. But the point hardly needs belaboring. States do not all assess threats in the same way. Nor do they draw the same conclusions, even when they do agree that they face a serious threat. The project of global governance supposes that there is (or can be) an underlying consensus that makes force unnecessary and therefore irrelevant.

Once one grants the initial premise, the whole vision may seem quite plausible. Citizens of a particular state must trust their government to exercise force on their behalf. They are almost always unwilling to entrust the same power to international bodies. But if force is irrelevant, this lack of trust won't be an obstacle to international authority. It does not matter that the International Criminal Court does not have force at its disposal, or that the bureaucracies mandated by the Kyoto Protocol have no force at their disposal. It does not even matter that the Security Council has no forces of its own. If force is irrelevant, then there is no reason the higher bodies should not direct each national government on its duties and limits in the name of the higher law of the international community.

The United States will not entrust its security to "authorities" that have no means of protecting the United States. The debate over Iraq should have made this clear. But many Europeans remain deeply enthralled by the new faith. Amid recriminations in the aftermath of the war, there were predictable calls for papering over differences, reengaging the United Nations, and restoring Atlantic and international ties.[8] But divisions that were so evident on the subject of the Iraq war did not simply arise from clumsy diplomacy or passing fits of ill temper. They did not simply reflect misunderstandings. They reflected opposing understandings of how international politics can be expected to operate.

Europeans remain attached to the notion that international cooperation can supersede the need for force, as well as questions about who gets to use force. The structure of the European Union reflects the new faith, as the EU can dictate policy to member states on a vast range of matters, though it lacks an army to provide security or a genuine executive (let alone a police force) to compel compliance. "Global governance" is essentially an extension of Euro-governance to the world at large.

There are many reasons to doubt that Euro-governance can be sustained in the wider world. There are good reasons to think we would not want to live in a world organized in this way, even if it were feasible. Almost all of the objections can be summarized in one word: sovereignty. It is a concept deeply embedded in America's political institutions and political culture. The United States can't go far in subordinating or delegating its sovereignty; it would be better for American diplomacy to acknowledge that fact more emphatically.

But it would also be well to recognize that sovereignty is neither an American invention nor an American idiosyncrasy. In asserting its own sovereignty, the United States has good reason to believe it is standing up for a principle that remains indispensable to any reasonable prospects for peace and freedom in the world at large. To understand this claim, one must start with some reasonable understanding of what sovereignty actually entails.

The Concept of Sovereignty

During the 1990s, when global governance was most in fashion, scholars sympathetic to the new vision argued that sovereignty was becoming less relevant to world politics. They insisted that the concept of sovereignty was, in any case, too confused or contentious to be meaningful. Even if this were true, it would not prove that talk of sovereignty should be "banished from polite or educated society," as the president of the American Society for International Law urged at the time.[9] No one proposes to stop talking about "liberty" or "equality" or "democracy" merely because these terms have been interpreted in quite different ways over many centuries. But, as it happens, the claim is not true. Sovereignty is a much more precise term because it came into general use only in the seventeenth century, when political thinkers sought to clarify political reasoning with more systematic terminology.

Hugo Grotius, the seventeenth-century Dutch jurist, was regarded by the American Founders and many others as the father of international law because his treatise on the laws of war offered the first compelling account of how the rights and duties of rulers could be understood without entangling them in medieval claims to papal supremacy.[10] Grotius gave a precise definition to sovereignty: the power to act without being "subject to the legal control of another."[11] Sovereignty is, in the first place, a legal claim—but, like any fundamental legal claim, it is one that rests on wider moral or political premises.

Grotius acknowledged that a sovereign government might be bound by constitutional limitations in its own state. He certainly acknowledged that a sovereign government could make wrongful decisions, so that the decisions of the sovereign might be subject to reasonable moral appeals, beyond any claim allowed by positive law within that state. Grotius also recognized that the actions of a sovereign government might provoke protest from other sovereigns, especially when the actions of one state worked direct injury upon another. What Grotius insisted on was that moral appeals could not carry the same sense of obligation to a sovereign as that which the sovereign's own law demanded of citizens. The citizen should see the threat of civil war or rebellion as among the worst evils; sovereigns were not bound, in the same way, to view conflict between sovereign states as more intolerable than the prospect of submission to a higher authority.[12]

Grotius urged that sovereigns could avoid occasions for conflict by respecting each other's right to exclusive authority in their own territories. He still assumed that war might remain a necessary last resort when one state threatened the sovereign rights of another. The right to declare war—and to exercise powers of taxation and mobilization to support war—thus remained an inextricable attribute of sovereign power. For a sovereign, to renounce the right to wield force was to renounce its sovereignty to whichever power could rightly exercise ultimate force.

Grotius took pains to argue that not even devout Christians should expect to see justice prevail without force. To believe that governments could dispense with force, one had to believe that all men would act reasonably, justly, and lawfully without coercion—one had to believe, as Grotius says, that "all men were living the Christian life." But this was a hope or prophecy of ultimate redemption which cannot apply "so long as there are men who do not suffer those that love peace to enjoy peace, but do violence to them." Christianity does not deny a right to defend one's self or one's community from violence.[13] Sovereignty was a proper device for ordering the necessary element of force or coercion in human affairs.

This outlook, developed and embellished in the works of early modern thinkers, proved immensely compelling. To Enlightenment thinkers, the doctrine of sovereignty seemed a necessary, initial corrective to what they saw as the most prevalent obstacles to reasonable politics. On the one hand, there was always the burden of fatalism or cynicism. Throughout history, ordinary people, in most circumstances, simply submitted to overwhelming force. It was hardly worthwhile for them to think of any political idea beyond the right of the stronger power to impose its will. But reasonable politics was also threatened by militant doctrines, or what we now call utopianism. From ancient times, visionaries and philosophers dreamed of transforming the world, if everyone would accept the right principles. And the right principles were conceived as necessarily universal. Down to the seventeeth century, even powerful local rulers were reluctant to proclaim their full independence and continued to embellish their authority by claiming to be agents of some larger, more inspiring entity—on the largest scale, by claiming to be faithful instruments of Christendom or of the Holy Roman Empire.

Of course, sovereignty itself is a principle or doctrine. It was conceived as a doctrine capable of wide acceptance because it was inherently modest in its claims. It relied on the commonsense idea that authority to rule must rest, in the first instance, on *the capacity to enforce*. A sovereign state was a state that exercised reliable control over its own territory. Grotius thus grounded his famous argument for freedom of the high seas on the premise that no government could control movement on the high seas as it could control activity on its own territory.[14]

But as a political doctrine, sovereignty was never simply a celebration of force. It was precisely about the *control of force*. If physical compulsion were required to make every person obey every law, then even the strongest government would find law enforcement an impossible challenge. Sovereignty is about establishing which authorities have the last word on the legal resort to force—that is, who is entitled to make rightful claims for compliance, at least among the citizens of a particular territory. Different constitutional arrangements might provide different answers to this question in different states. But any answer about the "domestic" side of sovereignty depends upon a prior agreement to exclude interference from outsiders. A sovereign entity would not be sovereign in its own territory if it could not exclude claims by outsiders against its own citizens—or if it could not rely on its own people to ignore such claims when raised against their own government. What authority is entitled to make law in this way?

Enlightenment thinkers did not imagine this was an easy question to answer. They emphasized the need to find an answer precisely because, in the wake of the Protestant Reformation and the discovery and dispersal of new kinds of wealth, it was no longer so obvious who was entitled to demand compliance with which laws. When Grotius wrote his great treatise, Europe was in the second decade of what came to be called the Thirty Years War. In the course of that conflict, Central Europe was devastated not only by armies of powerful kings but by private warlords, mobilizing their own armed bands who lived off local plunder. It was only the culmination of centuries of chaos and violence, wrought by feudal lords who conceived that they had the right to assault and plunder neighboring lands in the name of some higher cause. The most celebrated military expeditions of medieval Europe, the Crusades, were not launched by kings or governments but rather were preached by church authorities to barons who volunteered in the quest for salvation—or for plunder.

Sovereignty appeared as a way of ordering and constraining political life. It insisted that law and force must be joined, and that the power to command must be linked with the power to protect—especially against outsiders. Sovereignty would not answer every question, but it could narrow the range of plausible answers in political contests.

From the outset, the doctrine had strong appeal to Americans, along with so many other notions of the Enlightenment. The appeal should hardly be cause for surprise. The United States began its national existence by rejecting fatalism—which is what a revolution means, after all. Americans were then persuaded to replace an impractical confederation with the sober constitutional arrangements that remain in place to this day. By conscious design, the U.S. Constitution perfectly reflected the historic understanding of sovereignty.

Sovereignty Illustrated—The American Example

The Constitution crafted in Philadelphia in 1787 incorporated a number of innovations. In particular, the federal structure of the new government differed considerably from the forms adopted by earlier confederations. The willingness of the American Founders to experiment with new forms simply highlights the basic principles they retained.

Under the American scheme of federalism, the power to make and enforce laws is widely dispersed. But governing authority is not equally shared among different levels of government. State governments can make and enforce their own law, but the Constitution provides that federal law is "supreme." The Constitution stipulates that even judges appointed by state governments must adhere to federal law in case of conflict—even if the state's own constitution says otherwise. Nor does federal authority merely constrain the states in dealings with other states. The Constitution established a federal authority empowered to reach inside each state to safeguard individual citizens—to ensure that citizens retain federally defined rights, to protect them against rebellion from within as well as invasion from without, and to guarantee them a "republican form of government" within their own state. The federal government is equipped to enforce its own law, with its own officials and its own courts, so that it may make direct claims on citizens, without interference from or dependence on state governments. Along with the Constitution itself, federal enactments are not only "supreme law" but "law of the *land*"—not merely constraining the states, but going directly to citizens in every part of the national territory.

And to ensure that it can accomplish its aims, federal authority is provided with clear supremacy when it comes to the exercise of force. The federal government retains a monopoly of naval power and standing armies. States can retain "militia" units—what we now call, rather tellingly, state units of the *National* Guard—but Congress can regulate these state military formations, and the president can command them by calling them into national service. A government entrusted with legal supremacy must, the Framers assumed, be entrusted with paramount authority when it comes to the exercise of force.

Of course, the government of the United States can also make treaties with other nations. But the ratification debates made clear, and subsequent decisions of the Supreme Court always confirmed, that the federal government retains the authority to renounce treaties, even as it can repeal its own statutes.[15] Federal officials are required to take an oath to uphold the Constitution, not an oath to uphold treaties. Other nations may claim that the United States has violated its treaty commitments, but binding law within the United States is what U.S. authorities hold as such—not what outside powers think it ought to be on the basis of previous treaty commitments. Treaties may be made—and dissolved—by the president and the Senate, while the Constitution cannot be changed except through amendment.

Judges and other officials in every American state are bound by what federal authorities have construed the federal Constitution to mean, because, as the Founders insisted, the Constitution is not a mere treaty among states. By its own terms, the Constitution is "the supreme law of the land." For the United States to insist on its own interpretation of its treaty commitments—or on whether circumstances still allow these commitments to apply—is a matter of diplomacy. For the states to insist on their own interpretation of the federal Constitution is rebellion. And, as the Civil War proved, most Americans support the federal government's authority to crush rebellion.

The point of sovereignty is clear enough in this contrast. No international authority has the same claim over a sovereign state that the federal government has over states within the United States. International authorities cannot order the deployment of American troops (nor troops of any other nation) in the way the president can mobilize and deploy state National Guard forces. Since international authority cannot compel the deployment of force, it cannot readily protect nations when force may be needed. And if it cannot protect nations, it cannot readily control what they do to protect themselves—at least, not without their direct and continuing consent.

The point is not that sovereignty is "sacred and undeniable." Jefferson's original draft for the Declaration of Independence deployed that phrase to describe the rights of individuals, and would never have invoked it on behalf of sovereignty.[16] The Declaration itself insisted on the right of the people to "alter or abolish" their established "form of government"—if necessary by force. But a government challenged by force may often be in the right in resisting it, whether that force is launched by rebels at home or by enemies from abroad. When is it wrong for government to suppress rebellion or resistance to its own law? Would we want international bodies to have the authority to determine whether the rebels or the government were more in the right? Would we want to live in a country in which armed rebels could appeal to international authorities for authoritative vindication? Or where disputes between our nation and another would have to be settled, definitively and in every case, by an international authority? Why suppose that an international authority can be more trusted to come down on the right side?

The treatise of Grotius and a succession of later treatises on "the law of nations" acknowledged that states were bound, in their conduct, by a law that has higher moral authority, in some way, than any positive law of their own making. The American Founders did not dispute the point. Indeed, Jefferson's Declaration of Independence proclaims this doctrine: Natural law is "natural"—that is, attributable, as the Declaration says, to "the law of Nature and of Nature's God"—precisely because it does not derive from human will, and is not binding simply because human authority has decreed or endorsed it. For an outside power to instruct a sovereign state on its duties, as a matter of natural law, is to question the sovereign right of that state to interpret its duties, under its particular circumstances, for itself. It may be necessary for an outside state to insist on its own view of its rights in a dispute with another state—but the other state might well take a different view and resist the claims made upon it. A state that persists in demanding that another state submit to its view is asking for conflict. Such demands are well understood to carry the risk of war, because persistent demands imply a readiness to back them up, if necessary by force.

None of this means that the doctrine of sovereignty is incompatible with peace. Certainly, the historic American view was that sovereignty offered the best hope of preserving peace. No alternative arrangement seems a more assured path to peace, even today.

Sovereignty as the Path to Peace

For many people, it seems intuitively obvious that a world of sovereign states will be one in which peace is always in jeopardy. Governments have tremendous capacities for mobilizing force. Without a constraining superior, each government might well look like an armed adventurer in the international arena. Within their own territories, governments provide an overarching authority to secure peace. Why not, then, an overarching authority to prevent nations from resorting to war, just as national governments prevent individuals from resorting to violence?

But war is much older than governments or state structures. To have a structure that can secure peace within a particular territory—and all the more so, one that can do so without vast brutality and repression—is itself a considerable achievement. Even the terrible wars of the twentieth century caused fewer civilian deaths, relative to overall population, than medieval crusades or the marauding warlords of the Thirty Years War—or, indeed, as anthropologists now tell us, than tribal conflicts among primitive peoples.[17]

Even at the end of the twentieth century, people often preferred a brutal government with secure authority to the threat of chaos—especially when they had experienced chaos, as in many parts of Africa. International peacekeeping missions have often perpetuated conflict by nurturing truces and ceasefires and unstable provisional coalition governments, which have the effect of protecting insurgent forces, preserving their hopes and resources for renewing the conflict later on. Peacekeeping in Africa has a particularly terrible record—precisely because international interventions have been so focused on immediate humanitarian impulses and have given so little attention to the underlying requirements of civil peace: a secure sovereign authority.[18] Meanwhile, governments that cannot control their own territories may end up as unintentional hosts for terrorist organizations plotting attacks on others from "safe" retreats.

A government that is securely established in its own territory can still be terribly brutal to its own people and aggressive toward its neighbors. But sovereignty, as a doctrine, was not historically a way of exalting power. On the contrary, it was seen as a way of promoting peace by establishing boundaries. A government that wanted to live at peace with its neighbors had to respect their sovereign rights. A government that expected neighbors to respect its sovereign authority in its own territory had to exercise that authority in ways that made it a tolerable neighbor: it had to ensure its territory did not become host to guerrilla bands or pirate gangs—or, in our day, to terrorist organizations—that would attack its neighbors. This is still an essential obligation of sovereign states, and this obligation still has no more reliable means of enforcement than the demands of other states.[19]

The historic alternative to sovereignty was the crusading faith, demanding submission to the universal claims of Christianity or Islam— or more recently, of Communism or racial solidarity. Precisely because sovereignty focused on securing order in a defined territory—rather than saving humanity—a sovereign state could afford to be a more tolerant and liberal state. Even its claims on neighbors were more restrained.

Wars in the eighteenth and nineteenth centuries were indeed much more limited, though not less frequent, because they were seen as conflicts over the interests of the belligerent states rather than final struggles for ultimate stakes. No one imagined that a state could shield itself from all danger by waiving the word sovereignty. States might sometimes have conflicting claims that they were more willing to put to the test of war than to the diplomacy of compromise. Some compromises would only be accepted under compulsion of arms—when war proved that sustaining an earlier claim (most often to territory) was simply impossible.

Still, sovereignty was not conceived as an alternative to international law. By the eighteenth century, international law had acquired wide recognition in Europe, as a distinct body of law or at least of norms and practices, precisely by taking sovereignty as its starting point, in the way Grotius had done in his treatise on the laws of war. Other scholars sought to ground legal duties of states in practices which had come to be generally accepted. States would protect each other's ambassadors and each other's citizens traveling on recognized passports. They would observe certain restraints in land and naval warfare—as long as others did so as well.[20] By the nineteenth century, states were even prepared to submit certain disputes to international arbitration—though only on certain matters and only with the consent of both parties to the dispute.

What states would not accept was the imposition of outside determinations on matters they deemed of "vital national interest." Even the machinery of the International Court of Justice, established with the United Nations in 1945, did not require states to submit disputes to international arbitration. Historically, states which did entrust the most basic questions of security to an outside power were regarded as "protectorates" and not fully sovereign. Sovereign states might agree to many kinds of constraints, such as limitations on armaments, but they retained the right to renounce treaty commitments when they judged it necessary to do so. On vital questions of security, international law could offer only the most vague generalities. It could condemn aggression, but it did not presume to determine, in any particular dispute, which side was the actual aggressor.

Sovereignty offers its own answer: A sovereign state has the full right to respond to aggression with countering force. A smaller state might need allies to back up its resistance (or its threat to resist aggression). It might even seek assistance from other states with which it had no previous treaty but which had reasons of their own to fear the success of the apparent aggressor—even if there were not complete agreement as to which side actually was the aggressor.

It is, to say the least, not obvious that international bodies with no forces of their own can constrain aggression. Are potential aggressors more likely to be deterred—or more likely to be resisted—if their intended targets can act promptly and decisively to repel any threat, or if they must first gain the endorsement of all other states in the world before attempting a response? To believe that international organization can substitute for sovereignty, one must believe that international organizations can respond as promptly and reliably as sovereign states. It is, to say the least, a belief that cannot draw much support from past experience.

It is even more questionable whether extending purported international obligations into more and more areas is a reliable way of inducing dissident states to go along. To judge, for example, by the actual practice of European governments (in contrast to their internationalist rhetoric), it is prudent to not insist on China's compliance with international human rights standards. Even the United States has sought little more than to promote a "discussion" of China's human rights practices in international forums.

Such reticence still has an obvious point. In the early 1990s, Samuel Huntington warned that the conflicts of states were giving way to "a clash of civilizations."[21] Huntington's assumption that Western Europe and the United States shared a common "Western civilization" now seems rather optimistic, as it would have seemed to most American statesmen until after the Second World War.[22] His notion that Japan and India each represented a distinct "civilization" also seems rather superfluous, when these "civilizations" already correspond to the borders of sovereign states. But no one doubts that the Islamic world is agitated by claims to reawaken a transnational loyalty. Perhaps there may be threatening counterparts to this phenomenon in the future. Do we improve prospects for peace and stability in the world by insisting that a whole laundry list of policy claims that contemporary Europeans identify with "human rights" or "environmental security" are now universal claims which all states must honor?

If peace is our priority, we would serve that priority more effectively by focusing on the particular states that threaten peace, and the particular practices of these states that are most threatening—such as their sponsorship of international terrorism and their attempts to acquire weapons of mass destruction. It is entirely consistent with sovereignty for one state to pressure another in the name of security. It is not obvious that there is any better hope, even today, of preserving conditions of peace. Even if we have larger goals than peace, we are not likely to accomplish them peacefully— which means we are not likely to accomplish them reliably—without respecting sovereignty as the general norm in international affairs.

Further Fallacies

During the 1990s, advocates of global governance insisted that cooperation, indeed a broader and more enlightened understanding of "security" itself, required larger structures for coordinating the actions of states. With the growth of trade and interdependence, advocates argued, no state could any longer achieve its objectives by itself, so the authority of states must be shared with wider structures of governance. The idea still impresses many people today. But it rests, fundamentally, on a misunderstanding of what sovereignty is.

Certainly a state with ambitious objectives cannot achieve them all by its own fiat. That is not a new development. Throughout history, rulers have found their aims blocked by resistance from powerful neighbors, powerful subjects, or the sheer intractability of human affairs. Sovereignty came to be an accepted doctrine in the age of Enlightenment precisely as governments came to accept a more limited notion of their responsibilities. Sovereignty is the attribute of a state. The very idea of a state implies a distinction between its governing authority and the private lives of citizens, in what came to be seen as "society" in contrast to the "state." Enlightenment thinkers who championed the doctrine of sovereignty took it for granted that a sovereign state could not, and should not, want to control all aspects of society.

By the nineteenth century, when sovereignty was at the height of its prestige as a political doctrine, most European governments interfered far less in social life than they had in the past—or would seek to do in the twentieth century. By many measures, cross-border flows of trade and investment were relatively more important on the eve of the First World War than they were in the 1990s.[23] Borders were more open to immigration and cultural exchange than they have been since then. Few people seriously imagined that governments were therefore lacking in sovereignty.

But even the totalitarian governments of the twentieth century could not order everything according to their preferences. The Soviet Union, at the height of its totalitarian power, could not prevent crop failures. Decade after decade, bad harvests were blamed on bad weather—which apparently became much worse after 1917, since Russia had previously been a grain exporter. While totalitarian power could force farmers to submit to the dictates of central authorities, it could not ensure that central authorities knew how to farm productively.

Sovereignty is, fundamentally, about *the authority to establish what law is binding*—or will be backed by coercion—in a particular territory. It is not a guarantee of total control over everything that happens. Sovereignty cannot ensure that laws achieve their intended results. It cannot change the weather. It cannot change, by itself, what people in other nations will buy or sell or think, or what governments in other territories will do. But a sovereign state can decide for itself how to govern—that is, it retains the legal authority to determine what standards and laws will be enforced in its own territory, and what it will do with the national resources it can mobilize.

It may be true that larger states have advantages in bargaining (or in more direct conflicts) with other states. That may be an argument for joining a number of smaller states or entities under a common sovereignty. That was indeed an argument often advanced by the American Founders, as they urged the thirteen states of the original "Confederation" to yield some of their powers to a common federal government. It does not follow, however, that every small state must submit to a larger confederation, still less that all states would do better by yielding their sovereign powers to supranational structures. Some small states, such as Norway and New Zealand, have flourished without submitting to larger entities. They can make alliances to assure protection against possible aggressors. They can make treaties to secure favorable trade relations with other states or to cooperate in dealing with common environmental or public health concerns.

But states that want to retain their sovereignty will insist that they are not legally bound by determinations of outsiders. They will insist that they are only bound by treaties to which they have, in fact, consented. They may hold out for inducements to consent, such as pledges of reciprocal action by others or compensation for particular burdens entailed in a particular commitment. They may maintain safeguards—as the United States has always done and as most countries in the world still do—against allowing international claims to enter into their own legal systems without internal checks on their legal force.[24] Small countries, which may seem most at risk on their own, may also be most vulnerable to having their interests neglected in international organizations, where they lose the capacity to say no. The need for cooperation does not mean there is no longer a need to maintain safeguards against unacceptable interference.

If one views the challenge from the particular perspective of the United States, the claim seems even more questionable. The United States may want cooperation on a great range of matters. Sometimes it might be helpful to have other states seconding its claims on third states. To subordinate these claims to international authorities, however, means that even the agenda is set by others.

It is not at all obvious why the United States should care to see international compliance with treaties it is not itself willing to endorse. Sovereignty gives countries the right to insist that their policies not be subordinated to others. While citizens may have a stake in seeing that others honor the law, even when they do not agree with that law, no country has a stake in seeing that the schemes of other countries succeed out of some abstract devotion to "international law."

Some critics insist, however, that the United States has precisely that duty today, because it will otherwise face a world of enemies. Here the interdependence argument is turned on its head. The problem is not that states are too weak to accomplish their objectives, but that the United States is too strong to pursue its objectives without international chaperones.[25] Otherwise, we are told, the United States will be seen as a threatening "empire" and, as such, will encounter more and more resentment and resistance from other states. The premise is highly questionable, and the conclusion even more so.

If the United States were really so intimidating, one would expect the most intimidated state to be Canada. After all, Canada sits right next to the world's mightiest military power, sharing some 3,000 miles of undefended border with the United States. The United States is by far Canada's largest trading partner, so it might seem most vulnerable to American economic power as well. If Canada were intimidated, we would expect it to be among the first countries to endorse America's call to support the war against Iraq. In fact, Canada remained aloof, even when three dozen other states—including Canada's historic Commonwealth partners, Britain and Australia—did contribute to the American-led coalition against Iraq.

If America were viewed as an ominous threat, one would expect Canada to pursue a separate military alliance with Europe. One would then expect all the nations in that alliance to construct, in turn, a grand coalition with Russia and China to counter the American threat. Of course, nothing of the sort happened. To the contrary, Canada still cooperates closely with the United States on a range of issues where we share common interests, as in securing North America from infiltration by foreign terrorists—or taking a common stand with the United States against protectionist agriculture policies of the European Union. And the European Union shows no signs of developing military plans in coordination with Russia and China.

It may be true that the United States risks provoking adverse reactions if it abuses its power. It does not follow that nations that are fearful or jealous of American power will be reassured if U.S. policy is presented as "international" or world policy. China and the Soviet Union were unimpressed by the 1950 Security Council resolution that allowed the United States to characterize the Korean war as an "international police action." It hardly impressed Osama bin Laden and other terrorists when the UN condemned international terrorism in the wake of the September 11 atrocities. In August 2003, terrorists in Baghdad, who may have been connected to bin Laden's organization, showed themselves just as willing to bomb UN offices there as any American installation.

The United States has more capacity than most countries to enforce its rights. But as a superpower with many competing concerns around the world, it also has more distractions than almost any other state. If anything, the United States makes fewer claims regarding its sovereign rights than it did a century ago. In the early twentieth century, for example, America claimed that it had the right to use force to ensure that foreign governments honored their financial obligations to American citizens—a claim that powerful European states also advanced. The United States renounced such claims in the 1930s and has never seriously revived them.[26] Force, of course, was never the whole of diplomacy, and there are a range of lesser sanctions that states can apply short of force. But the states that the United States is most determined to influence—namely, those which might be involved with terrorism against Americans—are not likely to be moved by international counsels. To the contrary, they are likely to find protection in them, as American action is held hostage to international consensus.

The arguments for subordinating or denying sovereignty are so unconvincing on their own terms that one is bound to feel they respond less to actual analysis of costs and benefits than to an inchoate moral outlook. It is easy to identify what it is: sovereignty seems selfish, and its most determined critics are, in general, those who champion collective responses to other problems. In today's world, opposition to sovereignty is a cause that enlists the sympathies of the political left. Europeans have special reasons for denying the relevance or logic of sovereignty, but these reasons are reflected in—or reinforced by—the EU's enthusiasm for leftist causes in general. Any defense of sovereignty needs to address the moral qualms the concept now arouses for many people.

The Morality of Sovereignty

Most Americans hardly need to be persuaded that sovereignty is worth preserving. The doctrine of national sovereignty is an American birthright—literally. The opening sentence of the Declaration of Independence appealed to "the laws of Nature and Nature's God," which "entitle" independent states "to a separate and equal station . . . among the powers of the earth." National sovereignty, according to this doctrine, has the same moral claim as the "unalienable rights" of individuals, founded on the same enlightened understanding of natural law.

The doctrine had obvious appeal to the American Founders as they sought to launch a fragile new nation. But the attraction was far deeper than the particular diplomatic circumstances of the founding era. The doctrine was originally—and in some ways primarily—about the natural rights of individual human beings. The Declaration of Independence drew on the extended and intricate exposition of natural law in John Locke's *Treatise of Government*. By nature, according to Locke, all men have a "perfect freedom to order their actions and dispose of their possessions . . . as they think fit," as long as they remain "within the bounds of the law of nature." The law of nature obliges men to deal honestly, to fulfill their promises, and not to "impair the life" or "the liberty, health, limb or goods of another"—at least in dealing with others who have not offended against these same "bounds."[27]

If individuals start with these rights, limited only by these obligations to regard the rights of others, then something more is required to justify the imposition of more burdensome obligations—some scheme of consent. That is, of course, what the Declaration of Independence asserts: Rights are "endowed by the Creator," but governments "derive their just powers from the consent of the governed." But why assume that the "state of nature," in which men have no obligations beyond respecting each other's natural rights, is a reasonable starting point? Locke acknowledged it was "often asked as a mighty objection" whether the state of nature had ever existed; he answered with this confident response: "[I]ndependent governments all through the world are in a state of nature."[28]

In a memorandum to President Washington, Jefferson himself, then serving as secretary of state, took over the reasoning, which was affirmed by all the leading texts on the law of nations in that era:

> The Moral duties which exist between individual and individual
> in a state of nature, accompany them into a state of society & the

aggregate of the duties of all the individuals composing the society constitute duties of that society towards any other; so that between society and society the same moral duties exist as did between the individuals composing them while in an unassociated state.[29]

But Jefferson did not fail to note the proviso that obligations cease when they become "self-destructive," since "the law of preservation overrules the laws of obligation to others"; and when such "dangers" arise, "nations are to be judges for themselves, since no one nation has a right to sit in judgment over another."[30]

Of course, not everyone abides by the law of nature. Some scorn any constraint, and some honestly believe the law means one thing in a particular dispute while others take a different view. The built-in provision for exceptions—in the name of self-defense—opens many more opportunities for disagreement. Self-defense may be the primal right, but individual human beings would always be vulnerable to aggression if the law of nature relied on each person's own efforts to protect himself. So governments are instituted to provide more precision to the law of nature and more reliable enforcement. Government can make rights more secure.

But then government itself may be a threat to the rights of individuals. It makes sense, according to this theory, to consent to government if it is constrained by constitutional limitations, safeguarded by such institutions as elected legislatures, independent courts, and civilian control of the military. In the last resort, as Locke's treatise and the Declaration of Independence affirmed, the community may rightly rise in rebellion against an abusive government. The political community that forms itself under a sovereign government can be seen as resting on the agreement of the members to defend their rights in common. Seen this way, it can tolerate many differences among citizens, as long as they remain committed to this shared purpose: They agree to be regulated in common, to be taxed in common, and to accept other restraints and obligations imposed by government so they can all be more secure in their rights.

It does not at all follow that each of these communities must then submit to some higher authority. Each sovereign community holds its authority on the premise that its own citizens have agreed, in some way, to submit to governmental powers for the sake of their mutual protection. Why trust that some larger, more encompassing entity would care as much about the individuals in each community as their own government does? Locke's treatise specifically cites the transfer of legislative power to a foreign entity as a dissolution of the social contract, leaving citizens morally free to repudiate (or revolt against) their government (or, as he indicates, what has now become a new government).[31]

The objection is most obvious when a liberal state is asked to share power with illiberal or tyrannical states, responding to entirely different views of rights or justice. It may be quite possible for liberal states to live in peace with tyrannical states. But liberal states will not make the rights of their own citizens more secure by inviting illiberal states to share in the determination of what rights their citizens should have—or what powers should be entrusted to their government.

Even when it comes to states that share many common ideas about the purposes of state power, there are bound to be differences. In some ways, these differences are even more important when they arise among democratic and constitutional states. A dictatorship can promise anything it finds convenient at the moment. A democratic government rests on a constitutional structure, with a particular allocation of powers and rights. Different democratic communities have worked out different sorts of compromises among groups of citizens. Citizens within each community have agreed to submit to governmental constraints and burdens so they may have the advantage of a shared power to stand up for them against outsiders. Citizens of one community want their own government to act as effectively as it can to protect their rights, or to advance their shared interests in the community that does protect their rights.

If policies affecting the citizens are determined by international authorities, citizens lose the benefit of the constitutional safeguards and procedures they have agreed to accept within their own community. They also lose one of the central rationales for accepting such restraints—the idea that members of a community can trust each other enough to live together and stand together against outsiders. If international authorities can claim supremacy over national states, no state can fulfil its obligation to its own citizens: to protect their national community. International authorities cannot reliably appeal to the particular interest of particular nations.

International authorities must appeal to peoples of all or most nations for support or compliance in the name of abstract, universal claims. The appeal is not to civic spirit—the social compact among common citizens—but to general humanitarianism. It may not often be a sufficient appeal for opponents of an international policy to accept their disappointment and go along with the supposed international consensus.

If we all agreed on the same abstract ideals, we might accept that experts would always know how to implement them. If there were a world consensus, there could be world government—or, indeed, global governance, since the distinctive element of coercion (which distinguishes government from varieties of governance) would not be necessary. If we lived in such a world, we would not worry about the lack of constitutional safeguards in the bodies that established world policy. We wouldn't need to worry about whether world policies eroded constitutional safeguards in our own country. We would not need constitutional safeguards, because we would have reached global consensus on key matters of rights and governance.

By pretending that we already live in such a world, we would provide endless opportunities for self-serving insiders to manipulate credulous people on a global scale. To say that global governance would be undemocratic is to understate the problem. Under such a scheme of global governance, democracy as we know it—with constitutional safeguards for opposing interests—would be almost inconceivable. The whole organized structure of the world would already presuppose such deep and broad agreement that constitutional and democratic controls on government would seem superfluous. Genuine conflict would be unimaginable. Certainly, this would be a world in which competing approaches would be hard to envision, because all countries would be obliged to follow the same approach to policy challenges.

But these concerns only arise for the optimist. Human nature being what it is, global authorities would more likely be subject to constant challenge. The more likely prospect for a world governed by global institutions would be constant struggle by global authorities to repress rebellious jurisdictions. That is the history of all lesser empires, and would surely be the fate of an attempted world empire.

To start with, then, the moral case for the liberal version of the law of nature is that it allows different peoples to get along by not forcing them to agree. Nations that do not agree on much else might agree on this minimal notion of international morality. They might agree on this lowest common denominator in international affairs, even if they rejected any extrapolation from this version of "individual" rights (that is, the rights of individual political communities) to the rights of individual human beings in their domestic law.

We can say more than that, however, on behalf of sovereignty as the organizing principle of international politics. Sovereignty does more than just promote peace among states. A world of sovereign states can help to promote both liberty and democracy within states. At the most basic level, sovereignty is an inherently limiting principle. A sovereign state rules here—and not there. What is done "there"—in another country—may be an example for "us," or a dreadful counterexample. In the meantime, sovereignty allows people "here" to resolve their differences by focusing attention on what is needed to improve things "here"—in the here and now, where our actual political community operates, with all its unavoidable constraints. In this setting, people with quite differing views on what would be best in principle might still come together on what is most feasible within the confines of their shared political situation—as common citizens of a particular state.

To think globally is to think universally and encourage a focus on the most abstract principles—principles on which people are likely to disagree quite a bit within each state, just as states disagree with each other. A world of distinct or competing sovereigns is a world in which political debate is more constrained. For that very reason, sovereign states may provide a more durable forum for political life, by reminding citizens of the precondition of ongoing political debate: a stable political community.

A recurrent objection to this view is that sovereign states differ so greatly in size and wealth that the most powerful are bound to dominate the others. Sovereignty, then, may be no more than a mask for domination by the strongest. This charge is hard to reconcile with the observed fact that some of the world's wealthiest states, in per capita terms, are among the smallest in population, while some of the most populous states—including states with nuclear weapons and vast economies, in the aggregate—are among the poorest. What is true today, if one compares South Korea and China, or Australia and India, was seen to be true in the eighteenth century, when people compared the fortunes of, for example, the Netherlands with the Russian Empire. Governments of large states often feel they have more room for error, so they are more inclined to pursue futile policies. Governments of large, heterogeneous states often feel they have less capacity to rely on shared loyalties among citizens, so they proceed to rule with more brutality to keep their countries together. Either way, brutal and repressive policies often prevent citizens of large states from developing their productive capacities as fully as they might in a freer or more democratic state.

For many people, however, the issue is almost a matter of principle. A world in which each state pursues its own interests is one in which power—however one measures that or whatever it means—is not allocated equally. But it is very hard to imagine how power can be reallocated among states when they vary so much in wealth and population. Would we be better off in a world in which international authority could transfer wealth and military power to make all states perfectly equal? That seems entirely fantastical. Even with existing imbalances, no one nation—not even the United States—can dominate all the others. To suppose that sovereignty is empty because not all sovereign states have the same capacities, one must greatly underestimate the range of choice still available to independent states. It is a trend of thought that may appeal to people who think everyone must agree on the world's most urgent priorities and how to tackle them, as global governance supposes. But it remains a very implausible supposition.

Just the same sort of reasoning persuades many people that market competition is a hoax because competing firms are not equal in their resources, or that free speech is meaningless because not every person has the same resources to publicize his views. But competition still makes a big difference even to the behavior of the largest firms, because it drives cost control and innovation—and when it does not, potential rivals have a way of becoming very real rivals. Equal rights to free speech still make a considerable difference in blocking efforts to predetermine what will be said.

People may distrust sovereignty, much as they distrust private property or individual rights, because sovereignty does not ensure equality among states. But there is no good reason to assume that a world government or global governance would ensure equality, either. We can hardly even imagine what equality would mean, given all the disparities between different states. One vote for China (population: 1.2 billion) and one for Norway (population: 4.5 million)? Representation by population—so that China and India and a few others can vote to expropriate the wealth of Canada and Australia? Global governance might "address the needs" of poor countries, but there is no way of ensuring that well-meaning programs will work as intended, or even that affluent donor states will focus on the needs of poor people among the states supposed to be their beneficiaries. Poor countries may like the idea of an international authority empowered to siphon wealth from rich countries and redistribute it according to need—but that doesn't mean that, in practice, they are prepared to accept direction from international authorities. The experience of international lending programs, such as the World Bank or the International Monetary Fund (IMF), does not suggest that poor countries have limitless patience for international direction—or that their suspicion of manipulation or hidden interests is always mistaken.[32]

The deepest objection to sovereignty is that it is somehow an encouragement to selfishness: states think more about their own advantage than about the good of the world. That is a common objection to "rights talk" even in domestic settings. Few people pretend that respecting the rights of others is the whole of morality. Among other things, this formulation leaves out obligations that may not correspond to the rights of others but still constitute an important part of morality. It leaves out a duty that each individual may have to hold himself to certain standards of piety, dignity, or simple respectability, even when failing to do so causes no immediate or direct injury to other individuals but may still, in larger terms, prove demoralizing to others (and even destructive to the individual himself). It leaves out imperfect duties to help those in distress, even when they may not have a "perfect" right to assistance (that is, a right that can be readily determined by some general rule and insisted upon in all circumstances).

One can go some distance in talking about enlightened self-interest. Still, it is clear enough that moral life is sustained by larger concerns than self-interest. Religions appeal to something higher. A number of observers have noted that international environmental advocates often seem to make spiritual claims, or display a kind of spiritual enthusiasm for their policy claims.[33] Human rights advocates, as a prominent scholar warns, have begun to view their cause as a new religion.[34] The call for peace and brotherhood has always evoked religious enthusiasm. In the nineteenth century, as in the contemporary world, peace movements enlisted much support from churches. The Archbishop of Canterbury, the highest clerical authority in the Anglican Church, recently urged religious movements to take a greater role in global policymaking, since states seem increasingly preoccupied with narrower economic concerns.[35]

Reasonable people may wonder whether these new religious appeals do not hold out messianic visions at odds with the basic premises of older, biblical doctrines, by making international forums into instruments of planetary providence. People of differing faiths or spiritual leanings might still recognize that government requires force, as well as inspiration, and might see the point of caution when it comes to investing international bodies with coercive authority. If international authority cannot be trusted with genuine force, perhaps it is unwise to allow it to exercise a kind of moral authority that is beyond challenge. The strongest argument for sovereignty is that it is a brake on such authority.

Grotius invented the notion of "subjective rights" in order to make sovereignty more intelligible. He was the first prominent writer to give a clear account of rights from the standpoint of the claimant—"my rights," as opposed to "what is right."[36] The moral claim for sovereignty remains much the same as the moral claim for other rights. Yes, liberty can be abused, and property can be wasted, but such rights still have solid moral claims. To talk of rights is to distance the legal claim from the moral purpose—to imply that the rights-holder may still be within his rights, even if he exercises them in a poor way. To respect rights is to honor individual choice. More than that, it is to acknowledge that the political authority that defines and protects rights cannot be omniscient or omnipotent, so it cannot pretend to direct individuals in every detail of correct conduct. It must leave individuals to decide many things for themselves. The claim is much stronger when it comes to planetary authority, because its claims might, in principle, be so much higher than those advanced by an individual state.

The question is not whether states should be open to moral appeals, beyond their immediate self-interest. They are, and must be—among other reasons, because the self-interest of any state is not something that can ever be ascertained in isolation from its own ideals and aims. People argue, in a similar way, that domestic law should reflect more than the balance of selfish interests that happen to bargain their way to legislative majorities. No serious observer can doubt that higher or larger moral concerns often do influence legislators, as well as administrators and judges trying to interpret ambiguous laws. Some people say, with reason, that the background morality in America is Christian or Judeo-Christian, or at least that it necessarily pays heed to moral understandings that originally were inspired by biblical teaching. But few citizens argue that American law should therefore be determined by what the pope or the National Council of Churches or any other religious authority says it should be. Religious and moral advocacy—along with many other causes—can affect public opinion, which in turn affects the political incentives and constraints on governmental decision makers. But the government remains responsible for the decisions it makes and cannot plead that its decisions were required by outside advocates, however distinguished their spiritual authority. The moral argument for sovereignty is the argument for limited government—which means distinguishing the responsibility of any particular government from the claims of a universal faith.

The Appeal of Limited Government

Governments can lose their sovereignty altogether after total defeat in war, as happened in Germany and Japan in 1945 and in Iraq in 2003. But it usually requires an all-out war for one state or group of states to seize the sovereign authority of another. Few states are eager to engage in the kind of war this requires. Even fewer are inclined to accept ongoing responsibility for ruling the territory of another nation. The United States returned sovereign power to Germany and Japan after a few years of occupation, as it pledged it would do in Iraq, promising a restoration of self-government after little more than a year of occupation. America has always been wary of assuming permanent responsibility for territories it was not willing to incorporate into the Union in some form. There are political costs—as well as financial—in maintaining permanent colonies or protectorates.

To hector a government into compliance with preferred standards may seem far less dangerous than resorting to war, and far less costly than assuming ongoing direct control. Outside states can draw certain lines but are not always prepared to do what might be necessary to secure or defend them. It is more pleasing to imagine that some international authority could cajole or constrain states to go along with agreed-upon international policies, without resorting to war or to constant threats of compulsion. If such a thing could work, it would make sovereignty irrelevant by making the right to refuse almost impossible to exercise.

But would we really want such a scheme to work? A top official of the United Nations recently admonished Americans to recognize the UN's "invaluable" contribution to "legitimacy" since "the UN embodies world opinion": "When the UN Security Council passes a resolution, it is seen as speaking for (and in the interests of) humanity. . . . "[37] Is it really desirable to have one institution recognized as the voice of humanity? What if the voice of humanity is mistaken?

The victor in a war may force the loser to accept changes. The loser may often come to accept changes imposed by force. Germany and Japan have accepted many political reforms initially imposed on their countries by occupation governments. Most people in these countries may believe that these changes worked to their ultimate benefit. But it is something else to ask them to believe that everything done by the United States is just and right or that all changes imposed on them were imposed solely for their benefit. Germans may accept that the borders of Germany will never again encompass Alsace or East Prussia. It is something else to ask them to believe that Germany's current borders were determined by pure justice. It is in some ways more compatible with national self-respect to bow to irresistible force—to acknowledge new *power* realities—than to affirm that particular outside powers are the world's rightful instruments of *justice*.

The underlying problem does not disappear when the outside powers claim to speak for authorities who present themselves as detached from the interest of any particular state or coalition of states. Global authority does not wield direct force of its own. Certainly, the UN does not wield direct force of its own, and advocates of global governance do not now speak of any global authority with force of its own. For a global authority to compel a national government to submit, it must summon overwhelming moral authority. The state that is cajoled into compliance must in some way acknowledge that its past conduct was, after all, morally untenable, so the demanded change can be acknowledged as a moral exigency. Perhaps such moral bullying can sometimes prevail, but it will inevitably encounter disputes that prove more intractable, as some governments prove more obdurate in their stances.

For those with continuing grievances, the failure of global authority will be doubly insulting and humiliating. When global authority fails to remedy their claims, it implies that the status quo is somehow morally acceptable. How could the status quo otherwise be tolerated by a supreme moral authority? Precisely because they anticipated such problems, diplomats arranging international arbitration schemes, well into the twentieth century, always provided that states could demand that their "vital national interests" be excluded from the jurisdiction of arbitrators. No international institution, it was thought, could presume to settle the most impassioned disputes and still retain the respect of all nations involved. It was thought more conducive to peace to acknowledge that some disputes must simply be left to be resolved through ongoing tests of will and power.[38]

A global moral authority has much less ability to concede such limits on its own reach. What is right is right. What have questions of power or force to do with what is right? It is no answer for international institutions or advocacy groups to disclaim the highest moral pretensions and retreat to claims about international legality or technical expertise. Legal analysts in the UN Secretariat or the International Criminal Court and economic or engineering experts with the World Bank or the IMF may claim to have answers that are clearly right in some sense even if not morally right in all respects. Do such claims supply irresistible force to their international policy pronouncements? What if a national government disagrees? If international authorities can't control national governments, why should national governments submit to their directives? Why should national governments disclaim their own responsibility for deciding what they think best for their own nations?

Faced with obdurate resistance, the tendency of international organizations—and even of advocacy groups—is usually to temporize or compromise or obfuscate. All political entities may do much the same when they encounter hard political necessities. But why should international authorities then have any higher claim on anyone's compliance? Different people and different governments will make different assessments of what is feasible in particular circumstances. That is the historic appeal of sovereignty—that it preserves some room for political choice, between despairing fatalism and unyielding moralism.

The Federalist offers an apt admonition: "Responsibility, in order to be reasonable, must be limited to objects within the power of the responsible party."[39] In one way or another, global governance is a bid for authority without reliable control. Freed from the awkward responsibility of exercising actual power, it can always set its sights on high ideals and ambitious responses to global imperatives. It can imagine itself to be detached from the interests of any particular nation. In real life, of course, bureaucrats and advocacy groups have their own interests—including quite petty interests in income and office perks.[40] But even the most selfless servants of humanity cannot accomplish very much without the assistance or cooperation of powerful states. So international institutions are invariably entangled in the awkward realities of power politics. But international authorities still present themselves as something other than the agents of powerful states.

International institutions claim an authority that is, in some literal sense, irresponsible—because, by its own professions, it is not accountable to any state in particular. To be accountable to "humanity" is to be, after all, quite unaccountable, since humanity at large is not organized to hold anyone to account. It is not much different from the claim of revolutionaries or tyrants to be accountable to "history." Sovereign powers, with much less moral pretension, are likely to be judged by more tangible standards and preserve more reliable authority, because their authority makes more modest claims.

The controversy over Iraq illustrates the point quite clearly. There was much debate, in the months after the war, about whether Saddam's weapons or weapons programs really posed an imminent threat to the United States, or even to states in the region. No one could dispute that removing a murderous tyrant helped the Iraqi people tremendously. But critics insisted that America's commitment to democracy in post-Saddam Iraq did not legitimize the war, since the United States had acquiesced to various dictatorships in almost every other Arab country. The obvious answer to such challenges is that the United States and its coalition partners had gained control of Iraq and were responsible for organizing a new government. The United States is not responsible for the form of government in places it does not control. That is precisely what sovereignty means— that no nation is responsible for what happens in territories it does not control.

The better question is why the United Nations should be seen as "legitimate" by the Iraqi people, after so many years in which the UN allowed Saddam to remain in power. The inescapable and painful fact for Iraqis is that most states on the Security Council preferred that Saddam remain in place rather than see his murderous regime ended by American military action. Not surprisingly, observers on the ground report that Iraqis felt much distrust for the UN after its decades of support for Saddam's terrible tyranny.[41]

The world does not need to be told that the United States acts from a mix of motives, and that American self-interest figures largely in that mix. Countries that disagree with American policy may decide they do not have the capacity to alter it and so acquiesce, even when they do not approve. That is also part of the logic of sovereignty. Others are not responsible for American action. But many critics who distrust American power in principle are inclined to place great hopes in international organization or authority. In effect, international authority becomes a rallying point for opponents of American policy, masking a great many motives.

Perhaps it is not obvious to many governments whether they have more to fear from American power, applied to limited aims, or from international authorities, with potentially unlimited aims but little real power. It is, then, the challenge of American diplomacy to make clear that American sovereignty remains compatible with the sovereignty of other states, while a world of global governance is a world in which nothing is secure. Sovereignty is a way of institutionalizing the principle of distrust for overreaching authority.

Many states in the contemporary world may still find it easier to coast along with the pretenses of international authority, all the while keeping their fingers crossed behind their backs, hoping that, if push comes to shove, they can retain their freedom of action. To resist international authority in the open—to challenge the moral prestige of international authority—may be difficult. This is not simply an international phenomenon. "Every American," Mark Twain observed, "has the right to free speech and the good sense not to exercise it." If sovereignty requires some confidence and moral assurance to assert, that is all the more reason to embrace and encourage it as a principle. A world of sovereign states will never be a perfect world. But a constitutional government at home suffers the same limitation—and it is a limitation that Americans would not readily abandon.

Sovereignty remains the likeliest path to a world in which peace can be reconciled with human freedom. Its moral claims rest, in the end, on an underlying recognition of human limitations: As the Declaration of Independence says, independent states have an "equal station among the powers of the Earth"—no earthly power can direct the whole world because no earthly power can assume the omniscience or omnipotence of God. The Creator gave human beings the capacity to disagree. That is one foundation for the right to differ—a right that is best secured in a world of sovereign states.

President Lincoln famously described the United States as "the last best hope of earth."[42] He did not mean that every nation must adopt our specific political institutions, much less that America should impose its institutions on every other nation. In speaking of the "hope of earth," he implicitly distinguished political institutions from the spiritual hopes that transcend our earthly realm. But he assumed that in political affairs, "hope" depends, in the first instance, on the preservation of national sovereignty.

The American Civil War was, in a fundamental way, fought to preserve the sovereignty of the federal government. In calling the nation to renewed effort, Lincoln spoke of the war as a struggle to assure that "government of the people, by the people, for the people shall not perish from the earth." The thought depends on the initial premise that "the people" can indeed organize themselves as a distinct political community. Two years before he rose to address the crowd at Gettysburg, Lincoln himself formulated the legal claim of the Union as "a sovereignty," which he defined as "a political community, without a political superior."[43] Not every country may aspire to constitutional democracy as Americans conceive it. But Americans will never be alone in thinking that "the hope of earth" requires that sovereign political communities can continue to retain their sovereignty.

Perhaps the most momentous international political question of the coming decades is whether Europeans can be content with this hope.

2

Sovereignty Despite
Atlantic Community

It is one thing to say that the world would be better off with sovereign states. But by its very nature, sovereignty is not something that can be imposed on states. Standard treatises on international law might list prerogatives and characteristics of sovereignty, but no state is obliged to assert them all. Some states are not capable of doing so. At the end of the eighteenth century, neighboring empires annexed all the territory of Poland, extinguishing all claim to Polish sovereignty. Belgium retained control of its own territory in the nineteenth century by committing itself to a strict policy of neutrality—in other words, by forswearing its sovereign right to make alliances. Some states, like the princely states of India, were regarded as so beholden to a particular "protecting power" that others regarded them as "protectorates" rather than sovereign states—though British courts continued to acknowledge the "sovereign immunity" of Indian rajahs when their creditors or jilted lovers tried to sue them in London.[1]

And what are we to make of the dominions in the British Empire? By the end of the nineteenth century, Canada and Australia, for example, were entirely self-governing federations, but they continued until 1931 to acknowledge British supremacy in their foreign and defense affairs.[2] Even then, they retained the same monarch—literally, in the traditional phrasing, the same "sovereign"—as the United Kingdom. In 1919, American critics of the League of Nations protested that if British dominions were given separate seats in the League, the United States should receive a comparable number of seats—but they did not insist that the dominions must cut their ties to the mother country.[3]

From its inception, the United States has been particularly cautious about international commitments. It renounced all ties to Britain at the time of the Revolution and has been quite insistent in rejecting any sort of "external association" that might shadow its own independence.[4] Americans have seen their own national Constitution as defining the political community whose independence they have been so eager to defend.

But the United States has not been very dogmatic about how other states should define their sovereignty, as long as they did not seek to impose their political claims on Americans. Long after the Canadian provinces joined in a common confederation, the United States cheerfully continued to negotiate border agreements with Britain, as Canadian constitutional practice still required until 1931.[5]

Fascist aggression in Europe provoked a very different attitude. After the defeat of the Fascist powers in World War II, fear of Soviet aggression again stirred American defenses. The United States tried, unsuccessfully, to deny UN seats to Soviet-controlled governments in Eastern Europe, and continued throughout the Cold War to speak of Communist satellites as "captive nations."[6] But during the same era, America took a benevolent stance toward the efforts of nations in Western Europe to erect treaty structures to enhance "economic integration" among themselves.

With the collapse of previous threats, the United States now finds itself challenged by a different European project—one that seems more seductive because it is not backed by force of arms. As in previous efforts to organize the world according to ideological formulas, however, the European Union regards American independence as an unacceptable obstacle. Europeans have learned to live with supranational governance. By what right, they ask, do Americans reject such European projects as the International Criminal Court and the treaty on global warming?

Euro-governance is a far less immediate and disturbing threat than Communism or Fascism or previous forms of European imperialism were. But it is bound to be a source of continuing friction. The United States, given its character, cannot readily subscribe to the latest European schemes. The European Union, given its own character, can hardly avoid efforts to export its peculiar style of "governance." In that sense, Euro-governance poses a direct challenge to American ideas of constitutional government and national sovereignty.

Constitutional Obligations: Anchors or Ornaments?

The American position goes back to the founding of the United States. It turns, in a way, on what was founded. At the Philadelphia Convention in 1787, those who argued for a strong national government insisted that the thirteen states already constituted one nation. They had declared independence together, they had fought the War of Independence together, they had represented themselves to the world—through diplomatic endeavors and treaties—as one nation. The argument for the new Constitution was that, under the loose "confederation" which the thirteen states initially organized, the United States could not reliably function as one nation. The new Constitution would establish an effective national government for what the Declaration of Independence had already described as "one people."[7]

The text of the Constitution certainly went far toward nailing down the vision of those who thought this way. According to the Preamble, it is "We the People"—a single collective entity—who "ordain" the Constitution. Article I sets out powers for a national government which, as its advocates insisted, would be "sovereign."[8] Article VI expressly provides that the Constitution, itself, "shall "be the supreme law of the land." The same provision stipulates that "the Judges in every State [of the United States] shall be bound thereby, any Thing in the Constitution or Law of any State to the Contrary notwithstanding." So states cannot enforce their own law, even in their own courts, when it conflicts with federal law. The states are subordinate to federal law in the most fundamental aspect of authority—the ability to make and enforce their own law. Similarly, states are prohibited from maintaining standing armies or navies, making treaties with foreign powers, or exercising other traditional powers of sovereign entities.

What made this claim to supremacy acceptable to most Americans was the concomitant assurance that the federal government itself would be bound by constitutional limits. Limiting federal authority to particular enumerated powers, set down in Article I, Section 8, was one way of making supremacy seem less fearful. Lodging legislative power in a bicameral legislature, checked in turn by an independent executive and independent courts, was another assurance. Skeptics demanded still more assurances—and they got them. The first ten amendments to the Constitution, proposed by the very first Congress, were quickly ratified as the Bill of Rights.

Constitutional limitations on federal authority can only be secure, however, if the Constitution remains the highest legal authority. Everyone sees the point in regard to federal statutes or executive actions: If they can circumvent the Constitution and still claim binding force, then the Constitution is not a reliable limitation on federal power. So the Supreme Court has always insisted that federal legislation and executive action must bow to the Constitution.

The same reasoning was assumed to apply to treaties. Jefferson put the argument most succinctly: "Our peculiar security is the possession of a written Constitution. Let us not make it a blank paper by construction. I say the same as to the opinion of those who consider the grant of the treaty making power as boundless. If it is, then we have no Constitution."[9] The point was affirmed by such eminent authorities as Supreme Court Justice Joseph Story, in his *Commentaries on the Constitution*.[10] It was reaffirmed, time and again, by the Supreme Court: a treaty in violation of the Constitution must be void.[11]

The point is easiest to see in relation to the Bill of Rights. A treaty that, for example, required the United States to limit the free speech rights of Americans would not be constitutional. Accordingly, when the Senate ratified the International Covenant on Civil and Political Rights, it attached a formal reservation disclaiming any intention to abide by the requirements in that treaty to suppress free speech.[12]

In deference to such concerns, American presidents have generally refrained from signing any treaty whose constitutional validity might be questioned. The Senate has been even more reluctant to ratify treaties shadowed by constitutional doubts. In rare cases where international commitments have violated constitutional guarantees, however, the Supreme Court has insisted that the Constitution must take priority. In the most famous case, *Reid v. Covert*, the Court held that American civilians could not be subject to military justice, in circumvention of guarantees in the Bill of Rights, even though they were living on U.S. military bases (as dependents of uniformed personnel), and international agreements authorized trial by American military authorities in these circumstances. The Constitution, the Court insisted, must take precedence over any international agreement: "No agreement with a foreign nation can confer power on the Congress, or on any other branch of the Government, which is free from the restraints of the Constitution."[13]

The International Criminal Court raises precisely the same constitutional concerns. If ratified, it would subject American citizens to trial before a foreign tribunal that does not provide a jury or a number of other procedural protections guaranteed by the Bill of Rights.[14] Unlike ordinary extraditions to foreign legal systems, moreover, the ICC would claim jurisdiction over actions taken by Americans on American soil. Policymakers at the Pentagon, for example, could be liable for prosecution because they planned and ordered an air strike which the ICC's prosecutor regarded as a "war crime," even though the United States government took a different view.

If this sort of arrangement is accepted for what foreigners regard as "war crimes," then it can be applied to a range of other offenses. Early proposals for an international criminal court indeed focused on providing a forum for the trial of drug smugglers. If the United States government could extradite Americans to stand trial in a foreign tribunal, even for offenses committed in the United States, adherence to the guarantees in the Bill of Rights would be merely one of several legal options for the federal government. Either the government could abide by the procedural guarantees in the Bill of Rights, with all the difficulties that entails for prosecutors, or it could simply transfer Americans to foreign tribunals with fewer scruples and more "efficiency" when it comes to securing conviction.

The Bill of Rights is not the only part of the Constitution, however, that must constrain American treaty commitments. It has also been held, from the earliest period of American history, that a treaty cannot alter the governing arrangements set down in the Constitution. So, for example, the Constitution prescribes that treaties will be negotiated by the president and then ratified by the Senate. The requirement for a two-thirds majority in the Senate assures that treaties will rarely be ratified without broad agreement on their implications. Commentators have long insisted that a treaty cannot constitutionally delegate this treaty-making power to an international body.[15] If an international body could make binding regulations on its own, the Constitution's treaty-making power would be short-circuited, creating an independent body generating new law for the United States without going through the constitutionally prescribed process.

So, when the charter of the International Labour Organization was under negotiation in 1919, the American delegation insisted that the

United States could not, given its own constitutional obligations, adhere to a structure that gave the organization power to impose particular standards.[16] Each labor standard proposed by the ILO would have to be submitted to the Senate as a separate treaty. The United States eventually joined the ILO—and then ratified only a handful of the two hundred conventions the ILO proposed over the next eighty years. Similarly, the Reagan administration rejected the UN Convention on the Law of the Sea, and one of its objections was that, by delegating rule-making power to an international regulatory "authority" (for regulating seabed mining in international waters), the treaty would circumvent the constitutionally prescribed procedure for making treaties.[17]

The same arguments have arisen in relation to the Kyoto Protocol. It would require countries to delegate vast powers to specialized regulatory agencies to implement the general scheme set out in the treaty. In ratifying the treaty, the Senate would endorse a general set of aims and then allow international agencies to spell out what they actually entailed for the United States and other parties.[18] Nor would these be minor matters of detail. The policy discretion left to these agencies could, depending on how they decided, impose hundreds of billions of dollars in additional costs for the United States (while, in some cases, easing comparable burdens on other signatories on the same grand scale).

Constitutional objections to treaties are invariably entangled, of course, with other objections—as is true, as well, in most constitutional debates about domestic matters. As in domestic debates, constitutional challenges to international commitments may lie dormant for some period, and then suddenly reemerge with renewed force when the political context has changed. Questions about presidential war powers did not raise great passion in the late nineteenth century, when presidents launched a number of small military actions without congressional approval. In 1919, however, a major argument against the League of Nations was that it might commit the United States to war without congressional approval.[19] The argument was carefully evaded in 1945. Only a few years later, the Truman administration actually claimed that UN Security Council authorization was sufficient authority to take the United States to war in Korea, even without formal approval from Congress. By the early 1970s, however, the undeclared war in Vietnam raised all the old concerns again.

At the end of the Vietnam War, Congress passed the War Powers Act in an attempt to reaffirm limits on presidential war making. Among other things, this measure stipulated that no authorization from an international body could substitute for the constitutional authority of Congress, itself, to declare war.[20] There is much dispute about whether the War Powers Act is constitutional, particularly in its effort to subject military actions already in progress to an automatic congressional veto mechanism. But in its general approach, the legislation reflects—and indeed purports merely to clarify—wider constitutional standards already and separately binding on the executive. The weight of scholarly opinion now seems to embrace the doctrine that, whatever the president's independent constitutional authority as commander in chief, an authorization from an international body does not add to it.[21]

A treaty may commit the United States to pay certain funds, as, for example, in exchange for territory or basing rights. But ratifying the treaty does not authorize the president to withdraw money from the treasury without a separate and distinct appropriation. By itself, ratification of such a treaty cannot override the constitutional requirement that money may only be expended pursuant to appropriations agreed upon by the House and the Senate. So a promise to an ally may obligate the United States to go to war under certain circumstances, but a specific war does not become lawful without congressional approval.[22] Agreement to uphold some wider international peacekeeping scheme would not confer any additional power on the president, either.

What is true for the decision to commit to war would seem to be equally true for the deployment of troops before or even during hostilities. If the president can simply "loan" troops to foreign governments or to international authorities, then the president can no longer be responsible for the conduct of those troops—a condition that would circumvent the constitutional provision assigning responsibility to the president as commander in chief. It is doubtful that even congressional legislation can alter this allocation of governing responsibility in the Constitution. The Supreme Court has held that Congress cannot reassign implementing duties from the federal executive to state governments, lest this confuse lines of accountability set down in the federal Constitution.[23] It is very hard to imagine that the Constitution, while prohibiting delegations of implementing authority to state officials in the United States, actually permits such delegations to foreign governments or international authorities. Even more bizarre is the notion that, while the Constitution prohibits the delegation of routine regulatory tasks to state officials, it allows the president to delegate control of American troops—that is, delegate the president's own authority as commander in chief—to foreign governments or to international organizations. Actual practice follows this logic: No president has agreed to place U.S. troops under foreign command, except in carefully circumscribed tactical situations.[24]

There are other ways in which the Constitution limits what the government can do. To provide an exhaustive catalog of such limits might require a small treatise. But at least one further implication of traditional constitutional doctrine deserves notice here. If the Constitution imposes definite limits on treaties, it must also impose even more severe limits on international commitments that arise not from treaties but merely from "customary law."

The framers of the Constitution certainly recognized customary international law. The Constitution itself makes provision for Congress to "define and punish offenses against the law of nations"—and the phrase refers precisely to those standards generally agreed upon by "civilized nations," as evidenced by customary practice rather than formal treaties. From the outset, federal courts were thought to have jurisdiction to apply such customary practice, even when it was not directly "defined" by congressional enactment or treaty. But until quite recently, customary practice meant the practice of states in dealings with each other. Now many commentators insist there is a "customary international law of human rights" determining how states must deal with their own citizens, the evidence for which can be gleaned from resolutions of the UN General Assembly and other international forums.[25] If this can be law, enforced by federal courts, then traditional limits on the treaty power again seem to be at risk, along with constitutional checks and balances.

As some advocates see it, the customary international law of human rights can reach where treaties do not. So, for example, the United States can be bound by provisions of treaties it has refused to ratify, because the relevant provisions have already entered into "customary law."[26] This amounts to a wholesale delegation of lawmaking power to federal courts—or to federal courts working in association with foreign governments and international forums—in a way that goes beyond any claims about judicial activism under existing laws. It is doubtful this can be constitutionally acceptable, either. Certainly, it could not be carried very far before raising immense controversy.

Not all American commentators agree on the precise contour of constitutional limitations when it comes to international commitments, just as not all commentators (or Supreme Court justices) agree on the precise details of constitutional limitations that apply at home. But hardly anyone holds that the Constitution imposes no limits. If it imposes any limits, it can only do so because it is supreme law, taking priority even over international commitments that others may regard as binding or obligatory under international law.

This notion of constitutional supremacy as the underlying guarantee of constitutional limits on government may seem obvious to Americans. It does not seem at all obvious to contemporary Europeans, however. The kinds of constitutional arguments that have genuine weight in the United States do not have anything like the same force in European thinking.

Are there constitutional concerns about the ICC? Constitutional courts in Germany, France, and Portugal held, in separate rulings, that the ICC treaty would conflict with guarantees in their national constitutions. All three governments resolved the problem by amending their national constitutions. In contrast, even advocates of the ICC in the United States do not propose a constitutional amendment to resolve the doubts about the court's constitutionality. It would be unthinkable to resolve a conflict with the Bill of Rights by amending these protections out of the Constitution.

Are there problems with delegating governing authority to external bodies, which are not bound by the Constitution? At the heart of the European governing scheme is a set of very broad delegations of regulatory power to the European Commission. The commission has been empowered, under successive treaties of the European Community (and, since 1992, of the European Union), to make regulations that enter directly into the domestic law of member states. The commission is an independent bureaucracy whose commissioners are selected by secret negotiations among member states.

What if the commission gets out of control? Not to worry. The 1957 Treaty of Rome, which established it, also established a European Court of Justice to hear challenges to the legality of commission directives. Within its first decade, the ECJ determined that these directives must take priority over national laws—even national laws enacted subsequent to the regulatory directive of the commission; or even in response to it.[27] The Treaty of Rome said nothing about the supremacy of European law over national law. No one could have known that in ratifying the Treaty of Rome, each member state was, in effect, agreeing to major changes in its own constitutional form. The ECJ insisted that there was no cause for alarm because it would, on its own, safeguard human rights by requiring the commission to abide by international human rights standards. And it would do the same for member states—regardless of whether they had actually committed themselves to make international human rights standards binding in their domestic law and supreme over their own parliaments. The European Court would see to the details.[28]

The differences between American and European attitudes toward constitutional government are not merely differences over technical details. Europeans have increasingly come to embrace a notion of constitutional government that is fundamentally at odds with Americans' understanding of the concept. These are not differences over judicial doctrine, the sorts of differences that only lawyers might appreciate. Europeans are developing a whole constitutional culture in conflict with American ideas—or perhaps it would be more accurate to say that Europeans are reverting to a different constitutional culture.

Constitutional Cultures

If Americans find it hard to grasp European thinking, it is not because American constitutional thought rests on idiosyncratic American premises. The American Founders were steeped in English ideas of liberty—which is why the Constitution can embrace a common-law practice like "the writ of habeas corpus" without having to define what it is. In the ratification debates, both advocates and opponents of the Constitution made constant references to Blackstone's *Commentaries on the Laws of England*. And, almost always, Blackstone's treatise was invoked on the assumption that American practice would follow its guidance.[29] The early eighteenth-century French jurist, Baron Montesquieu, was also frequently cited for his exposition of the separation of powers—so much so that *The Federalist* refers to Montesquieu as "the oracle."[30]

Even the underlying notion of sovereignty was, as the Framers well recognized, a European idea. The first writer to give a systematic account of the concept was the sixteenth-century French jurist Jean Bodin, who in later times was often seen as a predecessor of Montesquieu. Bodin had performed diplomatic service in Elizabethan England, and his great treatise gives an account of sovereign authority that found an immediate audience in England, even among advocates of parliamentary supremacy.[31] Bodin advocated religious toleration, free trade, an independent judiciary, and the conditioning of taxation on parliamentary consent. He analyzed sovereign authority as a set of distinctive sovereign powers or attributes. Every one of Bodin's "marks" of sovereignty, as it happens, appears in the U.S. Constitution among the powers assigned to the federal government.[32] Bodin's main argument was that, when sovereign authority is firmly established, much else can be left to private choice. His treatise even admonishes, at several points, that providing security to the lives and property of citizens is the main purpose of government—a purpose required by the law of nature and the God of nature (an authority depicted in carefully nonsectarian terms). Like so much else in its reasoning, the memorable opening appeal in the American Declaration of Independence—to the "law of nature and nature's God"—seems to have been inspired by Jefferson's reading of Bodin.[33]

But the American Founders were quite aware that ideas they borrowed from European thinkers had not always prevailed in continental Europe itself. The opposite view had more often prevailed—that rulers would strengthen their claims against their own people by associating their governing authority with outside powers. At the time of America's founding, for example, the medieval Holy Roman Empire still retained a ghostly existence in Central Europe as the Holy Roman Empire of the German Nation. Prussia's impetuous and cynical king, Frederick the Great, had openly defied the empire and allied with foreign states to help him retain territorial seizures from the imperial dynasty. But even King Frederick found it convenient to pretend that Prussia remained a loyal adherent to the empire.

The Federalist gave special attention to the constitutional arrangements of the German Empire, which it described in a tone of visceral disgust: "The fundamental principle on which it rests, that the empire is a community of sovereigns . . . renders the empire a nerveless body, incapable of regulating its own members, insecure against external dangers, and agitated with unceasing fermentation in its bowels."[34] *The Federalist* explains that this ramshackle arrangement had "grown" from the "feudal system" which had, even in medieval times, "many of the important features of a confederacy." What sustained the "feudal anarchy" of medieval politics, according to *The Federalist*, was that "nobles and barons," while defying their nominal overlords, still disdained to enlist the support of "the common people"[35]—evidently because nobles preferred to conceive their own claims to rule as conferred from above or outside, and not in any way dependent on local consent.

The Founders retained sufficient concern about such attitudes that they inserted specific safeguards against them in the Constitution. Article I, which sets out the main lines of jurisdiction for federal authority, also includes an express prohibition against allowing American officeholders to accept "patents of nobility" or any other "title" or "emolument" from a foreign prince without the consent of Congress. Article VI requires all federal and state officeholders to swear an "oath" to "support the Constitution"—and then immediately proceeds to prohibit any separate "religious test" for office. Governing authority comes from the established constitutional structure for the American people, and not from outside.

And federal authority, to function effectively, cannot itself be something outside, merely superimposed on state governments. A mere league of states or confederacy, as the central paper of *The Federalist* points out, rests on a treaty among states and can be broken whenever some states regard others as having broken their faith.[36] To maintain its authority, the "government of the Union . . . must be able to address itself directly to the hopes and fears of individuals."[37] *The Federalist* famously argued that "faction" was inevitable in a republic, but it defined "faction" as a grouping "adverse to the permanent and aggregate interests of the community," presupposing a "community" which would have "permanent and aggregate interests."[38]

In effect, the federal Constitution constituted that community—in some ways, quite literally. The Constitution provides that its own terms can be amended when three-quarters of the state legislatures agree to a proposed amendment. But Article VII stipulated that the Constitution would initially go into effect only for those states that ratified it. Those that failed to ratify would, as *The Federalist* conceded, remain outside the United States.[39] Decades later, when eleven Southern states sought to secede from the Union, the majority of Americans rallied to federal authority and returned the secessionist states to the United States by force of arms. Thereafter, the Fourteenth Amendment to the Constitution defined who would be a citizen, clarifying that every state would be bound to accord state citizenship to permanent residents who obtained national citizenship, so that national citizenship would be decisive. Congress implemented the constitutional provisions for "naturalization" by requiring that immigrants could only attain citizenship by renouncing all allegiance to any foreign sovereign and swearing to "support and defend the Constitution and the laws of the United States, against all enemies, foreign and domestic. . . ."[40] Only one crime is defined in the Constitution itself—"treason"—and it is defined precisely in terms of "adhering to enemies, giving them aid and comfort."[41]

The idea that the United States might have "foreign enemies" was a large part of the argument for the Constitution in 1787. Even if America sought to withdraw from European disputes, it would need a national government with adequate resources—rather than an unreliable confederation—to defend its independence: "The rights of neutrality will only be respected when they are defended by an adequate power. A nation, despicable by its weakness, forfeits even the privilege of being neutral."[42]

From the outset, there was comparable concern about domestic disloyalty, stirred by foreign intrigue. President Washington urged the point in his Farewell Address: "Against the insidious wiles of foreign influence (I conjure you to believe me, fellow citizens) the jealousy of a free people ought to be *constantly* awake [original emphasis], since history and experience prove that foreign influence is one of the most baneful foes of republican government."[43] In the nineteenth century, much suspicion focused on Catholics. Misgivings were not grounded in theological objections, since closely parallel rituals and doctrines of the Episcopal Church passed without protest. But many Americans feared that Roman Catholic priests and bishops would mobilize their parishioners to embrace political programs laid down in Rome, at a time when the Vatican still refused to embrace modern liberal ideas.[44] In the twentieth century, populists and socialists of various stripes were largely tolerated in American politics, but Communists aroused particular loathing on the assumption that they took their direction from Moscow.

The premise has always been that the security of American rights rests on the willingness of Americans to constitute one political community, governed by the Constitution as "supreme law of the land." To most Americans, constitutional supremacy goes naturally in a package with individual rights and national sovereignty.

These ideas had not prevailed in Europe in the time of the American Founders; they did not always have great success there in later times either. As Alexander Hamilton and other acute American observers predicted, the initial constitutional enthusiasms of revolutionaries in France only paved the way for a more complete tyranny.[45] And the new tyranny established in France was spread, by force of arms and assiduous propaganda, to surrounding nations. Even in these new circumstances, rulers still sought to entrench their governing claims by associating them with some higher authority outside.

Napoleon Bonaparte ordered the dissolution of the Holy Roman Empire as a feudal anachronism—but then had himself crowned as "emperor" in a papal ceremony deliberately echoing the rituals of the medieval empire. The Hapsburg emperor in Vienna renounced his claim to be a holy or a Roman emperor, but then married his daughter to the new emperor in Paris. Bonaparte brothers placed on thrones throughout Europe did not need to secure proper in-laws to ground their local authority.

After Napoleon's defeat, the Romanov and Hapsburg empires recruited the restored kings of France and Prussia into a "Holy Alliance," which proclaimed its shared determination to suppress popular rebellions or liberal constitutions anywhere in Europe. Decades later, the Prussian Chancellor Otto von Bismarck succeeded in conquering or cowing neighboring states into associating themselves with a new empire (or "Reich," as the medieval empire was known to Germans). There would now be a Prussian emperor, but with vassal princes in Bavaria and Saxony and other ancient states, left with their own armies and their own control over local citizens. It was, as before, an alliance of princes against peoples.

But even peoples in Europe were not always anxious for what English-speaking countries came to understand as liberty and democracy. When the empires of the Hapsburgs and the Romanovs and the Prussian Hohenzollerns collapsed at the end of the First World War, successor states did not do well in maintaining constitutional government. Italians acquiesced to a bloodless seizure of power by Mussolini's Fascist Party, promising a higher unity based on the suppression of economic competition and personal liberty. Germans pined for a restoration of empire and voted themselves a brutal government, promising a Third Reich that would last a thousand years, like its medieval predecessor (the Holy Roman Empire). After its defeat in 1940, the National Assembly of the French Republic voted dictatorial powers to an aging hero of the First World War and proceeded to transform France into a Fascist state.[46]

German leaders spoke of reviving a higher unity among the peoples of Europe by suppressing dangerous competition between them, as between people within each state. The vision inspired quite willing and extensive collaboration in the early years of the war. French police duly cooperated in the roundup of non-Aryans, as did their police counterparts in Belgium and the Netherlands. Genocide proved as compatible with European traditions as collaboration with a supranational empire. It was almost logical: Since nationality could not be defined in terms of constitutional structures, it was left to be defined by "race"—in which Europeans imagined themselves to have bloodties and found it logical to "deport" those of "impure blood." Among other things, collaboration in this European project allowed people from small states, like Belgium and the Netherlands, to escape the burden of defending themselves while still maintaining an association with their conquerors. Many people in Western Europe eagerly embraced the new transnational scheme.[47]

In 1941, Roosevelt and Churchill tried to stir resistance by affirming their "wish to see sovereign rights and self-government restored to those who have been forcibly deprived of them."[48] There was not much response from Western Europe.[49] The attempt to reorganize Europe by "race" instead of by nation-states was finally ended by the victory of Anglo-American forces in the West. Under the Marshall Plan, the United States provided massive financial assistance to revive economic activity in Western Europe. Democracy was given a new chance, west of the Iron Curtain.

But millions of Europeans did not see their own governments as reliable guarantors of their rights—or still did not care much for liberal ideas about rights. Outside of Britain, the largest postwar parties were Catholic parties, which promised some vague sort of supranational understanding among people of common faith. Their most popular rivals were Socialist or Communist parties, that sought supranational solidarity by class.[50]

If European voters did not trust their own governments, their own governments did not entirely trust their national electorates. Less than a decade after the defeat of the German New Order, prominent figures in Western Europe were recycling German wartime slogans about the need to put aside "conflict" and "selfishness"and find a new "harmony."

A "confederation of European nations would [assure] collaboration in absolute harmony" and "would rule out the possibility of any internal war in Europe." Any of the architects of postwar European "integration" might have said it; Hitler's Foreign Minister Joachim von Ribbentrop happened to say it first, in an appeal for French collaboration with Germany in 1942.[51] Building on a "European customs union and a free European market," a European "Economic Council" would seek "the standardisation and improvement of employment and social security, as well as long-term production planning in the field of industry, agriculture and forestry," as a wartime German planning document asserted.[52]

These antecedents of "the European idea" did not repel European statesmen in the aftermath of the war. Many prominent figures in postwar European governments, including some of the leading figures in founding the postwar "European Community," had spoken quite respectfully of Germany's National Socialist system in the 1930s. Paul-Henri Spaak, for example, the Dutch premier who launched plans for the Common Market with the so-called "Spaak Report" in 1956, had spoken twenty years earlier of "Hitler's magnificent achievements" and described himself as a "national socialist." Robert Schumann, founder of the Coal and Steel Community, the precursor of the Common Market, had taken a direct role in collaborating with German plans for a New Europe during the war.[53] In the aftermath of the war, European leaders dreamed of a new Europe that would be quite different from the discredited past—and yet, in basic ways, eerily familiar.

Postmodern Syndromes

When first proposed in 1787, the new Constitution for the United States seemed a considerable innovation compared with the scheme of confederation adopted during the Revolution. Now the federal government would have direct powers of taxation and legislation, enforced by federal courts and a federal executive—none of which had previously existed. *The Federalist* sought to persuade Americans that the new scheme was a logical extension of previous practice: "To all general purposes, we have uniformly been one people. . . . As a nation we have made peace and war; as a nation we have vanquished our common enemies; as a nation we have formed alliances and made treaties . . . with foreign states."[54]

By the late 1940s, Europeans also had much common experience in war—but they had not always been on the same side. Even France, having spent four years in collaboration with Germany, subsequently thought of itself as among those powers always resisting Germany (which it did, nominally, for the last nine months of the war, as it had in the first nine months). By the late 1940s, it was obvious that Western European nations might all share the same vulnerability to Soviet aggression. That fact did not make them eager to share governing authority in matters of national defense.

General Dwight D. Eisenhower, as supreme commander of NATO in 1951, urged European defense planners to find ways of "rearming Germans without rearming Germany." Plans for a European Defense Community (EDC), with armies under joint command, were pressed forward for some years and then resolutely rejected by the French National Assembly as an intolerable threat to French sovereignty.[55] The French and others were content to see constraints imposed on West Germany but did not want to accept comparable constraints on themselves. Under American prodding, West Germany was then allowed to rebuild its own national defense forces—but with the understanding that these forces would be tightly coordinated with NATO, and with a sizable American force still maintained in Germany itself.

In practice, Western Europeans came to rely on the United States to provide security against Soviet aggression as well as any risk of German military resurgence. Much ordinary political deliberation about national defense—as well as much of the financial burden—was left to American leadership within NATO. By the mid-1960s, French President Charles de Gaulle protested that NATO was undermining the independence of European states and withdrew France from the military side of the alliance. No other NATO state followed this example. It is doubtful that even de Gaulle would have risked this assertion of independence if he had seriously thought that West Germany might follow the French example.

From the beginning, therefore—if we set aside the precedents from the era of Nazi collaboration—"Europe" had a peculiar political origin. It did not begin by grappling with the challenges of security or defense. Instead, European integration proceeded on two different levels, both conveniently abstracted from the hard policy decisions of traditional statecraft. One was moral or inspirational, and the other mind-numbingly technical.

The moral theme began with the founding of the Council of Europe in 1949 as a forum to articulate common values of European democracies. The council proceeded to establish a European Convention on Human Rights (ECHR), affirming shared devotion to freedom of religion, freedom of speech, freedom from discrimination, due process in the administration of criminal justice, and so on. The idea was to proclaim a shared opposition to the new forms of tyranny emerging on the far side of the Iron Curtain in Central and Eastern Europe. The convention was also supposed to lay to rest the demons of Fascism in Western Europe, where monstrous crimes had recently been committed with the assistance of governmental authorities in France, Italy, Belgium, and the Netherlands—and of course, in Germany, the principal sponsor of these crimes. Europeans would now reassure each other—and keep reminding Germans—that they were all opposed to such evils. Who could object to such good intentions? Britain, historically quite wary of continental commitments, joined as readily as any other state. There was scarcely any public debate in Britain when it ratified the European Convention on Human Rights in 1951.[56]

Britain initially held itself aloof from the more technical—and substantial—arrangements forged by the European Coal and Steel Community in 1953. The official purpose was to ensure that iron and coal deposits on different sides of the Rhine Valley would be equitably shared. From the beginning, it was said that such cooperation would remove one cause of traditional hostility between France and Germany and, together with Italy and the Benelux countries (Belgium, Netherlands, Luxembourg), would help build cooperation and trust in Western Europe. The Coal and Steel Community then became the model for the European Economic Community (Common Market), agreed to by the same six countries in 1958.

Perhaps these institutions did help to build trust among the nations involved. Certainly they helped to reduce trade barriers across European borders. But a major impetus for the effort was to insulate governments against political resistance to the lowering of trade barriers. So the Coal and Steel Community sought to reduce barriers to imports in a gradual way, while trying to ensure that particular mines or steel plants would not be hurt too badly by new competitive pressures.[57] The Common Market implemented a reduction in tariffs and border controls on agricultural products, while maintaining a complex system of price supports to protect farmers against excessive competition. Governments could indicate their priorities in regular meetings of relevant ministers from national cabinets, but day-to-day policy was left to a commission, which was supposed to be applying technical expertise to the challenges of "economic integration."

The term itself had no agreed meaning among economists.[58] It implied, however, that eliminating tariffs and subsidies was not sufficient to achieve the ultimate goal of "integration"; some larger, more active scheme of bureaucratic management would be required. So the European Commission gained more and more regulatory powers over more and more aspects of European economic activity over the ensuing decades. Meanwhile, the General Agreement on Tariffs and Trade—the predecessor to the World Trade Organization—focused almost entirely on reducing tariffs and subsidies by mutual agreement and required almost nothing in the way of a permanent staff to administer.

The two strands of the European project began to come together in the 1970s. The Common Market, like the Coal and Steel Community before it, was set up with a separate court to ensure that the bureaucrats in the commission stayed within the terms of the Treaty of Rome. Within less than a decade, the European Court of Justice had converted this arrangement into a system by which private citizens could enforce provisions of the treaty—and then regulations promulgated by the commission—against their own governments.[59] The ECJ insisted that such regulations must take priority even over contrary enactments of national parliaments. By the early 1970s, the ECJ was insisting that the commission's bureaucratic directives must take priority even over contrary rulings of national constitutional courts. To quiet protests that the commission would be operating without any serious constitutional constraints, the ECJ then announced it would improvise its own "European" safeguards for individual rights.[60]

One source of such safeguards, according to the ECJ, would be the European Convention on Human Rights. By the 1960s, the ECHR had acquired its own free-standing court, but its rulings were not directly binding in the domestic law of member states. The ECJ did not claim it would enforce every provision of the ECHR, nor even be bound by every ruling of the Human Rights Court. But once linked to the enforcement mechanisms of the Economic Community, the Human Rights Court acquired a new level of self-confidence. By the 1980s, it was challenging British police and military practices directed at terrorism in North Ireland. By the 1990s, it was insisting that Ireland must reform its law on abortion, that Britain must admit homosexuals into its armed forces, that school discipline in Britain must never include physical punishment, and so on.[61]

Quite a lot of policymaking authority had thus gravitated to authorities at the European level. But other institutions associated with normal states did not develop in parallel. Councils of ministers from member states were authorized to make decisions by qualified majorities, with weighted voting on some issues to reflect demographic differences among the member states. But the council decisions were negotiated in secret meetings, resembling diplomatic gatherings more than legislative sessions. Leaders of national governments took turns for six months, on a regular schedule of rotation, in conducting the "presidency"—essentially a power to host high-level summits.

An embryonic "assembly," composed of delegates from national parliaments and with a merely consultative or advisory role, developed by stages into a directly elected "European Parliament," with veto power over budgets and major regulations. But the Parliament can neither initiate legislation nor determine who will serve as commissioners or ministers in the council. Elections for the European Parliament have far lower turnout than national parliamentary elections within the member states.[62] The pattern is hardly surprising. Most voters can see that it makes some difference whether their country is governed by parties of the right or the left. No one can see that it makes any difference which party coalitions happen to hold the majority of seats in the European Parliament.

As a practical matter, most governing authority in Europe remains with bureaucrats and judges. No member state in the European Union (EU) has anything like this system for its own government. The problem is not just that it seems undemocratic—though that has been a frequent complaint against the EU. The problem is that it is systematically resistant to free political debate. Major innovations, like the introduction of a common currency, are packaged with other treaty revisions negotiated among the national governments. National parliaments are told that the whole package must be accepted for the sake of "Europe."

The very existence of the EU points away from inquiry into what is good for the political community. What is the relevant political community in Europe? Is it the members of the Council of Europe, now extended to forty-five countries reaching into Eastern Europe, including Albania and Ukraine? Is it merely the members of the EU? Even this smaller community had expanded to include fifteen members by the early 1990s, stretching from Portugal to Finland, from Ireland to Greece, and agreements for expansion will nearly double the number of members, as new states in Central and Eastern Europe and the Mediterranean region take their places in the European Union in 2004.

To speak of "common constitutional traditions"of these very diverse nations, as the ECJ does, is to escape from legal reasoning based on concrete provisions to a realm of spiritual contemplation regarding transcendent values that don't have to be concrete, don't have to be embodied in a particular tradition, don't have to be expressed in explicit acts or standards. In the end, if "Europe" has common standards, there is no reason to limit them to Europe, no reason not to see them as, after all, universal. What is "common" to Ireland and Greece—or, in the newly expanded EU, to Latvia and Cyprus—might as well be considered common to humanity. So the European Union has become a great champion of international human rights standards at the United Nations. The ECJ then purports to find guidance for concrete decisions in the vagaries of international human rights standards, as well as particular European agreements. And, of course, the EU has become a great champion of the

International Criminal Court, which may force European notions of justice on the world at large.

Something similar has occurred on the technical side of European governance. In the 1980s, the European Commission extended its regulatory reach into environmental policy and various areas of social policy, such as sex discrimination.[63] It made perfect sense that, just as European policy sought to compensate for the lowering of tariffs with new protective standards, so it would compensate for new economic burdens such as costly environmental controls by insisting that all trade partners had to follow broadly similar approaches. Germany, in particular, which was most ambitious for new environmental controls, wanted to ensure that the resulting burdens on its industry would not provide a competitive advantage to producers in other European states. So the European Commission gradually extended German standards to the rest of Europe.

In the meantime, however, the European market as a whole was becoming more exposed to competition from outside Europe. Europeans might react by putting up tariff walls, except that European states also wanted to export to other parts of the world. European states, bargaining as a bloc, participated in larger efforts to dismantle trade barriers worldwide. So the European Commission became an advocate for international environmental treaties and international trade standards that would allow something like the European compromise to be extended into the world at large—free trade, on condition that trade partners agreed to German or European standards for production. The Maastricht Treaty gave the European Commission the authority to participate directly in international environmental negotiations and make commitments for the member states, as it had already become trade negotiator for them. As it was already becoming a booster for international human rights standards, the European Union thus became a special champion for international governance in other fields.[64]

Not quite a state in itself, but assuming control over more and more activities of its member states, the European Union has been described as a "postmodern construction."[65] Other factors have reinforced its peculiar trajectory. At the center of a normal democracy, the parliament or legislature exercises considerable authority as the representative of its electorate. At the center of the European Union is a certain hollowness—as its "citizens" are not quite prepared to be governed by a parliamentary majority that might be drawn entirely from outside states.

Further, a normal state, at moments of crisis such as war or national emergency, looks to a single leader who can rally support for steps necessary to save the nation. Europeans have been unwilling to invest such authority in a single leader, because they are not quite sure they want to agree on a common approach to save Europe.[66] So Europeans have strong political incentives to believe that a crisis can never emerge: with no troops of its own, Europe finds it hard to confront security challenges that might require decisive action.

The run-up to the war on Iraq showed the result. Despite treaty provisions requiring that no state undermine the "common foreign and security policy" of the European Union, Germany immediately announced its opposition to a war against Iraq. France sided with Germany. Most other governments sided with EU member Britain and NATO ally America in support of the war, provoking bitter reproaches from French and German leaders. In a normal democracy, the turmoil might be settled at the next election. But nothing in the European Union is supposed to be settled by mere elections.

The inability of the EU's governing structure to reach decisive choices is one sign that "Europe" is not, at its core, a genuine political community. In fact, it is not easy to specify who or what "Europe" really embraces. It can keep expanding, because the electorate does not matter all that much. On the other hand, the moral authority supplied by elections is lacking. Increasingly, European bureaucrats and courts have looked to alternate sources of legitimacy.

One alternative has been to seek engagement and approval from nongovernmental organizations (NGOs). While the ECJ has given wide access to legal claims launched by NGOs, the European Commission provides them with extensive patronage in other ways. Environmental NGOs have been included in international delegations by EU representatives to lend enthusiasm and moral support. Human rights organizations have also been brought along to international conferences on relevant subjects, and European governments have become great champions of such conferences, in which NGOs usually play the most prominent roles. The EU allocates vast sums to subsidizing these organizations, which are not accountable to any particular electorate but tout their lack of responsibility as proof of their good intentions.[67] They are postmodern citizens of this postmodern construction.

Nationalist reactions are always a possibility. The European Union works hard to discourage nationalist feeling, however, by sponsoring regional and separatist identities within member states. Through special grants and regulatory concessions to recognized "regions," the EU provides reinforcement to Scottish sentiment in Britain, Basque sentiment in Spain—and a different sentiment for German speakers living beyond the boundaries of postwar Germany.

A more serious problem for national identification comes from immigrants. Until the end of the 1990s, German law, guided by ancestry criteria, withheld citizenship from longtime immigrants and even from children and grandchildren of "guest workers" who had been born on German soil. France and the low countries, despite nominally nonethnic criteria for citizenship, still experienced great difficulty in assimilating newcomers, particularly those from Muslim countries.

Part of the difficulty was economic: Highly regulated labor markets greatly restricted job creation, and immigrants experienced the highest levels of unemployment. But there may also have been a deeper problem. With so much political authority delegated to supranational bureaucrats, national identity came increasingly to be conceived in cultural or ethnic terms. If the French would always be French, even if increasingly governed from Brussels, "French" would mean something different than political participation in the French Republic.

The European Union tried to ease adjustment problems by providing special EU guarantees for immigrants not yet recognized as full citizens in their host countries. It has been called "post-national citizenship."[68] It did not assure social harmony, however. Instead, tensions have actually increased in Europe in recent years.

In the United States, assimilation of immigrants to civic allegiance is so taken for granted that almost no one considered it remarkable when, in 2003, an officer of Arab ancestry was placed in command of U.S. forces in the Central Command (by then encompassing occupation forces in Iraq). In France and neighboring countries, meanwhile, arson and bomb attacks on synagogues and street violence against Jews recurred with such frequency in the first years of the new century that the Council of Europe expressed concern. French officials insisted the problem was caused by Mideast tensions and was no reflection on France. Blaming outsiders was already a well-worn tactic for the French government. Two decades earlier, when a synagogue was bombed in Paris, France's prime minister at the time protested that disputes between Muslims and Jews should not be allowed to cause injury to "innocent Frenchmen"—by which he did not mean worshipers at the synagogue, though they happened to be, by birth and by law, citizens of France.[69]

It is not surprising that ancient hatreds have resurfaced in modern Europe. Common citizenship cannot mean very much when states are no longer organized around the idea of providing physical security to citizens— or when states are subordinated to a larger structure which is organized to serve larger and grander visions in which mere security plays no part. Meanwhile, a structure that is not trusted to exercise ultimate state power— with an army and police and criminal courts—is bound to promote the idea that actual conflict is unnecessary and unthinkable. It is bound to insist that seeming political conflicts are illusory—that everyone agrees at the highest level on universal principles, and that the details can be left to experts. It is bound to insist that government does not require parliamentary politics. It is bound to promote the notion that there is no essential difference between international conferences and legislative determinations, between international standards and national laws, between international advocacy networks and national electorates—or, finally, between government and nongovernment, all of which are bound up in the common abstract process of "governance."

The European Challenge

It would not have mattered to the outside world if Belgium and the Netherlands had at some point merged into a single state, or if Sweden and Norway had, or Portugal and Spain—combinations which have indeed existed as unified states in the past. As late as 1991, the United States supported the reunification of Germany, even while France and Britain expressed qualms about the reemergence of a Central European giant, which had given them cause for concern in the past. If all of Europe were united in a single state, it would be a formidable state, larger in population and wealth than the United States. Still, the United States might well live in harmony with a constitutional state that wanted to live in harmony with other states.

But the European Union is not even a state, let alone a constitutional state. It has acquired more and more regulatory power through a succession of treaties and agreements among ministers of member states. By 2003, a survey found that over half of the statutory standards of member states were imposed by the EU.[70] To address concerns raised by the growth of EU authority and challenges posed by the scheduled addition of a dozen new states, a constitutional convention was convened in 2002. After laboring for more than a year, it produced a five hundred page document, billed as a "constitution" which was, in fact, a new treaty. It was shelved in the fall of 2003, when the governments of Spain and Poland objected to its formula for reallocating voting rights in the Council of Ministers.

Yet even the proposed "constitution" would not have gone very far in clarifying the status of the European Union. The two things the American Founders regarded as central to a national government (as opposed to a confederation of states)—a military force of its own and a direct power of taxation—would still be absent from the European Union.[71] It would still operate in the background, relying on member states to enforce its directives, and it would still be largely unaccountable to European voters. The arrangement remains unique in the world.

But its oddness has a simple explanation: Europeans are prepared to cede vast governing power to "common" institutions, but the different peoples of Europe do not trust each other enough to organize themselves into a single state. Security is a serious matter. Tbe power to impose taxes to support retirement pensions and other benefits—that is also a serious matter, which rich states in the EU do not want to share with their less affluent neighbors. Living off the revenues of its common tariff, the EU is, in fiscal terms, a relative dwarf as modern states go—and the only one without military force or even police of its own.

For enthusiasts of this postmodern construction, the EU has squared the circle—it has learned how to coordinate without compulsion, taking over basic law-setting responsibilities from actual governments without any of the threatening aspects of state power. As it looks, in so many ways, like an international organization, the EU has become the great champion of international projects like the International Criminal Court. It is already so diverse, it can see its governance techniques as almost universal—or as an embryo of a pattern of governance that can be global. So France and Germany, the dominant states in the EU, expressed strong opposition to a war against Iraq which was not sanctioned by the universal authority of the United Nations. And public opinion in most European countries seemed to accept that this stance had nothing to do with power rivalries and everything to do with principle.[72]

But the EU is something more than a platform for moralizing. It is not simply a larger version of what Sweden was during the 1960s or what the Vatican has sometimes been in more recent times. After all, it is large enough to have major interests of its own (apart from its interest in saving mankind). French President Jacques Chirac, for example, when denouncing "American unilateralism," spoke not so much of universal standards as of the need to sustain a "multi-polar world."[73] Who might be prepared to lead the other pole?

While depending on American military spending to contend with serious security threats, Europe invests more than America in aid to developing countries—and in diplomatic initiatives to recruit developing countries into new structures of global governance. The appeal is seductive: No one is required to submit to international authority as to an actual sovereign power, but merely to coordinate, to share, to "pool" governing powers. After all, Europeans have learned to share in many ways. But for nearly fifty years, France, though among the richest EU states, has always been among the smallest net contributors to European integration in financial terms; French payments to Brussels have been largely offset by European expenditures for agricultural support programs designed to satisfy French demands.[74] Environmental and labor standards have had a way of tracking German standards. But everyone can share.

Or perhaps not quite everyone. Turkey is "alien to Europe," according to Valéry Giscard d'Estaing, former president of France and chairman of the European constitutional convention, and must never be admitted to the EU.[75] Turkey has held to the same constitution longer than most states in continental Europe. It has a record of religious toleration far better than most European states. But the majority of its people are Muslims. So Europe, which is not Christian, retains an identity as not Muslim.

Perhaps to compensate, France portrayed itself as the champion of Islamic states in the debate over the war in Iraq—as if Islamic states were a global counterpart to the EU. Even before recriminations over the war in Iraq, Christopher Patten, EU Commissioner for External Affairs, professed to see a new spirit of unity among Europeans, fueled by common resentment of American steel tariffs.[76] If that was not a sufficiently inspiring basis for European unity, French Foreign Minister Dominique de Villepin fell back on a more traditional source when he explained that the American war was the result of "a pro-Zionist lobby in Washington," composed, of course, of officials with Jewish names.[77] The recourse to such explanations seems to satisfy something in European thinking—some memory of racial pride, and disdain for America as a country where anyone loyal to the national Constitution might serve the nation in high office.

Of course, the American idea requires that we take our national Constitution seriously. For Europeans that seems an impossible commitment. It remains a source of fury that the United States, instead of submitting to European practices, honors its own Constitution—evidence, perhaps, that it has fallen under the sway of people who are not true Europeans. Europeans remain incredulous at the American assumption that no nation can dictate terms to another, if it is not prepared to risk war. Where would this leave France? What would it say to Germany? Better to say that Europeans simply know better—and pretend that what has been endorsed by Europeans and their clients in less-developed countries remains the standard of the world.

The pattern was noticed by the American Founders. *The Federalist* put it this way:

> Europe by her arms and by her negotiations, by force and by fraud, has in different degrees extended her dominion. . . . Africa, Asia and America have successively felt her domination. The superiority she has long maintained has tempted her to plume herself as the mistress of the world and to consider the rest of mankind as created for her benefit. Men admired as profound philosophers have in direct terms attributed to her inhabitants a physical superiority and have gravely asserted that all animals, and with them the human species, degenerate in

America. . . . Facts have too long supported these arrogant pretensions of the European. It belongs to us to vindicate the
honor of the human race and to teach that assuming brother
moderation. . . . Let Americans disdain to be the instruments of
European greatness![78]

Apart from Britain, European states have become far less able to use their
"arms" and "force." European governments have shunned the financial
burden and professional discipline required to maintain effective military
forces. On the whole, European security continues to depend on American
military capabilities. But Europe insists on projecting its aims into the
larger world, independently of the United States and often in direct and
conscious opposition to American aims. European diplomacy now must
depend much more on what Hamilton described as "negotiations" and
"fraud." In earlier times, the United States sought to secure its coasts from
European navies by building fortifications with powerful gun batteries.
Today, the United States must secure itself against European governments
wielding moralistic rhetoric or seductive assurances. This danger can be
faced without gun batteries. But it requires clarity of thought—a moral for-
tification of our national boundaries and our sovereign rights.

3

Sovereignty and Security

People of various faiths look forward to an era of ultimate peace, when all mankind finally comes to recognize God's dominion. History records many efforts to hasten the attainment of such prophetic visions by human action. Wars of religious conquest, however, did not bring universal peace. In the twentieth century, messianists claiming the mantle of secular science promised to end conflict by abolishing property or religion or nationality—whatever they diagnosed as the human root of conflict. Efforts to realize such visions brought tyranny and misery, but not peace.

Those who cherish sovereignty, by contrast, recognize that conflict is likely to remain an enduring element in human affairs. But sovereignty allows for the possibility that armed conflict can be constrained and often deterred by countering force, organized by sovereign states. It is a vision that fails to satisfy many people, particularly in Western Europe. As earlier generations of Europeans were drawn to other sorts of messianic visions, much opinion in contemporary Europe is drawn to the notion that the threat of war can be contained by international institutions. It is a particularly appealing vision to Europeans, who like to imagine that peace has been secured to Europe by supranational institutions.

Americans are less drawn to this vision, recalling that peace in Europe was made possible, in the first instance, by the military defeat of Nazi Germany, in which supranational institutions played no role at all. Americans are more likely to recall, as well—even if Europeans are prone to forget—that America's defense guarantees to Western Europe were rather more important in deterring a Soviet invasion than the regulatory schemes of the European Commission.

Still, people who imagine that the world can achieve peace by international organization are bound to think that the United States must join in the project. One problem with this notion is that it runs against the whole grain of American history and is, for that reason alone, unlikely to receive American approval. Peace through international organization has this additional defect: that it has no serious prospect of success. Most Americans know this instinctively, because American institutions have been built on this understanding.

American Traditions

The United States was created out of war—a war against a transnational empire. The Declaration of Independence argues that people are justified in resorting to war when it is necessary to protect their rights. If the American Founders had believed that peace should be preserved at any price, the American colonists would have remained subjects of the British Empire. In the very document declaring their independence, Americans asserted their right to "make war," and "do all other things which independent states may of right do."

This original assertion of national rights did not make America's founding statesmen disdainful of international law. To the contrary, they were keen to claim their full rights under the existing law of nations. One of the arguments for the new Constitution, given considerable emphasis in *The Federalist*, is that only a strong federal government can ensure that all states comply with American international obligations, and that other nations, in turn, honor their legal obligations to the United States.[1] Both Thomas Jefferson, as Washington's secretary of state, and James Madison, as Jefferson's secretary of state, sought to defend American shipping rights on the high seas with learned appeals to the law of nations.[2] The young United States was one of the most insistent champions of the rights of neutrals under the law of nations.

Still, the American Founders did not place great faith in treaties or in international law. John Jay's discussion of international law in *The Federalist* emphasizes that international legal claims must be backed by reliable force: "[I]t is well known that acknowledgements, explanations and compensations [for injuries committed by one state against another] are often accepted as satisfactory from a strong united nation, which would be rejected as unsatisfactory if offered by a State or confederacy of little consideration or power."[3] Hamilton notes that treaties in Europe, designed to ensure peace, "were scarcely formed before they were broken, giving an instructive but afflicting lesson to mankind how little dependence is to be placed on treaties which have no other sanction than the obligations of good faith. . . ."[4] The central paper of *The Federalist*—by Madison, as it happens—notes that the Articles of Confederation could not reliably bind the states, because it was only a "compact among the states," a special form of treaty; and the "established doctrine on the subject of treaties" acknowledges that "a breach of any one article is a breach of the whole treaty" that "absolves the others, and authorizes them, if they please, to pronounce the compact violated and void."[5]

So, far from regarding the confederation of the American states as a model for larger international ventures, the Founders regarded the Constitution—in establishing a firm, sovereign authority above the states—as a necessary guarantee against international encroachments. Nearly a decade after the Constitution was drafted, President Washington, in his Farewell Address, urged Americans to pursue trade with all nations but avoid any further entanglements with the aims of foreign governments: "The great rule of conduct for us in regard to foreign nations is, in extending our commercial relations to have with them as little *political* connection as possible"[6] (original emphasis).

Preoccupation with securing its independence did not mean, however, that the United States followed a policy of "isolation." In the course of a few decades, the young republic spread from the Atlantic coast to the shores of the Pacific, and by the end of the nineteenth century, America had planted its flag in Hawaii, the Philippines, and a score of islands in between. Such remarkable territorial expansion was not achieved by ignoring the outside world. In the course of the nineteenth century, the United States fought declared wars against Britain, Mexico, and Spain, and smaller naval actions in places as distant as the "shores of Tripoli" and remote South Pacific islands.[7]

But the United States did insist on an independent course. Even when it fought the Barbary pirates, it declined to link its efforts with European powers, who preferred to pay bribes to the pirates rather than fight them. Even when the United States went to war against Britain in 1812, to protect its rights on the high seas, it disdained to link its cause with Britain's major opponent, Napoleonic France. And the United States insisted on imposing its own terms after the Spanish-American War, rather than accepting European offers of mediation.

Continental expansion followed a similar impulse. Concerned about obstruction of American shipping on the Mississippi when New Orleans reverted from Spanish to French control, the Jefferson administration made no serious effort to secure shipping rights by treaty; instead, it sought full sovereignty over New Orleans—and ended up purchasing the vast wilderness holdings of France's Louisiana Territory. In the 1830s, when American settlers in Texas won their independence from Mexico, Congress hesitated to bring the new Republic of Texas into the United States. Annexation was decided upon, however, when Texas announced its readiness to negotiate a protective treaty with Britain instead. In Texas, as in the contemporaneous dispute over the Oregon territory, American statesmen wanted full sovereign rights rather than sharing control with an outside power.[8]

Until well into the twentieth century, the most emphatic and enduring American policy toward the world at large was the Monroe Doctrine, by which the United States sought to prevent the reimposition of European colonial control in the New World. Both in its origins and its operation, it was characteristically unilateral. The British government, happy to see Latin America detached from Spanish control (and thereby opened to British trade), offered to make a joint declaration with the United States, pledging support for the independence of Latin republics. President Monroe insisted on making a unilateral declaration of American opposition to European interventions in the Western Hemisphere. By the end of the nineteenth century, when the United States had more naval and military strength to back up its threat, the Monroe Doctrine was sometimes portrayed—even by Latin American statesmen—as a kind of alliance. But American policy was to protect the independence of Latin Americans, whether their rulers of the moment wanted American protection or not.[9]

By the early twentieth century, the United States deployed troops and gunboats to a considerable number of Caribbean states, to quell disorder or to ensure that local governments repaid their foreign debt, lest European gunboats arrive to collect the debts themselves. Certainly, the United States was not always scrupulous about whether local governments wanted an

American presence. On the other hand, a generation of American statesmen labored without success to win formal European acknowledgement of the Monroe Doctrine as an element of customary international law—and its absence did nothing to shake American commitment to the underlying policy of resisting European schemes for recolonization or the acquisition of protectorates in the New World.[10]

American policy sometimes verged on bullying and abuse, particularly in the chaotic and unstable states of Central America. The United States allowed itself a degree of involvement in the domestic affairs of Latin American states that it was determined to deny to European powers. Latin nationalists, even in the nineteenth century, and generations of left-wing critics ever since, portrayed the American posture as imperialist or neoimperialist. In fact, American policy showed the difference between actual claims of sovereignty and mere forceful diplomacy.

For four years, the United States faced a challenge to its own sovereign authority at home, when eleven states tried to secede from the Union because they would not accept the results of the 1860 presidential election. The Lincoln administration would not compromise on the supremacy of the Union, and the Northern states rallied to the federal government's aim of crushing the rebellion by armed force. Before it was over, the war had wrought vast destruction in the American South and inflicted more casualties than all American wars put together, including America's casualties in the world wars of the twentieth century. European military observers at the time were appalled at the scale of the bloodletting and carnage, made possible by railroads and industry that could sustain vast armies through extended battles. The war continued to total victory because federal authority was upheld by the support of most of the American people, which was finally and formally registered in Lincoln's reelection in the midst of the war.

The war was ennobled by the recognition that the Southern states had originally seceded to protect the evil system of slavery. The promised abolition of slavery, adopted as a war measure in 1863, made it a struggle for freedom in a deeper sense. But it remained a war to restore the constitutional supremacy—literally, the sovereignty—of the Union. The United States was quite unwilling to use force to end slavery in Brazil (where it continued until the 1880s) or anywhere else.

In fact, the United States was not willing to expend much force for any preference it might have had regarding the conduct of government in Latin American states. American military interventions sought to ensure that American investors and American travelers would not be arbitrarily seized by Latin governments—a resort still endorsed by international practice in the early twentieth century. The United States exerted other forms of influence to help establish stable and friendly governments in strife-torn countries in Central America and the Caribbean. But it was not prepared to pay much of a price to ensure its preferred outcomes—and it usually ended by acquiescing to a successor government not much to its taste.

When American philanthropists helped liberated slaves to establish a colony on the west coast of Africa—which became Liberia—the United States government formally disavowed any responsibility for the struggling settlement.[11] America's involvement in the Philippines is the one major exception to its general distaste for empires and colonies. The United States did invest considerable military resources to suppress a rebellion in the Philippines in 1900, after the islands were acquired from Spain in the peace treaty that ended the Spanish-American War. The United States claimed sovereign rights in the Philippines and was determined to maintain these rights with full military force. But barely three decades later, it grew tired of colonial obligations in the Philippines. Not willing to incorporate the islands into the Union, Congress pledged in 1934 to see the Philippines prepared for full independence, which was duly granted in 1946. The last major power to enter the scramble for colonial possessions, the United States was also the first to begin the process of decolonization.

To be sure, the United States has not always behaved generously or unselfishly or in ways that moralists would approve. But the point to notice is that it always made sharp distinctions between its diplomatic ventures abroad and its governing obligations at home. The United States was extremely serious about upholding the authority of American law on American territory. It did not seriously imagine that it could enforce American preferences on neighboring states, as if they were subject to American law in the same way as states of the Union. American diplomacy sought to shape the outside world, particularly in the Western Hemisphere, to American advantage. But the United States government was not prepared to incur great cost to impose its legal claims on the outside world, as it was at home.

Under Franklin Roosevelt's "Good Neighbor" policy of the 1930s, the United States even renounced the right to use military force to protect American investors in Latin America against expropriation or contract violations. The legality of such interventions had long been acknowledged by European states and practiced for decades by American administrations. But they no longer seemed prudent in a world where more ominous war threats were already visible on the horizon. The new American policy was vindicated when the United States went to war against Germany and Japan, and most states in Latin America followed suit, providing full cooperation with American hemispheric defense efforts.[12]

Still, the United States could not simply impose its will in Latin America as it could in California. If it could have done so, it would not have endured a pro-Fascist regime in Argentina during the Second World War. It would not have endured a Communist regime in Cuba, after 1958. It would not have endured a series of populist dictatorships or military juntas, often winning sympathy by railing against the United States in international forums.

During the nineteenth century, the United States participated in various efforts to promote cooperation among the republics of the Western Hemisphere. But it was always careful to cede no governmental rights of its own to the Pan American Union or its ultimate successor (after World War II), the Organization of American States (OAS).[13] During the late nineteenth century, the United States often acted as a mediator of border disputes and a champion of peace in the region. In the twentieth century, it often tried to promote transitions from dictatorship to democratic government. The Pan American Union and, later, the OAS were sometimes enlisted in these efforts. But the United States did not try to make these institutions independent guarantors, either of peace or of democracy.

The United States would not allow its own governing decisions at home to be subordinated to such institutions and would not even commit its foreign initiatives to strict compliance with policies approved by hemispheric forums. The United States encouraged OAS members to adopt an Inter-American Convention on Human Rights—but, given Senate objections, could not bind itself to observe its provisions. Direct American military interventions in the Dominican Republic in 1965, in

Grenada in 1983, and in Panama in 1990 were all undertaken without authorization from the OAS—and defended by U.S. administrations against subsequent resolutions of disapproval. The United States has maintained an embargo on Castro's Cuba, without OAS sanction and in disregard of the practices of most other OAS members.

American policy toward peace in Europe and the wider world proved not much different. And it probably could not have been.

Collective Security

In 1919, the United States Senate rejected the Covenant of the League of Nations, declining to participate in this first venture in what came to be called "collective security." American rejection of the League was met with surprise and consternation in Europe. Both reactions were misplaced.

Certainly, the Senate's rejection of the League should not have come as a total surprise, at least to anyone who had studied the Constitution and the history of American diplomacy. The Constitution provides a strong brake on international commitments, by requiring that treaties can only be ratified by a two-thirds majority in the Senate. And the Senate had not been hesitant in the past to exercise this check on presidential diplomacy. Only a few years earlier, for example, the Senate had rejected initiatives of the Republican Taft administration to commit the United States to an international prize court (to judge the legality of naval seizures) and to an open-ended scheme for settling disputes with Great Britain by arbitration. In both cases, senators protested that the proposed treaties would violate or compromise the governing scheme established in the Constitution.[14] Even President Woodrow Wilson had been careful with constitutional sensibilities when he persuaded Congress to endorse American entry into the World War in 1917. In the absence of any formal treaty with Britain and France, Wilson always referred to the United States as an "associate" rather than an "ally" in the coalition generally known as "the Allies."

Nor was there much serious ground for consternation at the Senate's rejection of the League. Leading critics of the League, including Henry Cabot Lodge, chairman of the Senate Foreign Relations Committee, announced their readiness to approve a more limited treaty, pledging American assistance to France in the event of renewed German aggression. By joining the League, however, the United States seemed to be pledging assistance to any nation facing any sort of military challenge—or any domestic insurrection. Critics found such an open-ended commitment alarming, as it seemed to prevent the United States from making its own choices, including the choice to remain aloof from a particular conflict.

In reply, defenders of American entry always stressed that the League would not commit the United States to any war or blockade, and certainly not without the consent of the U.S. Congress.[15] But if that was so, then American membership could not have made a decisive difference. If the League could not compel other countries to conform their security policy to its direction, then its mere existence was not likely to contribute much to the preservation of peace.

And so it proved. The League condemned Japanese aggression in Manchuria and Italian aggression in Ethiopia in the 1930s. The condemned nations simply withdrew from the League. Remaining members were not willing to take any serious action to punish them. In 1938, when Nazi Germany threatened to invade Czechoslovakia to secure control of border lands populated by ethnic Germans, Britain and France bargained directly with Hitler over new borders and then demanded that the Czechs accept them—as they did. Nobody bothered to consult the League. The question for the Czechs was whether Britain and France would help defend them against Hitler's demands. Another meaningless denunciation by the League could not compensate for the refusal of the British and French governments to pledge direct military aid to the Czechs.

The last important act of the League was to expel the Soviet Union from the organization, in December 1939, for its invasion of Finland. This gesture did nothing to protect Finland, which shortly sued for peace on Soviet terms. Still less did it deter Germany from further aggression. When Germany invaded the Soviet Union (in disregard of its previous nonaggression pact), it recruited Finland to its side—along with several other states that had been members of the League. By then, Britain and its dominions were only too ready to forget the League's condemnation and embrace a common, anti-Nazi alliance with the U.S.S.R. In a real war, the League had become entirely irrelevant. League officials packed up their records and retreated to Princeton, New Jersey.

With approaching Allied victory over Germany and Japan, the victorious powers developed plans for a new approach to "collective security." To judge from its charter, the United Nations might have seemed a more formidable organization than it was. It was to be supplied with its own "Military Staff Committee" and with an "air force contingent for combined international enforcement action."[16] Yet close readers might notice that all this apparatus was only for dealing with future aggression. Drafted in the spring of 1945, at a conference which opened in San Francisco in April of that year—when Germany had not yet surrendered and Japan still looked very formidable—the charter expressly exempted the "existing war" from its provisions.[17] For this real war, the major Allied powers did not want to be constrained or distracted by international forums.

Even for the future, the major powers hedged their commitment to "collective security." The charter proclaimed the "sovereign equality" of member states but provided for fundamental inequality in its own operations. Only the Security Council was empowered to make binding decisions, and most members of the council, elected from the general membership of the UN, would serve two-year terms. Five permanent members would remain on the council continuously, however: the United States, the Soviet Union, Britain, France, and China. And no resolution of the council could take effect over the opposition of any one of these powers.[18]

The great-power veto made it possible to persuade the Senate that the United Nations was no threat to American sovereignty; the UN would never act when the United States opposed its action. But of course this meant that the organization could be equally paralyzed by Soviet opposition—and so it was. In 1950, when the Soviet Union was demonstrating its pique over another matter by boycotting meetings of the Security Council, the council was able to authorize military action against North Korea's invasion of South Korea. The Soviets immediately recognized their mistake and never missed a council meeting again. Four decades passed before the Security Council again authorized resort to force—this time to repel Iraq's aggression against Kuwait in 1990. In the intervening period of Cold War, the UN was largely irrelevant to conflicts around the world, as the superpowers wielded the veto to protect their own actions, and those of their allies or clients, from Security Council condemnation. And the charter provisions for an international bomber command were never implemented.

The UN's paralysis over Iraq in 2002–3 was entirely in keeping with past experience. The Security Council demanded that Saddam Hussein cooperate with weapons inspectors, and then could not decide on a remedy when its own chief inspector acknowledged that Iraq was not complying with its obligation to account for its weapons programs. The Anglo-American coalition's unauthorized invasion of Iraq was also quite in keeping with past experience.

In the aftermath, there was talk of reforming the UN. Many American critics argued that France should not be allowed to wield a unilateral veto. A different arrangement might make the Security Council a more reliable and effective arbiter of international conflict.[19] In fact, there had been much discussion about reforming the charter a decade before. A reunified Germany sought a permanent seat on the council, which encouraged Japan to make similar claims, prompting India to demand a seat of its own, followed by Brazil. It had all come to nothing. Rather than see one or another regional rival advanced in rank, most states decided they preferred the existing stalemate. France would not hear of any reform that threatened its own position as one of the Permanent Five.[20]

And probably none of it mattered. It is doubtful that any change in the architecture of the United Nations could alleviate the underlying problems with collective security.

Fundamentals

The great-power veto is a symptom rather than a cause of the problems with collective security. To enforce its determinations, the Security Council has to threaten, at least in the last resort, to wield force to ensure compliance with its resolutions. If it cannot credibly threaten force, it is one more forum for windy exhortations rather than any assurance of actual security. Even without a formal veto, however, a major power might still oppose the council's policy. If the council tries to enforce its resolution, it might then be setting itself up for a war with a great power on the other side. So the council might have to rally half the world for a war against a great power—not exactly a pleasing prospect for an organization supposed to be securing peace.

Who would then fight this war? In a war against a major power, the council would need major forces. If the major powers did not have a veto on council resolutions, small states might, in principle, vote to organize a war that would then be fought with the military resources of the larger states. But it is unlikely that the major powers would allow their own military resources to be conscripted by other states. In effect, it would mean that their own soldiers might die in a war that their own government did not actually endorse. Even if this worked in a few cases, it could not be attempted very often before the major powers revolted at the absurdity of the arrangement. Why should major powers be ruled by a coalition of lesser powers?

The problem is not just that larger powers are likely to be too self-interested to support the right result. The problem is that the world does not agree on the right result. It is easy to say that aggression should be resisted. But it is not always easy to determine which side is the actual aggressor. Typically, each side in a conflict blames the other for the war, and there is often some genuine merit in the claims on both sides. The problem is even more complicated when the conflict arises within a state, as in a revolution, insurgency, or civil war. It is true that internal conflicts often draw in outside states and may thus present a serious threat to international peace and security. But this does not make it easier to decide what to do. Should the "international community" support the original government at all costs? If so, the most brutal and oppressive government could bolster its own tyrannical rule with the military resources of the whole international community. If, on the other hand, the international community limits itself to supporting only those governments that deserve support—because, let us say, they are not overly abusive to their own citizens—then it has set itself up as the judge of legitimacy for every government in the world.

It is not even plausible to claim that peace is, in every case, better than war. Many Europeans thought the Lincoln administration was wrong to continue fighting the southern Confederacy. Americans may be glad that there was no international forum to impose peace—and preserve slavery—in the 1860s. Perhaps some element of self-interested calculation inspired European sympathies for the slave-state Confederacy. But what international authority would not be distracted by self-interested calculations?

During the Second World War, Pope Pius XII repeatedly called on all sides to stop the conflict.[21] Had Roosevelt and Churchill heeded this advice, a Nazi regime would have remained in charge of vast portions of Europe. The Vatican might have regarded this outcome as preferable to allowing Catholic states in Eastern Europe to fall under Soviet control. Or perhaps the Vatican was not a good judge of strategic issues—a suspicion that received added weight when Vatican officials warned in 2003 that an American war on Iraq would have catastrophic consequences for civilians. (Actual civilian casualties numbered approximately 3,000.)[22]

Sometimes a compromise peace is indeed a good idea. Perhaps Europeans would have done better to heed President Wilson's call for a compromise peace in 1915 or 1916. But it is not obvious why leaders should heed the advice of any outside power—or why even a large aggregation of states should be heeded when local leaders think they are mistaken.

After all, other states might be quite prepared to let a small state or a small people suffer for what outsiders regard as the greater good. In 1938, Britain and France determined it would be better to let Hitler take the border regions of Czechoslovakia than to try to stop him—though this meant depriving the Czechs of boundary fortifications they might have held against a future German attack. If Britain and France were willing to impose such terms at Munich, they might well have persuaded the League of Nations to endorse the plan. The League would still have been in no better position to protect the Czechs thereafter, when Hitler indeed swallowed the rest of the Czech lands and Britain and France decided to do nothing. At the time, sacrificing the Czechs seemed a prudent concession for the sake of avoiding war.

Decades later, Israeli Prime Minister Ariel Sharon warned that Israel would not allow itself to become a new Czechoslovakia, forced into dangerous concessions to help European states appease Islamist terrorism. In 1981, Israel had launched a preemptive attack on the Iraqi nuclear program, knowing that its action would be condemned by the United Nations—as indeed it was.[23] Israel knew that if Saddam Hussein acquired nuclear weapons, the international community would do nothing to protect it from attack. After the United States fought its own preemptive war against Saddam Hussein, Europeans insisted that Israel must be forced to accept a Palestinian state on its borders, even if that state would not restrain terror attacks on Israel. It is clear enough why Europeans would find it convenient to offer up others as sacrifices to their own policy aims, as so often in the past. It is harder to understand why anyone would expect the Jewish state to jeopardize its own security to satisfy European conceits even if amplified by a hostile majority at the UN. The strongest argument for sovereignty is that no nation can trust others to care as much about its own security as it does itself.

Of course, sovereign states often behave abominably to their own people. This is sometimes a very serious moral challenge. But it is not answered by international organizations. The League of Nations was in no position to stop the genocide perpetrated by Europeans during the Second World War. Perhaps the United Nations was in no position to stop the mass killings perpetrated by the Khmer Rouge in Cambodia in 1975. In both cases, murderous regimes were finally brought down by successful invasions from outside—with no help from the UN and, in the case of Cambodia, over the UN's objections.[24] In Rwanda, there were UN peacekeeping forces in the country, trying to calm border conflicts with neighboring states. But when the Hutu government embarked on a campaign of genocide against the Tutsi people of Rwanda, the UN peacekeepers were hastily withdrawn. Nearly a million people were slaughtered, most of them hacked to death with crude weapons, before a Tutsi force sponsored by neighboring countries finally overthrew the government and put an end to the horror. The international community simply expressed its regrets. The UN official responsible for withdrawing the peacekeepers, Kofi Annan, was later promoted to secretary-general, and was subsequently awarded a Nobel Peace Prize—for peacekeeping!

Advocates of the United Nations insist that the organization remains essential as a guarantee of legitimacy. This is not a powerful point. It is, of course, better for a country to have the appearance of international support for its actions. It was presumably for this reason that when Nazi Germany invaded the Soviet Union, it took care to recruit separate divisions of troops from France, Belgium, the Netherlands, and other vassal states so that it could claim to be leading an "international effort." The tactic seems to have impressed many people in Western Europe, who regarded collaboration with Nazi domination as preferable to the triumph of "American materialism."[25]

But the game could be played by both sides. The United States and Britain referred to their allies as "the United Nations"—though few of these allies supplied actual troops on any relevant scale. When General Eisenhower addressed the troops invading Normandy, for example, he associated their efforts with "the United Nations," though there were only American, Canadian, and British troops in the landings.[26] Presumably, most people in Western Europe would have accepted their liberation by Anglo-American forces even if they had openly described themselves as "United Nations of the English-Speaking World."

The "legitimacy" supplied by the actual United Nations has often proven quite inadequate. In 1994, the Security Council demanded that Somali warlords stop interfering with UN food distribution. One of the warlords, Mohammed Aideed, promptly captured some U.S. peacekeepers, dragged their bodies through the streets of Mogadishu, and drove the whole operation out of the country. The prestige of the UN was not quite enough to persuade the Clinton administration to continue risking its troops in this venture. And without the American presence, the UN resolutions turned out to mean nothing. A year later, the Security Council demanded that Serb militia in Bosnia at least refrain from interfering with Muslim civilians in designated safe areas. In Srbrenica, the Serbs ignored this demand and slaughtered some 8,000 civilians. Dutch peacekeepers stood by, not only failing to protect their civilian charges but failing even to alert UN headquarters to the carnage occurring on their watch.[27]

Faced with a genuine threat, no state would let its security be determined by a show of hands among others that have no commitment to protect it. In 2003, the United States decided it could not accept the risk that Saddam Hussein would share weapons of mass destruction with Islamist terror groups. In the end, it acted without UN authorization. Most Iraqis were grateful for their liberation, even if it lacked the endorsement of Saddam's former sponsors in Moscow and Paris. Twenty years earlier, the United States had intervened against Grenada in a similarly unauthorized, preemptive attack and was denounced by the UN for "flagrant violation of international law."[28] This clearly made no difference to the United States or to the people of Grenada, who cheered the arrival of American forces.

The question is whether it is even desirable for bystanders to determine the rights and wrongs of wars. Wars sometimes pit good against evil—or at least relative good against very great evil. But the world often disagrees about which side is good and which is not. Should the world be organized to decide which is right? Should the majority of states or peoples, simply because they are the majority, determine which others can defend themselves? The idea is morally untenable—as well as impossible to implement. To insist that no one is authorized to act without international approval is to give great advantages to those who will disdain to seek approval in any case—such as terrorists and aggressor states.

How International Law Can Strengthen Security

The machinery of the United Nations cannot guarantee peace. It is doubtful that an organization that embraces nearly all the nations of the world—with all their differences and divisions—can even contribute much to the maintenance of peace. It is quite wrong, however, to think that international law is useless or irrelevant in matters touching on security. International law is much older than the United Nations and has, over the course of centuries, developed on the basis of much sturdier premises than the collectivist conceits associated with the United Nations.

First of all, security often requires cooperation. In an actual war, allies can sometimes be of crucial assistance. In diplomatic calculations it therefore may matter a great deal whether a prospective ally will keep its word. It can matter, too, when a pledge of neutrality will be honored. In 1914, Britain was persuaded to enter the World War because Germany had invaded neutral Belgium, violating treaty guarantees stretching back to the early part of the previous century. The Germans promised to restore Belgium afterward, but such a blatant violation of treaty guarantees made it impossible to believe this new German promise.

In June 1940, France decided to repudiate its alliance with Britain and make its own peace agreement with Nazi Germany. Having betrayed its word, France could not be trusted when it promised to prevent its fleet from falling under German control. The British decided they must disable the French fleet and proceeded to bomb warships of this unreliable former ally in July 1940. When British and American forces landed in North Africa in 1942, they took pains to secure every part of French colonial territory not under direct German control on the same reasonable premise: French promises could not be trusted. Spanish Morocco was left untouched by Anglo-American forces, because Spain seemed more likely to respect its pledge of neutrality.[29] Similarly, today, a promise not to develop nuclear weapons means something different when made by Argentina than when made by North Korea, which has repeatedly violated such promises.

Just as it can be valuable to have a reputation for keeping promises, it can be important to maintain a reputation for respecting limits, even apart from treaty guarantees. Britain decided against sending troops to occupy neutral Ireland in 1940, despite concerns over Ireland's vulnerability to German invasion and its potential as a launching base for attacks on Britain. The British refrained because they were afraid of losing the sympathy and cooperation of neutrals—above all, the still-neutral United States. The United States, in its turn, ended up accepting Ireland's refusal of American basing rights. Such restraint helped to win local consent for the basing of American troops in Iceland and Greenland later in the war and in many parts of Western Europe after the war. Germany, having displayed utter contempt for neutral rights, was regarded with great wariness, so Franco's government resisted Germany's pleas in 1941 to allow the Wehrmacht to pass through Spain to attack the British base at Gibraltar.[30]

Even between nations at war, international law can preserve some elements of mutual restraint. Even Hitler and Stalin allowed each other's embassy staffs to depart their respective capitals at the outset of the German attack on the Soviet Union. Each country was able to recover its own diplomats in this way and perhaps encourage respect for the customary rules protecting its remaining embassies in other countries. Germany and Russia then proceeded to treat each other's war prisoners with horrifying brutality. But even Germany treated Anglo-American prisoners with some respect, allowing the International Committee of the Red Cross to make regular inspections of German-run POW camps to confirm their compliance with internationally agreed-upon standards. The difference was that Germany and the Western Allies were parties to the 1929 Geneva Convention on war prisoners, while the Soviet Union was not. German generals deliberately evaded the Führer's demand for the execution of Allied bomber crews, fearing this step would lead the Allies to disregard international standards in their treatment of German prisoners.[31]

German commanders had no expectation that the Soviets would spare German POWs, especially after the way Germany had treated its Russian prisoners. But there remained considerable incentives to humanity in the treatment of American and British prisoners.

Countries have an incentive to observe internationally agreed-upon standards, even in the midst of war, when they have reason to fear the consequences of not doing so. The most direct and immediate consequence is that violations by one side can trigger reprisals. One reason German generals feared retaliation against German prisoners in Allied hands was that Britain had already shown its willingness to shackle German prisoners to their prison bunks in reprisal for German action of this kind against British prisoners.[32]

Reprisals of this sort have been the main means of enforcing international standards in war. Historically, restraints in war were not codified in treaties but developed in response to mutual accommodation—and were often ignored where no reciprocal restraint was expected. British and French troops treated each other with considerable courtesy during the Peninsular campaign in the Napoleonic war, while French troops adopted savage methods against Spanish guerrillas, who fought the French with equal savagery.[33] Even after the Second World War, efforts to foster more restraint in war, codified in the Geneva Conventions of 1949, began with the stipulation that such restraints—on the treatment of wounded, shipwrecked, and captured combatants—would only apply to regular combatant forces which themselves observed these restraints.[34]

Where the accepted rules of war were thought to apply, violations could be punished by the home army to demonstrate good faith and avoid retaliation. Sometimes, captured soldiers from an opposing army could be punished for war crimes. But abuses on both sides were often forgiven in the subsequent peace. During the Civil War, for example, President Lincoln threatened that Confederate commanders who ordered the killing of captured black troops would be subject to execution if captured by the Union army.[35] But perpetrators of such atrocities were subsequently pardoned.

Until quite recently, no treatise on international law proposed that violations of international standards in war could be punished by third parties to the conflict. That approach could generate obvious difficulties for the belligerent states when they tried to reach agreement on the terms of peace. The sort of punishment or reparation that should be imposed on the losing side was often a significant element in bargaining over peace terms.

The advent of the United Nations did not change this underlying reality. It was not designed to ensure any rule of international conduct, unless all the great powers were in agreement on the response to a particular violation. The idea that justice could be achieved in abstraction from force did not appeal to the international coalition that had just defeated the Axis powers—by force. So the Statute of the International Court of Justice, appended to the UN Charter, stipulated that only states could be parties to disputes before the court and then only with the consent of both parties to the particular dispute.[36]

At Nuremberg and Tokyo, the victorious Allies organized criminal tribunals to punish Axis leaders for war crimes. The victors did not ask the UN for permission (or even for advice or assistance) in organizing these tribunals. And they took care to limit their jurisdiction to nationals of the defeated Axis powers. They would not allow actions of Allied war leaders to be challenged. The tribunals were not presented as organs of the international community but as instruments of the victors. In its very first ruling, the Nuremberg tribunal insisted that its charter derived entirely from "the exercise of sovereign legislative power by the countries to which the German Reich unconditionally surrendered."[37]

The Nuremberg tribunal introduced a new term: "crimes against humanity." But prosecutions were limited to atrocities that took place after the outbreak of war and generally on foreign soil. The difference between "war crimes" and "crimes against humanity" remained quite vague. None of the four governments wanted to establish a precedent for international criminal claims which might later be turned against the domestic practices of Allied states.[38]

The United States remained quite resistant to any international interference in its domestic affairs. When the Senate ratified American participation in the UN's International Court of Justice, for example, it included an express reservation against allowing the ICJ to judge matters of U.S. domestic policy.[39] The Soviet Union was even more determined to exclude international inquiry into its practices—many of which, after all, were not much removed from those charged against the Nuremberg defendants. But the Soviet Union's participation in the tribunal was considered essential to its prestige.

During the ensuing decades of Cold War, on the other hand, Soviet participation was viewed by most Western policymakers as an obvious objection to international tribunals. Various studies were undertaken by groups of jurists, occasionally with UN sponsorship, on the proper arrangements for a new international criminal tribunal. The 1948 Convention on the Punishment of Genocide refers in vague terms to possible future tribunals authorized to judge such horrible crimes.[40] But there was no serious possibility that the Soviet Union and the Western nations would find mutually agreeable standards for such a venture.

The issue did not seem of much relevance since, in the postwar era, no war by an international coalition was actually carried through to total victory. The UN war in Korea was ended by negotiated truce in 1953. Even this level of peace could not have been achieved if the American-led coalition had demanded that Chinese and North Korean leaders turn themselves over to a war crimes tribunal. The UN war against Iraq in 1991 was also ended without taking top Iraqi officials into custody.

But the end of the Cold War generated new visions of international cooperation. The UN soon began to toy with the idea that actual control of territory was not really necessary to assert criminal jurisdiction. Hopes for a higher version of international justice quickly went far beyond anything previously attempted.

Justice from the Sky

In 1993, the Security Council established a special war crimes tribunal for Yugoslavia, the International Criminal Tribunal for the former Yugoslavia (ICTY). Yugoslavia had crumbled into competing ethnic states, with multiethnic Bosnia set upon by both Croatian and Serb paramilitary forces. Successive resolutions from the Security Council demanded an end to conflict and to ethnic atrocities. These resolutions were disregarded. Sending lawyers to investigate seemed easier than sending military forces on a scale that might actually ensure peace. The tribunal put no stop to the fighting, either, but then even NATO forces in the region did not make serious efforts to capture indicted war criminals—among other reasons, because they sometimes needed their cooperation to maintain fragile cease-fires.[41]

In Rwanda, one year later, the Tutsi minority was threatened with genocide. The UN withdrew its peacekeepers and nearly a million people were
slaughtered. The Security Council mobilized its conscience only when Tutsi
forces managed to overthrow the genocidal Hutu regime with an organized
military effort of their own. The Security Council then decided that what
Rwanda most needed was an international team of lawyers to administer
justice—by European standards, including elaborate trials and a guarantee
that capital punishment would not be imposed. After years of desultory
effort, less than two dozen perpetrators had been tried for crimes that had
involved the slaughter of nearly a million civilians.[42]

Occupation governments in Germany and Japan had not been squeamish about executing the worst war criminals. But home governments
retained control of the proceedings. In Germany, Western governments
subsequently directed that scheduled prosecutions should be abandoned
and sentences against convicted war criminals should be commuted. As
Cold War priorities made it more vital to enlist German support, justice
for war crimes was curtailed to conciliate German opinion.[43] In Japan,
Emperor Hirohito was never accused of any wrongdoing, although several
of his closest advisers were hanged for their involvement in war crimes.
American policy was eager to retain the emperor as a symbol of continuity,
all the more so because Hirohito urged his people to submit unreservedly
to the occupation authorities.

The Balkan and Rwandan tribunals were on automatic pilot, entirely
cut off from any accountability to any actual government. They were supposed to impose justice for humanity. But humanity, it seemed, did not
have high expectations. Humanity was not concerned if Rwandans raged
at the idiosyncratic priorities of international prosecutors, who shielded
most perpetrators of genocide from any trial and shielded all from capital
punishment. Humanity was not concerned if an extraordinarily bureaucratic procedure allowed trials to drag on for a decade. Prosecutors strove
to establish new precedents to establish that sexual humiliation could be
classified as a "crime against humanity," while allowing mass murderers to
remain unprosecuted.[44]

Nor was humanity concerned if different Balkan peoples came to see
the tribunal as blantantly biased, opportunistic, or capricious in its prosecution priorities. The Yugoslav tribunal allowed the leader of a particularly

nasty guerrilla force, directly responsible for mass slaughters in Bosnia, to plea bargain for a light sentence in return for testifying against Serbian President Slobodan Milosevic—deemed a "partner for peace" when these atrocities were occurring.[45] To establish the rule of law, the tribunal demanded and eventually won the extradition of Milosevic—after the Serbian Supreme Court had pronounced the extradition unlawful (based on historic Serb practice which was exactly parallel to the historic practices of Italy and Germany and other European states).[46] The prime minister who defied Serbian law to deliver Milosevic was subsequently assassinated, amid continuing instability in the struggling new democracy. By the fall of 2003, Serbian voters gave Milosevic's party a plurality of seats in the national parliament—with a seat reserved for Milosevic himself, even while he remained a prisoner in The Hague.

Those who spoke for humanity were not concerned to determine whether these modern exercises in international justice had contributed to peace or stability in the countries involved. At the urging of human rights activists, plans were developed for a permanent criminal tribunal which could operate on a global scale. A conference in Rome in the summer of 1998 agreed on the main provisions for a treaty to establish an International Criminal Court. By the terms of this treaty, the ICC would be served by a permanent independent prosecutor, answerable only to judges elected by parties to the organic treaty for the court. The court would have jurisdiction over "genocide" and "crimes against humanity" and also over "war crimes" and the crime of "aggression." Its independent prosecutor could launch prosecutions against nationals of ratifying states. The prosecutor was also authorized to indict nationals of nonratifying states if their crimes had involved victims from states that had ratified—or even from states that had not ratified but had sought the court's assistance for particular prosecutions against nationals of another non-ratifying state.

The Rome conference could not reach agreement on defining the crime of "aggression." So the definition would be left to future determination by states that ratified the Rome Statute. Presumably, the judges of the court would then offer further clarification through accumulating case law. Whether a state has been so threatened or so provoked that it is justified in resorting to war—or whether full-scale war is an excessive response, amounting to aggression in itself—has occupied the attention of diplomats and moral philosophers for many centuries. Now it might all be settled by a small panel of international jurists impartially determining the right answer in conflicts around the world.

If this seems fantastical, the existing provisions for "war crimes" were not much better. There had certainly been much experience with restraints in war. It had, for example, been accepted by professional armies, at least since the seventeenth century, that enemy prisoners should not be massacred or enslaved and that civilians in conquered territory should also be protected from massacre and even from looting.[47] The Hague Peace conference in 1899 had sought to ban weapons considered unusually destructive, but these constraints had been largely disregarded in the world wars of the twentieth century. Conventions to protect prisoners of war, negotiated in Geneva after each of the world wars, codified a considerable list of requirements for proper treatment, but stipulated that these standards would apply only between uniformed troops, belonging to states that conformed to these standards themselves.

Following the Vietnam War, the International Committee for the Red Cross organized an international conference to consider additional restraints in war. In a conference dominated by Third World countries, an "Additional Protocol to the Geneva Conventions" was proposed, which for the first time would protect guerrilla forces (like the Viet Cong) and simultaneously impose restrictions on aerial bombardment, siege warfare, and other methods of war to ensure minimal harm to civilian lives and even civilian property.[48] The protocol contains many provisions purporting to hold military decision makers to a precise balance between "objective military advantage" and collateral harm to noncombatants—as if commanders could always know in advance what might be gained by each military action. The evident purpose of the protocol, over all, was to constrain nations with advanced military technology in their conflicts with insurgences that did not have access to advanced weapons. The United States refused to ratify. And, at the time, most of its NATO partners also remained aloof. With the ending of the Cold War, however, almost every European country felt free to subscribe to the protocol.[49]

The definitions of war crimes in the ICC Statute were largely drawn from provisions in the Additional Protocol. In effect, countries that did not expect to be engaged in war would now dictate the tactics permitted to those that might still be engaged in combat operations. The protocol prohibited retaliation in kind for violations of the laws of war and made no other provision for reprisals. It could not be readily enforced, then, by combatant states. It would have to be enforced outside the arena of war itself—presumably by separate and subsequent prosecutions. The ICC, detached from any particular state, seemed the obvious vehicle.

The project looked particularly unpalatable to American military planners after the attacks of September 11. President Bill Clinton had signed the Rome Statute during his last weeks in office but recommended against Senate ratification until the treaty was substantially amended. Six months after the 9/11 attacks, President George W. Bush announced that the United States should no longer be listed among the signatories. Congress, meanwhile, enacted a law not only prohibiting American cooperation with the ICC but authorizing the president to use all means necessary, including military action, to secure the release of any American held for trial by the ICC.

The prospects for the court did not look promising. But even after September 11, European states remained extremely committed to the project. Russia, China, India, Pakistan, Japan, Indonesia, and other major states refused to ratify the Rome Statute, as did a majority of UN member states. Israel declined to ratify, as did all Arab states except Jordan. Nonetheless, European Union officials lobbied countries in Eastern and Central Europe to ratify, along with former African colonies of Europe. African states had been notorious for permitting their armies to massacre and rape civilians, to slaughter prisoners, and, in general, to display total disregard for all customary laws of war. If one took the project seriously, one had to believe that these states would be qualified to select and sustain a court equipped to judge the war measures of the United States.

Nonetheless, European governments vetoed efforts by the United States to secure exemptions from ICC jurisdiction for UN peacekeeping operations (a particular concern for the United States, since American troops sometimes took part in these operations). Europeans insisted that the Security Council lacked the authority to interfere with the ICC—even though the council was supposed to have supreme responsibility for peace. It was, in a way, a perfect encapsulation of the moral vision underlying the court.

Democratic party has used courts to further their
agenda when legislative action would have failed
SOVEREIGNTY AND SECURITY 95

Unlike the Security Council, the ICC is not subject to veto by permanent members of the Security Council. That is reason enough for states like Germany, which does not have a permanent seat on the council, to favor a shift in international authority from the council to the court. Germany has announced that it will provide 20 percent of the ICC's budget and, according to its foreign ministry, expects to secure at least a comparable proportion of staff appointments in the prosecutor's office.[50]

The court is even less well equipped than the council, however, to ensure compliance with its own rulings. Without an army or a police force of its own—or even a foreign aid budget—it has no reliable means of forcing even signatory states to carry out the arrests and extraditions its prosecutor might demand. Signatories to the Rome Statute are pledged to cooperate in extradition efforts, but this is merely a moral obligation backed by no obvious sanction for noncooperation. During the 1970s and 1980s, Germany and other European states allowed Palestinian terrorists, wanted for the murder of Israeli athletes at the Munich Olympics, to slip out of their territory—even from their police custody.[51] It is doubtful any state can be made to cooperate with criminal justice merely because it now claims to be international.

But the ICC still has a more sinister potential than the Security Council. UN resolutions are easily ignored; indictment of a particular individual speaks more loudly. The ICC cannot possibly punish any but a tiny fraction of "war criminals." It is not designed to secure justice. It is designed to highlight particular "crimes," or what the ICC prosecutor chooses to consider as "crimes." Criminal trials in a national court system are, among other things, devices to ensure that the overwhelming power of the state is not abused—to ensure, that is, that the accused receives due process. Since the ICC has no real power, it can only dramatize the guilt of particular defendants—essentially, by mounting international show trials. Since moral authority is all the authority it can muster, the ICC will try to earn more of it by showing that it can humble the strong. If that does not work, it can try to serve the agendas of its main state sponsors.

Germans and other Europeans may be cheered by the prospect of mounting their own Nuremberg trials of American and Israeli "war criminals." It may be all the more satisfying as they imagine they do not have to duplicate the achievement of the powers that organized the Nuremberg tribunal:

defeating the national forces of the accused in an all-out war. The moral authority of European states is supposed to be enough to cow the guilty ones.

Of course, it cannot work. But it is not even a noble ideal that happens to be impractical. It is, fundamentally, a quite bizarre idea. That may be why nothing of the sort has ever been attempted in the modern world—nor, for that matter, even in medieval Europe, which was not exactly scrupulous about notions of national independence.[52]

The moral authority of the ICC rests on its claim to be removed from the aims of any one nation. That is, it seeks to abstract the issues it is asked to consider from their diplomatic context and from dominant political realities. While this may be attractive for Europeans, it is not plausible to imagine that a court in The Hague can produce genuine international justice in instances where the Security Council has failed.

Under the terms of the Rome Statute, the United States could, in principle, have been subjected to ICC investigation for its military actions in Iraq, if only Saddam Hussein had had the wit to ask the court to assert jurisdiction. That is all that would have been required, despite America's rejection of the treaty. In fact, within weeks after the toppling of Saddam's government, legal advocates began petitioning the court to indict British Prime Minister Tony Blair for "war crimes" committed by British forces. The petitioners argued that British military tactics were unlawful, because they generated excessive civilian casualties.[53]

Despite enormous care and precision in the Anglo-American bombing effort, some civilian casualties were inevitable. Apart from other crimes, Saddam's government systematically placed Iraqi military forces in the vicinity of civilian residential settings to make civilians into unwilling "human shields" for the Iraqi military. Overall, however, the Anglo-American intervention surely saved Iraqi lives—civilian war deaths were less than 3,000, while casualties of Saddam's tyranny had numbered in the hundreds of thousands. The statute makes no provision, however, for viewing possible "crimes" in their larger context.

The court may very well shrink from involvement in such a controversial case during its first few years. But a prosecution of this kind would not be absurd. It is something to be expected—if not immediately, then a few years from now, when the court gains more self-confidence. The court is certainly entitled to abstract from the context of any particular conflict;

the Rome Statute encourages a juridical perspective that does so. The court is supposed to be impartial. It is supposed to blind its eyes to the fact that one side is vastly more culpable, so long as the other side might also be found guilty of infractions. The court will find it hard to resist demands to acknowledge a share of guilt on both sides. Otherwise, it risks being attacked as a tool of American power, and so disappoint its main backers in Europe.

What if a new government in Iraq decides it does not want to pursue the charges against the British? Something similar happened when a new government came to power in Nicaragua in 1990. The previous government, of the Marxist Sandinista party, had pursued claims against the United States at the International Court of Justice, arguing that the Reagan administration's policy of support for anti-Sandinista rebels violated international law. The new government, organized after internationally supervised elections, agreed to drop all previous legal claims against the United States—and the United States offered financial assistance to the new government without reference to earlier disputes.

But a criminal prosecution by the ICC would present quite a different challenge. If, for example, the ICC decided to prosecute British officials for "war crimes" in Iraq, the new government in Iraq would have no say in whether to continue prosecution of forces that most Iraqis see as liberators. The decision would be left to the ICC prosecutor—or the judges reviewing his decision. Nor would there be anything the British government could do about the matter. The ICC Statute provides that national pardons or amnesties will not be binding on the international court.

Does this scheme risk inhibiting the good guys in international conflicts more than the bad guys? Saddam Hussein was willing to defy eighteen resolutions of the Security Council, endorsed by all the great powers in the world. He would not likely have cared whether he was also indicted by an international bureaucrat in The Hague. He was not going to be arrested in Baghdad while he remained in power, and an indictment was not going to drive him from power. Terrorist leaders do not care about indictments, either, as they have proven again and again by ignoring indictments by national courts.

But citizens in a democracy may be shaken when international law pronounces their leaders "criminals." That is the only plausible way the

ICC can have effect—by working on public opinion in democratic countries. Should we worry about a system that may encourage people to think General Richard Myers (chairman of the U.S. Joint Chiefs of Staff during the Iraq war) is somehow the moral equivalent of Uday Hussein? That is, in a way, the central point of the ICC—to prove that there is impartial justice, so liberators may be condemned along with tyrants.

In a domestic setting, where a government has full control of its territory, it is reasonable to think that law should be enforced without regard to the larger context. It is reasonable to insist that law be enforced even against those who, in general, have been contributors to the public welfare. In an international context, it is hard to separate particular complaints from general reputation. No country that denounced the American action in Grenada in 1982, for instance, really imagined that the United States would next invade Canada or even Jamaica. In an international context, the larger pattern matters, because international standards can rarely be enforced to everyone's satisfaction in every case. Reliable enforcement of international obligations can only be achieved by states, none of which is morally perfect, none of which is constrained by reliable institutions in the same way as a domestic prosecutor is.

The general conduct and reputation of each state must matter, because force, at some point, may be necessary and can only be wielded by a state. It is obvious to Americans. But Germans may ask, why should national reputation be so important? Belgians may wonder, why is it necessary to deploy force? After all, what harm did it do to Belgium when Belgian peacekeepers allowed a million innocents to be slaughtered in Rwanda?

Law must have a moral and political context or it is mere ideological assertion. That is true in domestic settings—at least, it is the principle of constitutional states, which require that laws have some basis in consent. It is even more true in international affairs, when there is no reliable constitutional system to coerce those who do not consent to a particular standard.

Plainly, the United States cannot cooperate with the International Criminal Court. The only relevant question is whether it can coexist with this bizarre institution. The answer to that question will depend on whether the international bureaucrats who staff the ICC are prepared to coexist with the United States and the majority of other states that have refused to ratify the ICC Statute. The first test will be whether the ICC can establish true international credibility, or whether it will succumb to European political biases. The record so far gives little reason for optimism: When the UN Human Rights Commission voted to endorse Palestinian suicide bombing—little more than six months after the attacks on the World Trade Center and the Pentagon—most European states on the commission joined with the majority of representatives in affirming this grotesque view of human rights.[54]

For similar reasons, it is likely that the ICC will be turned against Israel, since condemnations of Israel are the crowd-pleasing highlight of most international circuses—and the ICC has no bread to offer.[55] It is easy to demonize Israel, since there is only one Jewish state in the world. And apart from various diplomatic calculations of advantage in joining the condemnation, Europeans seem to take particular satisfaction in associating Israel with "crimes against humanity." Psychologists have various theories about why this is so.

But having whetted its appetite on a small scapegoat, sooner or later the ICC will be turned against the United States. French leaders have repeatedly warned that the United States is a "hyperpower" that needs to be "balanced" by international resistance. The ICC remains the most plausible instrument for humbling the United States. Prominent voices in Europe seem unable to forgive the United States for using military force to end the careers of mass murderers—most recently in Iraq. Commentators in Germany now insist that Britain and America committed war crimes against Nazi Germany. Endorsing this view, the German President, Johannes Rau, assured a German audience in September 2003 that "Hitler's criminal policies do not exonerate anyone who answered terrible wrongs with terrible wrongs."[56] If the statute of limitations has lapsed on those crimes, others may still be prosecuted. Nongovernmental advocacy groups will also be major constituencies for the court, and they have many reasons of their own to insist that international law must be shown to cover even the United States.

France and Germany provide the most funding for the ICC and will be in the best position to highlight its "achievements." The judges are unlikely to forget that fact.[57] The court may be even more brazen than the foreign ministries of these countries, since it is more insulated from retaliation. The United States cannot impose economic penalties or diplomatic reprisals on a group of freestanding international civil servants. It is unlikely that such independence will make the court more cautious in appealing to its likeliest constituencies—among nations or among NGOs.

But much of the world—certainly much of Europe—does not see the court as an institution operating in a political context, with constraints and incentives of its own. The European Union itself has conditioned Europeans to think power can be wielded safely by mysterious bureaucrats in small, low-lying countries in Northwest Europe. The idea of the court also echoes larger currents of opinion that appeal particularly to Europeans. The moral force of law can subdue even powerful governments. If it were not so, then how could the European Court of Justice be trusted to provide impartial justice among the states of Europe? If it were not so, how could Europeans entrust their security to a union with no force of its own to deploy in their defense? If it were not so, how could the institutions of the new Europe have succeeded in subduing the evil tyrannies of Hitler and Stalin? To question the court would be to risk opening too many awkward questions. To believe in the reign of justice is far more edifying.

4

Holy Empire of Human Rights

In the last decades of the twentieth century, scholars, advocates, and even many judges began to speak about an "international law of human rights" as a serious body of law, already in place, already binding on sovereign states. Some scholars insisted that this law drew on long-standing constitutional traditions of nations like the United States. Some courts even identified human rights standards with "the law of nations," a term that appears in the U.S. Constitution in a provision authorizing Congress to "define and punish offenses against the law of nations."[1]

Such claims are meant to be reassuring. They happen to be quite implausible, however. Medieval commentators, borrowing the term *ius gentium* from Roman law, had often identified that term with universally accepted standards or with natural law. The Framers of the Constitution probably invoked the English version of the term as they found it in Blackstone's *Commentaries*, which had a separate chapter on "offenses against the law of nations." But Blackstone used the term in a much more restrictive sense. His account treated only those "offenses" involved in failing to protect foreign ambassadors, failing to protect foreign nationals traveling under approved passports, and failing to suppress piracy.[2] From the early seventeenth century onward, treatises on the "law of nations" had emphasized that the term should apply only to obligations of sovereign states. It was precisely to emphasize this restrictive understanding of its reach that the English legal reformer, Jeremy Bentham, coined the new term "international law" in 1789: "International law," he insisted, would clearly indicate that this was a law governing the "mutual transactions between sovereigns"—a law that was entirely *between* nations, rather than reaching into their internal affairs.[3] One of the first treatises to invoke the new term, in the early nineteenth century, was the work of an American diplomat.[4] The term quickly spread to almost all European languages, however, because the thought behind it was already familiar and widely accepted, at least in nations of Western Europe and the Western Hemisphere.

Prior to the last decades of the twentieth century, then, talk of an "international law of human rights" would have seemed puzzling. In fact, it would have have seemed oxymoronic.[5] Earlier generations were certainly familiar with claims under international law by which one state might protest the mistreatment of its own citizens when they traveled into the territory of another state. But human rights law purports to apply to human beings, as such. It purports to protect individuals, even in dealings with their own government. There is nothing international about such a claim.

The idea that governments are bound by an international law of human rights seems to imply that governments which violate this law can be subject to correction by some higher authority. Who could serve as that higher authority? Can one state lay down proper standards for the way another state treats its own people in its own territory? States ordinarily resist efforts by outside states to impose their own favored policies in this way. If there really were an international law of human rights, however, each state would be bound to accept the views of external human rights authorities, and could not resist such claims as foreign intrusions. Obviously, this is not how states actually interact with each other. International human rights law, therefore, seems to float in a realm altogether removed from interstate conflicts, championing the claims of human beings, as such, on behalf of humanity at large.

In some sense, this vision of international affairs seems more religious than practical or political. Yet it does not even claim to be political. It claims to be a system of law, presumably to be determined by lawyers and judges like any other body of law. Of course, it is an unusual body of law in that it is separated from police and armies and other ordinary requisites of enforcement—not to mention a sovereign state with the clear authority to write the laws itself. It is a body of law that does not assure protection to those who try to adhere to its requirements, or punishment to those that ignore it. In more than one way, it starts by rejecting some of the most fundamental presumptions in modern thinking about law and politics.

Law That Isn't

Even for some decades after the establishment of the United Nations, textbooks still expounded the traditional view that only states could be "subjects" of international law, claiming rights and holding obligations under it. This view, which was well known to the American Founders, had obvious advantages.

In the first place, this approach limited the reach of international law. If only another state could press a claim under international law, then claims could only be made when there was some injury to the territory or nationals of another state. A law that made fewer claims was more likely to gain general acceptance. Until well into the nineteenth century, most of international law was based, in fact, on customary practice, on what states already acknowledged as obligations in their dealings with other states.

The second advantage was equally important. If international law only addressed injuries by one state against another, then any violation of it would, by definition, provide at least one other state with the incentive to protest the violation. And a protest from a state would likely carry some weight. Even a small state could usually impose some retaliation on the offender, such as expelling ambassadors and consuls or limiting trading privileges. And a small state might take care to have allies or protectors who were stronger.

By the end of the nineteenth century, there had already been several ventures in submitting individualized claims to international arbitration. The practice was further encouraged by the establishment of a Permanent Court of International Arbitration in 1899. But such arbitrations always began with carefully negotiated agreements between states, defining the claims to be reviewed—and assuring some parity in the number and scale of claims on each side. Arbitrations usually involved claims for financial compensation. States often advanced them on behalf of their own nationals, regarding some injury inflicted by another state, in situations where businessmen or other travelers of one state had been operating in the territory of the other. But states remained in charge of ultimate payments to individuals and often settled such claims by compromise or by subsequent proceedings in the home state.[6]

An international authority empowered to hear complaints brought by individuals against their own governments would be quite a different thing. Defining and enforcing the rights of citizens are not, after all, peripheral or merely technical governmental services. According to the Declaration of Independence, it is the very purpose of government: "to secure these rights, governments are instituted among men." Most of the complaints against British abuses in the body of the Declaration accordingly protested British interference with colonial institutions of *government*— courts and legislatures—that were supposed to protect the rights of individuals, in the American understanding. One could say that Americans fought a revolution to assert their right to follow their own understanding of rights. It was only after much debate that the new American states were persuaded to accept a federal government that could reach into their jurisdictions and enforce its own laws and standards, regardless of what the states might wish. Even with apparent justification in the text of the federal Constitution, the Supreme Court often provoked intense controversy when it sought to enforce its own understanding of particular constitutional guarantees. Complaints about "activist rulings," of course, remain a source of controversy to this day.

Is the whole world now prepared to entrust such determinations to the direct authority of some international body? In the United States, the appointment and confirmation process assures that the Supreme Court has some continuing connection to the tides of American public opinion. What could assure such connection—from the perspective of any one nation—for an international authority? The Supreme Court interprets constitutional guarantees in the light of a much wider body of established law and practice within the United States. Can an international human rights authority draw on any comparable body of law? The Supreme Court can appeal to "lessons" taught by "national experience"—to the experience of the great constitutional crisis of the 1930s, for example, or the experience of racial segregation in the era of states rights or of the successful campaign for civil rights in the 1950s and 1960s. Such references, frequently encountered in Court opinions, appeal to memories of shared experience, to shared commitments to honor past sacrifices or atone for past wrongs. What can an international authority say to bolster its conclusions in this way?

These remain good questions regarding the authority of the European Court of Human Rights, which has, in recent decades, developed a quite active case law based on abstract treaty provisions and the changing moods of the multinational collection of judges who serve on it. In fact, they were never very serious questions for the United Nations. Certainly, they were not questions which the architects of the UN Charter took very seriously.

When the charter was negotiated, in the aftermath of a horribly destructive war, the immediate concern was preserving the peace. Even for this purpose, the major powers were not willing to empower the UN to override their own national decisions, as the veto provisions in the Security Council showed. Was it plausible that the Soviet Union, which would not submit to international checks on its own use of force abroad, would actually submit to international checks on its use of force at home? Western states had acquiesced to Stalin's imposition of Communist governments in Eastern Europe and his extensive, essentially unilateral, redrawing of boundaries in Eastern Europe. Would these same Western states really risk confrontation with the Soviet Union by demanding that Stalin's government comply with international human rights standards in its treatment of Soviet citizens inside the Soviet Union? The architects of the UN Charter had struggled to find formulas that could allow both the United States and the Soviet Union to cooperate in a common framework for maintaining some degree of international order. Was it at all plausible that this organization could uphold human rights, when its existence rested on the support of one of history's most relentless mass murderers?

The United Nations dealt with this problem by evading it. The charter's preamble spoke of "promoting respect for human rights" rather than enforcing rights. Any serious claim to enforce human rights seemed to be excluded by the stipulation in Article 2 that the organization's authority would not extend to "matters essentially within the domestic jurisdiction of member states." The Security Council was authorized to make binding resolutions for the "peaceful settlement of international disputes." Nothing about human rights was included in the provisions outlining its powers. References to human rights appear in very vague statements about the general aspirations of the United Nations organization as a whole. Somewhat more specific references appear in charter provisions

on the General Assembly and the Economic and Social Council, authorizing these bodies to "recommend" policies in various areas to member
states.[7] In fact, these organs have no other powers beyond such powers
to "recommend."

For many decades the UN followed this strategy of evasion. The
General Assembly immediately established a Human Rights Commission.
The commission immediately devoted its attention to drafting a Universal
Declaration of Human Rights, which was duly endorsed by the General
Assembly in December 1948. But the Declaration achieved consensus
support because it did not purport to be binding and made no provision
for enforcement. It was filled with platitudinous affirmations of individual
rights, which countries were free to interpret as they chose. On the issues
most in dispute between Communist nations and the West—such as the
right to hold private property, the right to engage in private commerce, or
the right to organize competing parties to challenge a government at the
polls—the Declaration was so ambiguous that Communist dictatorships
could easily claim to be acting in conformity with it.[8]

Subsequent treaties did not change the underlying pattern. After
decades of negotiation, the UN achieved widespread ratification of what
was grandly styled a Covenant on Civil and Political Rights, along with a
companion Covenant on Economic and Social Rights. They were essentially restatements of ambiguous formulas in the Universal Declaration that
retained the same ambiguity regarding Communist practices. The Covenant
on Civil and Political Rights did establish a monitoring committee, called
the Human Rights Committee, composed of elected representatives from
ratifying states. But this committee was given no authority to enforce the
terms of the covenant, nor even to establish definitive interpretations of its
terms.

The same approach was taken with subsequent international conventions, purporting to define prohibited practices of race discrimination,
sex discrimination, torture, and failure to protect "the rights of the child."
All these new conventions included provisions for monitoring committees, none of which gave any definite authority to these committees. The
committees had so little authority that they were not even able to enforce
reporting requirements, under which states submitted accounts of their
compliance with the treaties; most states submitted only the most cursory

and unrevealing reports, while many simply failed to submit anything.[9] International authority was not empowered to do anything to enforce even formal compliance at this level.

If it seems quixotic to imagine that international human rights standards could be enforced by actual international authority, it might seem more attractive to regard human rights standards simply as treaties, whose terms might be insisted upon by other states. But international human rights conventions are not ordinary treaties. A normal treaty is a kind of contract, in which one state agrees to make certain concessions or commitments in return for certain concessions or commitments by the other state or states involved.[10] The usual means of enforcement is to withhold promised concessions if the other side reneges on its commitment. Human rights treaties are very hard to conceive in these terms. Canada and Saudi Arabia might both sign the Convention to Eliminate All Forms of Discrimination Against Women (CEDAW), as they have. But if, by some chance, the Saudi government fails to live up to its pledge to eliminate sex discrimination against Saudi women, Canada cannot very well retaliate by withdrawing such protection from Canadian women.

Because nothing is exchanged, it is not even necessary for the various parties to agree on what it is they have actually promised. The conventions do not, by their own terms, obligate signatory states to adhere to the interpretations UN committees or other international authorities—or even other states—may give to the conventions. Technically, each state agrees only to adhere to its own understanding of the convention, allowing other signatory states to adhere, each in its turn, to its own interpretation. It is a very odd sort of contract. One might reasonably question whether a rhetorical exercise of this kind deserves to be regarded as an actual treaty, in the sense in which the U.S. Constitution refers to "treaties."[11]

Since the conventions have no binding force, the most brutal regimes in the world have readily signed human rights conventions. There is very little cost to them in doing so and considerable advantage. Among other things, signing these conventions makes them eligible to serve on human rights monitoring committees. Brutal regimes are often quite eager to serve on such committees, to ensure that the committees do not criticize or embarrass them. And, of course, they hardly ever do. A recent study finds that ratification of human rights treaties is often accompanied by a worsening of human rights violations in the ratifying state, because the paper pledge reduces pressure to do anything more than offer a meaningless signature.[12]

What is true for brutal regimes is also true for other states. As the treaties do not commit murderous governments to adhere to any particular standard, they do not commit other governments to demand serious compliance. The mere existence of a treaty does little in itself to ensure that signatories will care about the compliance of other signatories. After all, Saudi Arabia's conduct does not prevent Canada from adhering to its own notions about sex discrimination within Canada. And there is not much evidence that states put much priority on encouraging other states to comply with international human rights standards. They may deplore brutality in others' domestic policy, but they often find it convenient to maintain good relations with states that are brutal. Canada, for example, has sought to cultivate good relations with Cuba, the most repressive regime in the Western Hemisphere. Most countries have preferred to maintain good relations with Saudi Arabia and not make too much fuss about its approach to sex discrimination.

The game is quite out in the open. Saudi Arabia ratified CEDAW with the reservation that it would not adhere to the terms of the convention when they were in conflict with Islamic law, or *shari'a*—as determined by Saudi Arabia itself. Many other Islamic states ratified with the same reservation. The traditional approach to treaties was that any reservation by one party had to be approved by others, since they would not otherwise be parties to the same treaty. This approach was relaxed to encourage wider adherence to multilateral conventions, most especially human rights conventions. Still, the 1970 Vienna Convention on the Law of Treaties, which was supposed to codify the modern approach to treaty interpretation, provides that a state may not claim to have ratified a treaty if it did so with reservations that are "incompatible with the object and purpose of the treaty."[13] Few states bothered to raise any questions about the *shari'a* reservations, and no one claims that Saudi Arabia is not a full party to CEDAW.[14] Saudi Arabia attached the same reservation to its ratification of the torture convention. When challenged by the monitoring committee to justify its practice of cutting off the hands of convicted thieves, Saudi Arabia's representative replied that the practice was required by the Saudi government's understanding of *shari'a*.[15] Next case?

Does China respect the rights of free speech and religious freedom, as set down in the Covenant on Civil and Political Rights, to which it claims to be a party? China says it adheres to these standards, but according to its own interpretations of their meaning. These interpretations are, evidently, somewhat different than those of Western states. The United States made repeated efforts in the late 1990s to persuade the UN Human Rights Commission to initiate an investigation into China's human rights practices. China made it known that it would cut off contracts with European states that voted in favor of initiating such an inquiry. Year after year, European states voted against it.[16]

In 2001, the European states made things easier all around by voting to exclude the United States from a place on the Human Rights Commission, for the very first time since its establishment in 1946. European governments were irritated at the Bush administration for "unilateral" policies. Registering this resentment toward the United States took higher priority than preserving the credibility of the Human Rights Commission. The regional voting bloc (which encompasses North America and Western Europe) decided to replace the United States with Austria—at a time when other EU states had imposed diplomatic sanctions on Austria for allowing the somewhat xenophobic Freedom Party to join the new coalition government in Vienna. Other regional blocs at the UN elected China, Syria, Pakistan, Cuba, and Sudan to the Human Rights Commission. In 2003, Libya was elected to chair the commission.

Since there is no international authority to enforce human rights standards, and governments that ratify human rights treaties do not seem to take them very seriously as treaties, the whole business might seem an exercise in symbolism. But not all symbols are empty; it depends on how people view them. The great hope of the "international human rights movement" has been to appeal over the heads of governments to the people who are supposed to benefit from these standards.

This was, in fact, the hope from the outset. The preamble to the Universal Declaration calls its provisions "a common standard . . . for all peoples and all nations" which "every individual and every organ of society, keeping this Declaration constantly in mind, shall strive by teaching and education to promote respect for. . . ." Presumably, this exhortation was meant to echo—or perhaps to supplant—an earlier admonition:

"[T]hese words . . . shall be upon thy heart; and thou shalt teach them diligently unto thy children and shalt talk of them when thou sittest in thy house and when thou walkest by the way and when thou liest down and when thou risest up" (Deut. 6:6–7). But the Bible, in demanding such diligent attention for these "words," does not hesitate to characterize them as "commandments" (Deut. 6:6). The Universal Declaration does not "command" but exhorts "all peoples and nations" to "strive" by "progressive measures, national and international, to secure . . . universal and effective recognition and observance" for provisions of the Declaration.

The Bible could demand faithful and unceasing attention to the Ten Commandments because they speak to the personal conduct of individuals. Faithful Jews and Christians have adhered to them—honoring their parents, refraining from theft, adultery, coveting, and so on—under a great variety of governments and circumstances over many centuries. Most of the "observance" that the Universal Declaration seeks to "secure" can only be provided by governments—due process in criminal trials, free public education, laws assuring paid vacations to all employees, and so forth. The General Assembly of the United Nations was not in a position to issue commandments to governments, however. In effect, it appealed to "every individual and every organ of society" to persuade governments to comply with its agenda. Subsequent conventions have added some elaboration to the Universal Declaration but no additional enforcement authority.

One could say, with only slight exaggeration, that instead of an international regulatory authority or a serious treaty structure, the human rights conventions sought to found a new church. The conventions appealed to the faithful to believe. Medieval Europe had much experience with religious authorities claiming higher legal status than mere governments. Medieval popes and bishops claimed, for example, the authority to absolve believers of their vows of allegiance to local rulers when those rulers had angered the church. Medieval notions about natural law, however, were not always in keeping with modern ideas about individual rights: Pope Innocent III, having incited rebellion against England's King John, turned around and absolved that scheming monarch from his sworn oath to uphold the Magna Carta when John promised to place his kingdom under papal control.[17] The medieval church was often embroiled in complex political disputes, and the experience was not remembered in later centuries as a credit to religious teaching. But advocates for universal human rights standards assumed that modern international authorities would never become entangled in politics. How could these inspired modern principles possibly lend themselves to political abuse?

Evangelism

Private advocacy groups attended the San Francisco conference that formulated the final text of the UN Charter in the spring of 1945. By some accounts, their advocacy helped persuade diplomats to include favorable mentions of "human rights" in the charter. They also secured favorable mention for themselves: Article 71 stipulates that the Economic and Social Council may consult with "non-governmental organizations." The phrase would, at the time, have seemed disorienting to most Americans: Wouldn't any organization at all be "non-governmental" if not itself a part of the government? Like many UN phrases, this one was inspired by Communist rhetoric. In the 1930s, the International Labour Organization had rejected a Soviet delegation of "trade unionists" as not properly representative of actual workers. Stalin's government insisted that Soviet labor organizations were "non-governmental."[18] The term from then on had the connotation of an organization devoted to public policy but not accountable to any actual electorate.

For some decades after the founding of the United Nations, diplomats had little use for nongovernmental organizations. The Human Rights Commission adopted a self-limiting rule prohibiting any comment on the particular practices of any particular state. The rule was relaxed in the mid-1960s to allow private advocacy groups to present information about racial oppression in South Africa. But into the 1970s, groups with wider concerns found UN forums closed to them.[19] The General Assembly passed resolutions proclaiming the "right" of states to expropriate private property, particularly when owned by foreign investors. Other resolutions proclaimed a "right to development," by which rich states would somehow be obligated to provide assistance to poor states.[20] The UN was not much interested in the rights of individual human beings, who remained subject to torture and brutal repression throughout Africa, Asia, Eastern Europe, and much of Latin America—that is, in the majority of UN member states.

Yet talk about human rights began to gain momentum in other forums. Academic specialists in American law schools, with counterparts in some European universities, began to argue in the 1970s that human rights obligations had become part of customary international law. So the Universal Declaration of Human Rights, though conceived as nonbinding in 1948, must now be seen as "legally binding." The proof that it had entered into "customary international law" was that it had become the custom of the General Assembly to mention the Universal Declaration in subsequent resolutions. By 1980, professors at the Yale Law School announced that "activities of the General Assembly" provided "what is in effect a new modality of law making" and "a closer approximation to par-liamentary enactment" for international law.[21]

That same year, a federal appeals court in New York was persuaded to endorse this vision when it approved federal jurisdiction for a Paraguayan man to sue a Paraguayan official for the torture of the man's son in Paraguay.[22] The claim could go forward, the court ruled, under the Alien Tort Claims Act, a 1789 statute authorizing federal courts to hear tort claims for "offenses against the law of nations." Amicus briefs from legal scholars had persuaded the court that "the law of nations" had now come to embrace prohibitions on torture founded on General Assembly resolu-tions. It therefore did not matter that Paraguay had not ratified any actual treaty prohibiting torture, nor did it matter that the United States itself had not done so, either.

By 1987, a prestigious academic commentary, the *Restatement of Foreign Relations Law* (3d) devoted a whole chapter to the "customary law of human rights." The *Restatement* insisted that this law could be enforced by American courts—even, it seemed, against American officials. Custom-ary law had already embraced prohibitions on "genocide" and "slavery," but might eventually reach other offenses as heinous as sex discrimina-tion; the customary law of human rights, as the *Restatement* explained, was still "evolving."[23] By the mid-1990s, this law was thought sufficient to establish jurisdiction in U.S. courts for a suit against a Serb militia leader for atrocities committed against Bosnian civilians in Bosnia. More imaginative lawyers invoked customary international law to file lawsuits

No legitimacy but UN — and it's our courts profiding it

(in U.S. courts) against private corporations for complicity in environmental crimes and human rights abuses in Bolivia, Indonesia, Burma, and other places rather removed from the usual jurisdiction of federal courts.[24] By the early 1990s, Professor Louis Sohn of the Harvard Law School acknowledged that the relevant law could not be left to governments to establish: "States never really make international law on the subject of human rights. It is made by the people who care: the professors, the writers of textbooks and casebooks, and the authors of leading articles in leading international law journals."[25]

By then, however, there were already many more "people who care." In the 1970s, a public interest advocacy movement came to play a substantial role in American domestic policy debates. Relaxed rules of standing allowed public interest advocates to demand more regulatory controls for environmental protection and workplace and consumer safety, and protections for racial and ethnic minorities and women and the aged and infirm. By the 1980s, public interest advocacy began to flow into international advocacy efforts. The Environmental Defense Fund, for example, which had been based in Washington close to federal regulatory agencies, opened an office in New York and began to emphasize global environmental threats, such as depletion of the earth's ozone layer. Leading figures in the American Civil Liberties Union helped to organize a series of international human rights advocacy efforts that emerged in the 1980s as a well-funded new organization, Human Rights Watch. Foundations began to pour money into international advocacy efforts. Law schools opened new programs in international legal advocacy, with heavy emphasis on international human rights claims.

The trends found echoes in Western Europe. As the Cold War began to wind down in the late 1980s, a "peace movement" there, organized to resist deployment of new American missiles a few years before, began to turn its attention to environmental causes and the threats posed by industrial development to aboriginal peoples in various parts of the world. The new organization, "Greenpeace," which developed a considerable following in Western Europe, symbolized the merger of earlier protest movements into new currents.

Finally, even the United Nations began to take notice. The proliferation of "nongovernmental" organizations was registered at the UN. The

Economic and Social Council had accorded "consultative" status to thirty-nine NGOs in 1948. By 1991, there were 395 such organizations registered with the UN. The UN's "Earth Summit" at Rio de Janeiro in 1992 drew 1,400 NGO representatives who organized their own parallel conference ("Global Power") while actively lobbying and monitoring government delegates involved in negotiating a series of new environmental agreements. The following year, the UN hosted a World Conference on Human Rights, which drew even more NGO delegates.

A series of conferences on such topics as "population" and "women's rights" and "human habitat" drew nearly comparable crowds of NGO observers and lobbyists to Cairo, Beijing, and Copenhagen. NGO involvement was sustained in subsequent conferences to monitor progress in implementing past conference resolutions and add precision to previous platitudes. Seemingly divergent concerns converged at these UN forums, so that "human rights" and "gender equality" and "sustainable development" came to look, at least to many advocates, as mutually supporting causes in a single great movement, which advocates called "global civil society."

UN officials were only too happy to play hosts and partners to "global civil society." Secretary General Boutros Boutros-Ghali explained that a new "world system" had undermined "the exclusive claims of the state to jurisdiction over the lives of its citizens," but international institutions could not take up necessary new responsibilities on their own: "NGOs also carry out an essential representational role, an essential part of the legitimacy without which no international activity can be meaningful."[26] Kofi Annan, who succeeded Boutros-Ghali as secretary general, enthused about a "global society" held together by "common values" and a new common language: "The language of global society is international law."[27]

Even states took up the call to speak this new "common language." In 1998, a Spanish prosecutor sought to prosecute former Chilean president Augusto Pinochet for "genocide" of "political opponents" after the 1973 military coup that brought Pinochet to power. Acting on a Spanish warrant, British authorities arrested Pinochet after he had entered Britain on a Chilean diplomatic mission. British judges trimmed the charge back to violations of the UN's Convention Against Torture during the last eighteen months of Pinochet's time in office (by which time both Britain and Chile had ratified the convention). The European Parliament endorsed the prosecution of

Pinochet, and governments throughout Western Europe offered to host their own prosecutions if Britain or Spain declined to act. Advocacy groups mobilized to present information about human rights abuses in Chile during Pinochet's rule, and put forward legal arguments and moral appeals before the courts, legislatures, and the media. One of the British judges who ruled in favor of extraditing Pinochet turned out to be a fundraiser for Amnesty International—a fact he had not thought important enough to disclose. When Britain's lord chancellor found out, he ordered a new appeal before a new group of judges (although the ultimate result remained much the same).[28]

Throughout this process, the elected governments in Spain and Britain insisted that this was a matter that must be resolved by courts— until Pinochet's appeals were exhausted and Britain's home secretary decided that the aging dictator was too sick to stand trial. That final diplomatic evasion provoked much protest from human rights advocates. The case had otherwise been a perfect reflection of new ideas about international law: "Global civil society" would be empowered to demand justice from international outlaws, while states became either dutiful servants of this cause or passive bystanders to these actions. The will of the Chilean people—whose democratically elected government demanded Pinochet's release—could be simply ignored. International human rights law promised to be something universal, standing above and outside the mere political concerns of governments.

Human rights advocates saw the Pinochet case as setting an important precedent (regardless of its final outcome), and looked to build upon this success with a free-standing international criminal court. When plans for the ICC were fleshed out at a 1998 conference in Rome, NGOs again played a prominent role, advising and lobbying as government officials tried to sort out the implications of conflicting proposals. The result was something much closer to the NGO vision than the proposals advanced by the American government: The prosecutor would be entirely independent, subject to control only by the court itself. Bylaws specified that failure of the prosecutor to act on evidence of crimes could itself be appealed—in effect, by the human rights advocacy groups seeking to organize a prosecution.[29]

Barely two years later, prosecutors in Belgium, urged on by advocacy groups, announced that they were preparing to file criminal charges against Israeli Prime Minister Ariel Sharon for the murder of 800 Palestinian civilians in refugee camps in southern Lebanon twenty years earlier. The killings had been perpetrated by Lebanese Christian militia forces. Sharon had commanded the Israeli Defense Forces and did not have reliable control over the Lebanese militia, nor did he know about these terrible revenge killings at the time they took place. But advocacy groups were not interested in finding the actual perpetrators of the massacre. They focused on Sharon, and Belgian prosecutors were ready to press the case. The Belgian government claimed to be powerless—this was a matter of "law." Belgian courts staved off embarrassment in 2002 by deciding that Sharon could not be prosecuted while he was in office.

Pro-Israel advocates tried to persuade Belgian prosecutors to consider action against Yasir Arafat for his decades-long sponsorship of terrorism. Arafat had little to worry about. One of the British judges who voted to extradite Pinochet candidly explained that it would be imprudent to assert "universal jurisdiction" over crimes committed by leaders in Islamic countries, since Muslims might retaliate with terror attacks on European cities.[30] The Arafat inquiry did not make much progress.

In spring 2003, Belgian courts were faced with a claim against former president George H. W. Bush for "war crimes" ostensibly committed by American forces in the 1991 Gulf War. American officials then speculated that if Belgium insisted on holding Americans hostage to its global ambitions for justice, the United States might urge the removal of NATO headquarters to a safer location. The Belgian Parliament then acted swiftly to limit the jurisdiction of Belgian courts to crimes involving Belgian nationals or territory.[31] Perhaps the International Criminal Court will be equally reticent about confronting the United States: Legislation enacted in 2002 authorizes the president to use all means, including armed force, to ensure the release of U.S. personnel held for trial at the ICC.[32] But what about dangers at home?

Sovereignty as a Constitutional Brake

The most obvious problem with human rights standards is that they are not the result of a constitutional process. In various ways, they promise—or threaten—an end run around the domestic lawmaking process. That is inherent in the goals of international human rights law. Political advocates of varying views often advance moral appeals for their causes. But if there really is an international *law* of human rights, then it has more status than mere arguments about moral duty. International human rights advocates, now backed by a sizable contingent of legal scholars, insist that their preferred standards really are binding law. How do these standards come to attain the status of "law"? Almost any route to legalizing international human rights standards, within the United States, implies an alternate constitutional process—a different way of making law for the American people.

Even claims based on treaties that have been ratified by the Senate raise serious constitutional questions. One obvious consequence is that matters which, under the Constitution, would ordinarily be left to the states can now be handled by the federal government, under the claim that it is merely implementing international obligations. In the 1950s, critics of human rights conventions raised just this concern. Constitutional criticism was advanced by some distinguished legal scholars, including the president of the American Bar Association. The Senate came within one vote of endorsing a constitutional amendment, proposed by Senator John Bricker of Ohio, which would have specified that no treaty could authorize congressional legislation which would not be constitutional for Congress to enact in the absence of a treaty. The Bricker Amendment was derailed in the early 1950s when the Eisenhower administration promised that it would not submit any human rights treaties to the Senate.[33] President Jimmy Carter urged a different approach in the mid-1970s, but the Senate still refused to ratify these treaties.

The Senate finally ratified a handful of human rights conventions after the Reagan and George H. W. Bush administrations urged ratification with appropriate reservations. So the United States became a party to the International Covenant on Civil and Political Rights (ICCPR) and the Convention against Torture and the Convention Against Race Discrimination. But in each case, ratification was accompanied by reservations designed to ensure that the conventions could not be invoked in domestic law or to justify any measure contrary to limitations in the Bill of Rights. The Covenant on Civil and Political Rights, for example, demands that adhering states prohibit hate speech and "propaganda for war," and

Senate reservations specifically exempted the United States from taking any action that might violate First Amendment guarantees.[34]

If Congress has a duty to implement other aspects of the conventions, however, it would still seem to have handed itself authority it would not otherwise have. So, when the Supreme Court struck down the Religious Freedom Restoration Act on the grounds that it improperly interfered with matters reserved to state governments, at least one legal scholar argued that legislation could be justified regardless of constitutional limitations on congressional authority, since it was required to implement an international obligation. Others have argued that accepted interpretations of the First Amendment must be revised in order to ensure that the Constitution does not interfere with American international obligations.[35]

Senate reservations might seem to have put such appeals to rest in most areas. But the monitoring committee for the Covenant on Civil and Political Rights insisted, in the mid-1990s, that no reservation could be valid if it interfered with the "object and purpose" of the treaty—or with some larger principle established by customary law as a "peremptory norm." The committee insisted, moreover, that if a reservation were found to be improper, this would not invalidate the ratification but would simply nullify the legal validity of the reservation. Who would determine the validity of any particular reservation? The committee suggested that it could act as the register of evolving international opinion on such questions. The whole argument was denounced at the time by American representatives, but once one enters the shadow world of customary international law, it is hard to say what rules apply.[36]

Perhaps the greatest danger is that American courts might come to embrace the customary international law of human rights as an independent standard of law. That has already happened in a series of lower court opinions dealing with actions by foreign officials or American corporations operating in foreign territory. But if this approach can be applied in these settings, there seems no logical reason why it could not be applied to American officials—or indeed American corporations or citizens—operating within the United States. Many legal scholars have urged such an approach. Something quite similar has happened in Europe, where national courts have readily subscribed to rulings of the European Court of Justice, including rulings that have invoked international human rights standards. For judges, it opens the prospect of new realms of activist policymaking without the awkwardness of having to justify innovations using provisions in the U.S. Constitution that have long been interpreted in a different sense.

Indeed, national courts in other countries have been prepared to interpret their own constitutions in light of rulings by courts in other nations, dealing with different constitutions but addressing similar issues. Robert Bork calls this process "international constitutional common law."[37] It is the logical extension of conjuring new standards in the name of customary international law of human rights and might even seem to have more credibility than appeals to resolutions of the UN General Assembly.

Even the U.S. Supreme Court is not deaf to the appeal of this approach. In spring 2002, the Court ruled that imposing capital punishment on a murderer with subnormal intelligence would constitute "cruel and unusual punishment." The Court had ruled just the opposite barely a decade earlier; in the interim, it noted, many state legislatures and foreign governments had decided that capital punishment was improper in these circumstances. The Court's decision cited an amicus brief to this effect filed by the European Union.[38] Similarly, in 1987, the Court had found no constitutional bar to state laws against sodomy. In 2003, the Court reversed its ruling, finding that the Constitution did, after all, contain an implied guarantee of sexual freedom; the proof for this claim was that the European Union had endorsed the same doctrine. Needless to say, the EU had not based its decision on an interpretation of the American Constitution.[39]

The objection to this approach was stated with some succinctness by Justice Antonin Scalia. Dissenting in the capital punishment ruling, he dismissed the relevance of "practices of the 'world community'" on the ground that the latter's "notions of justice are (thankfully) not always those of our people."[40] This was not an expression of xenophobia: Whether the American people are entitled to have their own standards, different from those of Europeans or other people, is the central point in dispute.

Many constitutional provisions are framed in such general terms that their meaning is uncertain. The Supreme Court has often changed its mind about the meaning of particular provisions. Why not be guided by the opinion of other courts in other countries? The Council of Europe expressed the point when it argued, in opposition to American practices on capital punishment, that to defy the conclusions of other democratic states is "undemocratic."[41]

One reason to doubt the wisdom of this approach is that, compared with most countries in Europe, the United States has somewhat different priorities in its understanding of rights. If one looks at comments of UN forums, the United States seems even more unusual. American opinion and American law are somewhat more insistent on property rights and commercial freedom, whereas European and UN opinion is more sympathetic to government controls and government redistribution programs. European and UN opinion is more in tune with feminist aims, so that, for example, the European Court of Justice has insisted that women must not only be paid the same as men when working in the same jobs, but that governments must ensure that jobs in which women preponderate must be compensated at their "comparable worth"—something which government is supposed to be able to determine.[42] UN committees are so sensitive to feminist opinion that they have criticized countries for maintaining Mother's Day as a holiday.[43] A UN conference even insisted that the United States must enact more gun control legislation to assure security to citizens because European opinion is convinced, contrary to the view of most American legislatures, that private gun ownership is a threat to others, offering no compensating security to owners.[44]

Not surprisingly, many Americans balk at the idea of accepting moral instruction on human rights from countries in Europe that, only a few decades ago, were accomplices to genocide. Human rights advocates consider that a parochial view. Within Europe, British law was made subject to correction by judges from countries that had been Fascist dictatorships or Communist dictatorships not long before. And of course, some people in Britain like the idea of subscribing to the more cosmopolitan views of the European Court of Human Rights or the European Court of Justice, rather than their own government's policies. Constituencies in the United States might also prefer European standards—listeners to National Public Radio, for example, of which the European Union is a paying sponsor.

There is an additional difficulty, however: While European standards are international (that is, foreign), they are not at all universal. One of the most objectionable features of international human rights law is that its sponsors do not enforce it uniformly. What diplomats vote in the UN is no guide to what actually happens in their home countries. It is all too easy to endorse standards that do not have to be complied with. For this body of law to make any headway in American courts, it will almost certainly have to be applied selectively—which is precisely what the system invites.

In the end, this project may not get very far without provoking political resistance. But resistance to this trend will bring new dangers. International human rights law threatens to entangle the American legal system, grounded in American practice and American constitutional structures, with legal phantasms that float in the intellectual ether of international law. Experiments in this direction threaten the stability and authority of American law. If they are allowed to gain momentum, these experiments may be hard to constrain and efforts to do so may simply provoke greater cynicism and squabbling about all aspects of the American legal system—including those that ought to be safeguarded from partisan sniping. International human rights law introduces a vision of law not based on consent, not based on national traditions, not even based in abstract moral philosophy—but based on policy claims put forward by activists and foreign institutions responding to activists. This is not a particularly attractive approach to law in a country that seeks to sustain public respect for constitutional government.

From an American perspective, international human rights law might look like a dangerous import. Still, advocates insist the United States ought to cooperate more extensively in order to encourage other countries to comply with international human rights norms. In fact, the risks that may be posed by international human rights law may be greater for other countries than for the United States itself.

The Risks of Global Justice

There are two obvious problems with the idea that human rights can be protected by outside powers. One is that the world does not agree on how human rights should be protected—that is, on how human rights guarantees should really be enforced. The other more fundamental problem is that the world does not agree on what human rights are—either in their ultimate, ideal form or in transitional situations, where pressing exigencies require some degree of compromise. Both problems pose quite serious challenges, if one takes the notion of universal rights protection at all seriously. The world as a whole is simply not constituted to reach inside states and impose genuine legal claims on behalf of individuals. It is not obvious that half-measures make things better; they can certainly make things worse.

The enforcement problem is the most obvious. Whatever one thinks about the best way to define particular rights, almost everyone sees that mass murder is terribly wrong. What to do then about regimes that perpetrate mass murder on their own people? Some early theorists of sovereignty argued that liberation from terrible oppression was a legitimate basis for one state to attack another. The most influential scholars in the eighteenth and nineteenth centuries were much more cautious about acknowledging a right of "humanitarian intervention."[45] The problem was that third parties were not always ready to acknowledge that a particular intervention was "humanitarian" rather than self-serving, and were often willing to take sides with the supposed oppressor in the name of resisting aggression. Through much of the nineteenth century, for example, British policy sided with the Ottoman Empire, notwithstanding concerns that the Ottomans were oppressing Christian minorities in the empire.

Does international organization make it easier to gain support for humanitarian intervention? So far, the reverse has been true: The Security Council has never authorized outside military intervention solely to protect people from slaughter at the hands of their own government. To the contrary, when the Hutu government of Rwanda commenced mass murder of Tutsis, UN peacekeepers were immediately withdrawn, and nearly a million people were hacked to death. Every government on the Security Council bears some blame for standing by amid this horror. But governments looked to their own priorities. The UN official responsible for peacekeeping, who should have been looking out for humanity at large, might be judged most worthy of blame—if anyone took UN professions of concern for humanity at face value. In fact, Kofi Annan was promoted to secretary general of the UN for siding with the governments in this tragic episode.

No government is prepared to take very great risks to liberate people from terrible oppression in another country unless that country poses a threat to other states. And it is not obvious that this policy should be a subject of censure. A war to liberate the peoples of Russia and Eastern Europe from the horror of Stalinist rule would have been a brutal and terrible war with many innocent victims of its own. The same could be said of a war to liberate the people of China from Maoist tyranny in the 1950s or 1960s. It is not even certain that the supposed beneficiaries in these countries would have welcomed liberation at the price of such a war or recognize the motives of outside interveners as genuinely humanitarian.

The point is not that war never solves anything. That viewpoint appeals to some people who aspire to moral seriousness, but it is almost certainly mistaken. The war against Nazi Germany clearly made an enormous difference to Western Europe. But success in that war required an alliance between Anglo-American democracies, on the one hand, and the murderous tyranny of Stalin on the other. A morally serious policy often requires morally serious compromises.

Similarly, in the postwar era, the United States led a coalition of states opposed to the spread of Soviet Communism. This coalition was called "the Free World," but it included, of course, a great many states whose democratic credentials were, at best, highly questionable. The UN was not in a position to rally moral opposition to the most oppressive regimes on either side. By the 1970s, a solid majority of UN member states called themselves "nonaligned"—that is, not aligned with either the Soviet Union or the United States—but generally voted with the Communist states in UN forums. If there were not going to be wars of liberation against Communist tyrannies, there might at least have been some serious effort to isolate and condemn Communist regimes. But the UN was neither equipped nor inclined to condemn individual states, even in its human rights forums. It never condemned the Soviet Union.

What the UN did, instead, was to focus obsessive attention on countries that Communist and Third World states found most objectionable. South Africa was condemned, over and over, for apartheid, entrenching the notion that racism could only be perpetrated by whites against nonwhites, so that tribal slaughter in the rest of Africa—far beyond anything ever perpetrated by the white racist regime of South Africa—was met with indifference.[46] Chile was endlessly condemned in the 1970s and 1980s because its reformist military government had come to power in a coup against a Socialist government aligned with Fidel Castro, a particular darling of the Third World in that era. And, of course, Israel was endlessly condemned for racism, colonialism, and other sins, as Communist and Third World states endorsed the demonologies most favored by Arab tyrannies.

There were certainly strong grounds to criticize the white minority government in South Africa and the military government of Chile. And legitimate criticism might well have been directed against particular Israeli policies. To target these three states as the world's most serious abusers of human rights, however—while ignoring mass slaughter in other countries—was quite bizarre. Or would have been, if one supposed the exercise had anything to do with universal human rights standards. Most government at the United Nations had quite different priorities.

If Western democracies were not going to overthrow despotic regimes by force, they might at least hope to isolate and condemn the worst of them. What the UN actually did was to provide a forum in which all such elemental distinctions could be obscured and displaced into alternate themes about white oppression or capitalist oppression, or Jewish conspiracy. It was not just that human rights failed to receive a high priority. It was that human rights, from the outset, were presented in a void, without any sense of perspective, strategy, or priorities.

It may be that talk of human rights helped to weaken Communist authority in Eastern Europe in the late 1980s. If so, however, the UN deserves no credit: It never condemned the Soviet Union's barbaric human rights practices. And this did not change much in the decade following the end of the Cold War. Transitions to full democracy in Chile and other Latin states, along with a transition to full democracy in South Africa, meant that pariah states of old became fully respectable. There was very little disposition to focus on remaining despotisms.

The issue is not whether the UN needs to address everything before it can speak with authority in any particular place. The issue is whether it can speak with authority anywhere when it is so utterly corrupt. The idea of a Human Rights Commission to which the world's most oppressive regimes are elected implies that the electorate—member states—are not very concerned about human rights, at least as Western countries understand them. In effect, the UN remains a forum to bolster the self-confidence of tyrannies.

NGOs, which might be free of many of the selfish or short-term calculations of member states, have their own agendas. During the Cold War, leading human rights advocacy organizations were keen to promote the idea of a human rights law transcending differences among states—that is, in particular, Cold War divisions. In much the same way, the Vatican presented itself as a neutral mediator between Nazi Germany and the Western democracies. Now Amnesty International sought to present itself as neutral and nonpolitical during the Cold War. The wartime pope has been criticized (perhaps excessively, given his circumstances) for not condemning Nazi genocide more forthrightly. Amnesty International, with far less excuse, refrained from criticism of the Soviet Union during the 1970s. Even when the Communist regime in Cambodia perpetrated the mass slaughter of civilians, Amnesty International refrained from comment, for fear of seeming to provide retrospective justifications for U.S. war aims in Vietnam.[47]

Meanwhile, Amnesty International found other issues. Capital punishment in the United States was high on the list. Mass murder of innocents in other countries might be overlooked for the sake of political detachment—but the execution of convicted murderers in America provoked a sustained protest campaign. The Council of Europe, sensitive to NGO opinion, announced in 2001 that one of its top priorities in human rights advocacy would be to persuade America to abolish capital punishment.[48] Amnesty International, meanwhile, had moved on to new causes. Early in the new century, it announced that it would make U.S. ratification of CEDAW its top priority. It also embraced gay rights.[49] It is hard to take such endeavors seriously. Is feminist advocacy a way to persuade governments in Muslim states to abandon torture as an instrument of state policy?[50]

It is natural for people suffering from brutal repression to look to outside advocates for help. There have certainly been cases where Amnesty International and similar groups have helped to secure the release of improperly imprisoned people by focusing publicity on particular abuses. But few human rights advocacy groups have been able to remain focused on the worst abuses.

It may be most charitable to explain their distractions as an ideological compulsion. If human rights are what UN conventions and declarations say they are, then they cover so many claims that it is hard to stay focused on fundamentals. To focus on the worst abuses might imply that there is some natural or reasonable ranking among rights claims, contrary to the official claim of UN and NGO advocates that "human rights are indivisible."[51] The original purpose for lumping so many diverse claims together in human rights declarations and conventions was precisely to blur distinctions between different governments. The Universal Declaration came to be "universal" by avoiding any focus on the abuses most characteristic of Communist regimes.

A human rights movement that can't focus on the worst abuses will be more devoted to ideological abstractions than effective policies. And human rights advocacy organizations often seem to be indifferent to effective policy. The problem was cast in sharp relief by the response of human rights groups to the challenge of Saddam Hussein's regime in Iraq. Whatever its motivation, the Anglo-American invasion of Iraq certainly liberated the Iraqi people from a murderous tyrant. Nonetheless, Amnesty International denounced the war and protested that Prime Minister Blair had only spoken about human rights abuses in Iraq as a belated tactic to justify it. For Amnesty, purity of intention did indeed seem to rank higher than actual achievement. Human Rights Watch subsequently issued its own formal condemnation of the war that liberated Iraqis from Saddam's monstrous tyranny.[52]

One need not be overly cynical, however, to suspect that ideological compulsions are not the only factor driving priorities of international human rights advocates. Human rights organizations derive the vast bulk of their funding and support from sympathizers in Western countries. Many supporters and donors are more interested in advancing causes in their own countries—feminism and gay rights, or scoring points against America or its allies, for example—than in developing realistic strategies for alleviating suffering in remote places. People who believe that American imperialism or American capitalism is the main scourge of the planet—as readers of mainstream publications in Europe might well be led to think—will see no important distinction between attacking the United States and alleviating suffering in other parts of the world. It would take heroic self-discipline for human rights advocacy groups to ignore the priorities of their donors and sympathizers.

Meanwhile, human rights groups find at least symbolic ways to connect with the enthusiasms of non-Western countries. They can often do so by taking stands that do not at all put them at odds with major constituencies in Western countries. Amnesty International and Human Rights Watch issued loud and insistent condemnations of Israeli responses to terror attacks. Both organizations insist that international law requires Israel to accept a full "right of return" for three million Palestinians—a position more extreme than anything endorsed by any European government. Amnesty International did not bother to issue a major condemnation of suicide bombing until 2002—after two years of such bombings.[53]

Despite such pandering, it is doubtful that Western NGOs can do much to settle the very difficult issues local leaders face in struggling toward some form of acceptable government in the aftermath of war or terrible repression. Just as outside powers have difficulty establishing a new government in a foreign territory, human rights advocates from outside may also be distrusted. They do not have more authority merely because they lack military power. The crucial thing is to establish a government which can be accepted by its own people—otherwise, that government does not have great prospects of remaining in power without continued repression, contrary to the demands of human rights advocates.

In almost every country where transitions to democracy have taken place in the last two decades, the transition agreements included provisions for the amnesty of officials in the outgoing dictatorships (and often of those who resisted them by terrorism or other extreme methods). Terrible crimes were pardoned in this way in Latin America, Eastern Europe, and even South Africa. New democracies thought it more important to reconcile supporters of the old tyrannies than to deliver perfect justice. Sometimes there were exceptions for particularly odious crimes. Often there were truth commissions, charged to provide at least an accurate record of past crimes as an admonition to the future.[54]

Characteristically, human rights advocates sought to leap over these local accommodations with legal instruments that could be operated from outside. The argument for universal jurisdiction for crimes against humanity was that such crimes were so terrible that they could rightfully be punished by any country which sought to do so. This argument originated with human rights advocates, and was strongly pressed by NGOs to support the prosecution of Pinochet in Europe over the protests of the democratic government of Chile. The International Criminal Court bears the stamp of NGO advocacy in its endorsement of national prosecutions under such theories of universal jurisdiction.[55] And, of course, not only in that.

Perhaps the most telling feature of the Rome Statute is that it makes no provision for amnesties or pardons. The ICC is authorized to act in disregard of local amnesties but is not empowered to grant its own pardons. This is perfectly logical in its way. The power to pardon is usually exercised by a supreme executive official, while amnesties may be granted by a national legislature. The granting of pardons or amnesties is a political act, entrusted to authorities responsible for making political judgments on what is best for the particular community involved. An international court has no claim to make political decisions for particular communities. The ICC is not supposed to worry about the well-being of any particular community. It is there to serve humanity.

And if its prosecution upsets a fragile peace in a particular country? If its threat to prosecute makes it hard to persuade a brutal dictator to relinquish power? If its approach to defining lawful combat makes other nations more reluctant to commit their own troops to a humanitarian intervention? If the court ends up provoking more bloodshed, if it ends up inhibiting or undermining political efforts to constrain bloodletting— will it still look like a good idea? None of this may happen if the prosecutor ignores the actual terms of the Rome Statute and exercises a prudent discretion which the treaty does not grant him. Should we assume an international bureaucrat in The Hague will know what each situation requires?

It is not in the spirit of the human rights crusade to ask these awkward questions. Consequences are not the point. Justice is the point. And eighteen judges in The Hague will know what justice requires. The best motto for the enterprise might be the Latin saying embraced by the Prussian philosopher Immanuel Kant: *Fiat justitia, pereat mundus*—Let justice be done, even if the world perishes.[56] It is the perfect motto for advocates and institutions that take pride in answering to no one. Humanity—the cause of human rights advocacy—is above all nations. The cause of humanity, as human rights advocates see it, is so exalted that it fails to notice the most basic attributes of actual human beings.

Human rights advocates fail to reckon, for example, with human weakness or human limitations—the sorts of things that make people insist on constitutional structures to constrain state power. As a cause, human rights advocacy has this in common with other crusading faiths.

5

Trade Rights and Sovereignty

No aspect of international law stirred more controversy in the 1990s than the body of trade agreements supervised by the World Trade Organization (WTO). Some of the opposition to the WTO bordered on paranoia or demagoguery. Some protests passed far beyond such border regions.

The antiglobalization movement, which mobilized large protest rallies at successive WTO meetings in various world capitals, seemed less concerned with the WTO itself than with "trade"—that is, commerce, which the protesters seemed to regard as an enemy of the world's poor. For such critics, the WTO was a threat to poor countries because trade itself was a threat to the world's poor, and also to its endangered plants and animals. Other critics acknowledged that trade might after all benefit both parties to an exchange, but insisted it must be properly managed to ensure it delivered its potential benefits, without placing our own producers at a systematic disadvantage. Trade could be good, but only if "fair."

For the Left and the Right, competing claims about sovereignty were readily embraced as rhetorical clubs to wield against opponents. The rhetoric was often so heated or so reckless that serious analysts were tempted to throw up their hands in despair. Some prominent trade scholars indeed succumbed to the temptation and dismissed appeals to sovereignty in this context as mischievous abstractions or empty "mantras."[1]

But there are serious issues involved for anyone concerned about the safeguarding of national sovereignty—even for those who hold, with the American Founders, that trade is not in itself a threat to sovereignty. The Founders favored diplomatic agreements to facilitate international commerce. Efforts to conclude such agreements were among the earliest ventures of American diplomacy. But a trade agreement is one thing; it is something else to view trading privileges as one element in an all-encompassing system of international controls. That is, in fact, how top officials of the World Trade Organization now see the WTO's purpose—as a body that can anchor trading rights in a larger and more comprehensive system of international law. Those who share this vision seem to think that trading privileges will be more secure if connected to international standards protecting the environment, labor conditions, and an expanding array of "social and economic rights."

But the WTO cannot go very far down this path before it, in effect, promotes constraints on trade as part of a package with the right to trade. A WTO strong enough to enforce such a notion would be enforcing conditions not merely for the exchange of goods and services, but also for the exchange of regulatory standards. Or rather, it would be enforcing a common embrace of common regulatory standards. To that extent, the WTO would be promoting the opposite of trade. And if it could succeed in this project, it would indeed be a serious threat to the sovereignty of participating states.

Beneath the demagoguery, then, are serious questions regarding the terms on which the United States can continue to participate in the international trade organization. And the questions are all the more serious if one starts from the constitutional premises of the American Founders that trade in itself is not a threat to independence, but that independence itself is valuable because it allows us to decide for ourselves in what ways we choose to regulate or organize economic activity at home.

Reasonable Premises

Trade with foreigners implies a need for what foreigners have to offer. In earlier centuries, governments that sought to limit foreign influence also sought to limit foreign trade. Down to the middle of the nineteenth century, for example, Japan imposed very sharp limits on foreign access to its home islands, lest its people develop a taste for foreign products and a dependence on foreign providers. In the twentieth century, Communist governments in Russia and China sought for decades to limit foreign trade to the barest minimum so that central planners would not be constrained by the claims of foreign buyers, sellers, or investors.

But this is hardly a reasonable view of sovereignty. If it is dangerous to allow people to trade with foreigners, it may seem equally dangerous to allow unrestricted exchange among citizens within a state. Domestic trade patterns can also generate political demands to maintain or protect particular economic relationships, complicating the calculations of government planners. Totalitarian governments were suspicious of foreign trade precisely because they were already determined to exercise complete control of all economic activity (and, indeed, all social life) in their own territories.

From any reasonable view, however, a government is not less sovereign because it chooses to leave most economic activity to find its own path. It is not less sovereign because its laws allow private individuals or firms to find and pursue market opportunities on their own, whether these opportunities arise at home or abroad. Jean Bodin, the first great theorist of sovereignty, published a treatise on the value of coinage in which he devoted many pages to criticizing the self-defeating effect of most restrictions on imports and exports. Restrictions on imports, he argued, would impose needless burdens on poor people at home, while also depressing the profits and wages of people producing goods for export. A policy of free trade, he concluded, would, over time, generate more contentment and loyalty among citizens—and more taxable wealth for public purposes, such as the support of national defense against armed aggression.[2]

Two centuries later, Adam Smith made the same point at greater length: A policy of free trade would produce more national wealth, which could then assure more adequate financing for "the first duty of the sovereign . . . that of defending the society from the violence and injustice of other independent societies."[3] Smith argued for free trade among nations on the same grounds that he urged governments to leave each one of their own citizens at home "perfectly free to pursue his own interest in his own way." Otherwise, governments would "always be exposed to innumerable delusions" in taking on a task for which "no human wisdom or knowledge could ever be sufficient"—that of "directing . . . the industry of private people . . . towards the employments most suitable to the interest of society."[4]

The American Founders did not have to read Smith's treatise to see the point. It did not occur to them to think that national independence required unlimited government control over the American economy. In fact, America's first treaty—concluded barely a year after its Declaration of Independence—was one of friendship and commerce with France. Both countries promised to eliminate almost all restrictions on the flow of goods between them, so that exports from each could compete on equal terms with domestic production. More importantly, at least in the American view, the treaty pledged each to extend to the other whatever trade terms they might subsequently offer to any other nation. Each party to the treaty would thus remain the other's "most favored nation" in trade, though not necessarily its exclusively most favored nation. The Articles of Confederation, while not prohibiting the states from regulating commerce with foreign nations, did expressly prohibit any scheme that would interfere with the most favored nation provisions of the treaty of commerce with France.[5]

In the first years under the new Constitution, Secretary of the Treasury Alexander Hamilton proposed a protective tariff to encourage the development of new industries in the United States. He offered arguments that even Adam Smith had considered plausible.[6] But Hamilton's proposals were fiercely resisted. By the early part of the nineteenth century, congressional leaders had come to regard a tariff for protection of industry (rather than revenue) as constitutionally improper.[7]

Five decades after the signing of the first commercial treaty with France, Secretary of State John Quincy Adams celebrated the treaty's underlying policy as one of the twin pillars of American independence, ranking just below the Declaration of Independence itself: "The two instruments were parts of one and the same system." The United States would continue to work toward "the general establishment of this most liberal of principles of commercial intercourse," since "the fairness of its operation depends upon its being admitted *universally*." [8]

Adams, serving under James Monroe and taking the leading role in formulating the "doctrine" that bears Monroe's name, was not naive about the potential for permanent harmony among nations. He advocated restraints in war on the assumption that war would still remain an instrument of national policy. He advocated treaties protecting the "liberty of conscience and of religious worship" for Americans in foreign countries, along with treaties guaranteeing commercial access. Adams linked "commercial and religious liberty" as "but various modifications of one great principle, founded in the unalienable rights of human nature."[9] He seems to have envisioned a world in which, whatever their other disputes, more and more nations would agree to self-limiting rules when it came to interference with commerce. Nations could agree to exclude trade from their political disputes, even as they had come to agree that religion should be left free from political interference.[10]

Adams did not imagine that, by forswearing restrictions on foreign trade, a nation would be less sovereign, any more than the United States lacked sovereign authority because it was, by its own Constitution, constrained from retaliating in kind against religious discrimination in other states.[11] After all, the United States was already constrained (by another express provision in the Constitution) from imposing duties on exports or giving preferential treatment to commerce entering through ports in different states.[12] No one claimed that this constitutional safeguard diminished the sovereignty of the United States. Constitutional limitations of this kind were seen, instead, as an expression of national sovereignty—as legal standards that the nation agreed to establish for its own reasons.

The hope to exclude trade from political conflict was spurred by unhappy experience. Economic warfare had been a central tactic of both Britain and France in the Napoleonic wars of the early nineteenth century. Both sides tried to exclude not only enemy commerce but neutral commerce as well, unless neutrals complied with restrictions on trade with targeted enemies. The United States had protested vigorously, insisting that such restrictions were contrary to the customary understanding of the law of nations. Seeking to enforce respect for its own trading rights, the United States had then imposed an "embargo" on trade with nations that did not allow American access to their own ports. The embargo brought immense hardship to American merchants, however, without actually forcing Britain or France to change its policies.

The United States ultimately went to war against Britain in 1812 to prevent Britain's Royal Navy from interfering with American shipping on the high seas. The war proved injurious to both sides and seemed all the more questionable when the defeat of Napoleon removed the need for British trade restrictions. Britain ceased its attacks on American shipping, even though it did not make any commitment to do so in the peace agreement that ended the War of 1812. The next generation of American statesmen had reason to hope that restrictions on trade could be removed from international politics.

Most European states did, in fact, open their doors to wider commercial exchange in the course of the nineteenth century. Impressed by the wealth Britain secured from open trade, one country after another tried to expand its own trade with outside states. The young American republic thus was able to negotiate trade agreements with reactionary governments in Russia, Prussia, and Austria, as well as feudal monarchies in China and Japan and an assortment of military governments in Latin America. Improvements in transportation brought by canals, railroads, and steamships dramatically lowered shipping costs and made it feasible to trade not only luxuries or essential materials but also a wide range of manufactured goods and agricultural products. The nineteenth century proved a golden age of commerce, drawing more and more of the world into a global trade network.

At least two important limitations remained, however. First, when conflicts between states reached the stage of open hostility, governments still found trade restrictions an irresistible supplement to military coercion. The United States itself imposed a wide-ranging embargo on the Confederacy during the Civil War. It proceeded to build one of the world's largest naval forces to ensure that European shippers complied with the blockade—even restricting European shipping to Mexico to prevent supplies from reaching Confederate states by that detour. The United States again imposed a wide-ranging blockade, this time of Cuba, during the brief American war with Spain in 1898. When Britain proceeded to enforce a still more encompassing blockade on Germany during the First World War, the United States protested on behalf of its neutral shipping rights. For various reasons, however, the United States did not let its exasperation with British restrictions on trade overshadow its deeper indignation against German submarine attacks on American shipping and against German intrigues designed to draw Mexico into war with the United States.

The military implications of trade dependence were one reason governments sought to ensure they would have domestic sources of manufacture. There turned out to be others that found a receptive hearing, even within the United States. Congress had initially rejected the principle of protective tariffs, but there was already intense politicking before the Civil War on which kinds of imports should be subject to what level of duties for revenue needs. During and after the war, as Congress came under the control of Republicans who drew their strength from manufacturing states in the North, tariffs were increased on more and more goods. Protection came to be accepted as a reasonable policy, now conceived as a guarantee of higher wages. By the late nineteenth century, as increasing numbers of countries began to raise their own tariffs, advocates in the United States often argued that raising American tariffs would provide a bargaining chip for diplomacy—a barrier which might be lowered if other countries would do the same.[13]

Beginning in the 1890s, Congress experimented with schemes that would authorize the president to lower tariffs against imports from any country that would agree to parallel reductions on its tariffs on American goods. The Supreme Court endorsed the system on the grounds that delegation of tariff-setting powers to the president in this context was reasonably confined by overall legislative tariff policy.[14] These schemes were favored by some advocates as a first step toward freer trade overall, and by many others as an alternative to free trade.[15] In fact, the general trend of American tariff rates remained upward. It was hard to mobilize reliable political opposition to the trend, when technological improvements still allowed for a continual rise in American exports.

Despite the immense dislocations brought about by the First World War, the United States in the 1920s continued to build ever-higher tariff walls against industrial imports. The policy depressed European exports to the United States at a time when European countries desperately needed to rebuild their export trade to earn foreign exchange to repay debts incurred during the war—which the United States, as the principal creditor, insisted on seeing repaid. A further round of American tariff increases, in the Smoot-Hawley Tariff of 1930, seems to have aggravated panic over the plunge in stock prices on Wall Street in the fall of 1929. European countries suspended debt payments on their accumulated borrowings from American banks. Many countries then proceeded to raise their own tariff rates to protect their struggling industries. Many also imposed restrictions on the exchange of national currency to compensate for the difficulty of earning dollars or other foreign currencies amid the collapse of their export trade.

Prolonged economic crisis provoked desperate remedies, as countries sought to prop up faltering industries and failing farms with new kinds of government controls—and to soften the effect of unemployment and dispossession with new kinds of government social programs. After 1934, the United States sought to revive trade with a new program authorizing tariff reductions with any nation that agreed to a reciprocal set of reductions. The Reciprocal Trade Agreements Act also took an important step beyond previous programs of this kind. This time, the agreements were authorized to incorporate most-favored-nation clauses. The president was authorized to lower tariffs on any nation that made comparable agreements with any RTA partner, without having to negotiate a separate American agreement with such partners. The hope was that the impulse to reduce tariffs would, in this way, ripple outward, reaching a wider range of trading states than the slow-moving procedures of formal American trade negotiations.

The program achieved only limited results during the 1930s, however.[16] Some of the largest trading states were never covered by agreements, and those that were concluded often set relatively modest or highly selective targets for tariff reduction. The Roosevelt administration was reluctant to see imports interfere with its own highly interventionist economic programs at home, which aimed at boosting prices by substituting regulatory standards for market competition.[17] Strange as it now seems, this general policy of suppressing competition attracted support at a time when the economy suffered from ongoing deflation, and a desperate nation was willing to try any expedient to promote recovery.

Meanwhile, in Asia and Central Europe, Fascist governments drew different lessons from the economic crisis. In Japan, Italy, and Germany, dictators looked to revive their economies by mobilizing for war, and hoped to sustain new ambitions with territorial conquests. By the early 1940s, Washington policymakers looked back on the collapse of trade in the 1930s as having exacerbated international rivalries in ways that speeded the world's descent into a new world war. In the midst of that war, Washington officials began to think seriously about how to ensure economic conditions for a more stable postwar world.

The Diplomacy of the GATT

The institutional foundations for postwar recovery were negotiated at a 1944 conference of Allied states, convened at a resort hotel in Bretton Woods, New Hampshire. An International Monetary Fund (IMF) would help to stabilize currency fluctuations and facilitate the phasing out of currency exchange controls by lending foreign currency reserves to central banks. A Bank for Reconstruction and Development (or "World Bank," as it came to be called) would pool resources to lend money for development projects in poor countries. And an International Trade Organization (ITO) would provide an institutional forum for the negotiation of mutual tariff reductions.

The IMF and the World Bank came into existence, according to plan, in 1946. The ITO ran afoul of mounting doubts in both the American Congress and the British Parliament, as the former worried that it would not go far enough in dismantling British Commonwealth trade protection and the latter worried it would go too far.[18] Instead, an agreement intended as a stopgap measure, the General Agreement on Tariffs and Trade (GATT), became the framework for tariff-reduction negotiations over the next forty years.

Despite its unpromising beginnings, the GATT proved to be a quite effective and enduring forum for trade negotiations. Essentially, it tried to generalize the experience of the Reciprocal Trade Agreements of the 1930s. All participating states would grant each other the same tariff rates provided to other participants. Participants agreed to phase out import quotas and other restrictions and rely only on tariffs, and then to lower tariffs by successive agreements. Within this framework, initial agreements gave the participants the confidence to embark on new agreements, providing deeper tariff reductions on a wider range of products.

Within each country, demands for protection against imports could be answered by promises to secure wider export markets. This had been the theory of the RTA program in the 1930s. But GATT rounds, based on simultaneous negotiations among all participating states, offered more incentive to make concessions: What state A might not be prepared to offer state B, given their existing trade balance, each might be prepared to offer if assured comparable concessions from states C, D, and E, with which they had different trade prospects.

Every few years, GATT participants would thus embark on a new agenda of trade liberalization, called a "round" and usually named for the site of the conference where the bargaining was launched—as with the "Tokyo Round" of the 1970s and the "Uruguay Round" of the 1980s. Bargaining in this way, through successive rounds, made it possible to reach agreement on very steep and broad-ranging reductions in barriers to trade. Over five decades, GATT rounds reduced tariff levels by almost 90 percent, compared with average rates in effect at the end of the Second World War.

The sanction for noncompliance remained what it had been under the RTA and, indeed, under nineteenth-century trade agreements. If a state did not live up to its obligations to other GATT members, any state that claimed to be injured in consequence (because, for example, its exports to the delinquent state had been reduced as a result of this noncompliance) could retaliate in kind, by withdrawing some of its own trade concessions to the offending state. The technical term, "withdrawal of concessions," captured the reciprocity on which the whole system rested. The GATT added no new sanctions. It did not require other states to retaliate for infractions by a GATT member. It did not even require an injured state to retaliate. It allowed states to do what they had always had the right to do—change their own trade policies toward other states. All the GATT added was a forum in which to air complaints, in the hope that conciliation would satisfy both sides before any particular dispute degenerated into a series of tit-for-tat retaliations that worked real disruption. GATT members promised not to retaliate before seeking to settle a dispute (regarding compliance with GATT standards) in this way. The mechanism proved so successful that retaliation in kind was almost never attempted.[19]

One important reason for the success of the venture was that the GATT did not aspire to be universal. Communist countries refused from the outset to have anything to do with the institutions that emerged from Bretton Woods. Some two dozen countries which had participated in negotiations over the proposed International Trade Organization decided not to join the GATT when it was launched in 1947. Most of the holdouts were countries in Latin America and other places where economic development had lagged behind. Now they wanted assurances against export subsidies by more advanced states. At the time, no serious effort was made to recruit these countries to the GATT system. The twenty-three states that did subscribe in 1947 were nations in Western Europe and the British Commonwealth which, along with the United States, wanted to see a return to the beneficial trade patterns they had enjoyed before the 1930s.[20]

Remaining outside the GATT meant that a government did not have to lower its tariffs or dismantle other trade restrictions. The GATT did not prevent states from liberalizing their trade policies on their own, however. Nor did it prevent participants from reducing trade barriers more than the agreement required—or reducing trade barriers with nonparticipants. But in practice, trade reductions did follow GATT rounds, providing incentives for nonparticipants to join, if they wanted the assurance of comparable access to GATT-covered markets. Over time, more and more countries did decide to join. By the 1990s, over a hundred had chosen to take part in GATT negotiations.

New adherents may have had many motives for joining the system, but the simplest explanation is probably the most important: Countries that opened themselves to trade experienced continuing economic growth in the postwar era, while countries that sought to protect themselves from engagement in a growing world economy experienced stagnation. The growing respect for trade was related to a growing respect for markets. The GATT did not prevent states from "socializing" industries in their own territories and operating them as public enterprises. It only required that such public enterprises not be provided special tariff protection against foreign competitors. By the 1970s, GATT rounds had considerable success in reaching agreement on reducing even nontariff subsidies to domestic industry (though it still placed no direct limits on public ownership). The GATT prospered along with policies of market competition.

What began as an attempt to revive pre-1930s patterns of trade blossomed into a scheme that built confidence in still older notions about where government could or could not exercise its power with reasonable effect. By the 1980s, the success of deregulatory initiatives in Britain, the United States, and other countries brought new credibility to market economics. The GATT reduced American tariffs to levels not seen since the mid-nineteenth century, while at the same time deregulatory initiatives brought a dismantling of many market controls on particular industries which had been accumulating through most of the twentieth century. And the American economy enjoyed the most sustained period of robust economic growth in all of American history.

The World Trade Organization was launched in 1995, in the midst of this economic expansion. The new organization, agreed upon by participants in the Uruguay Round of GATT negotiations, was intended to provide a more formal structure for developing new rules. Many observers viewed the new forum as a guarantee of increasing liberalization. But liberalization was not on everyone's agenda. And the WTO, it turned out, could be turned to purposes other than liberalization.

Rival Agendas

The GATT may have flourished on the premise that trade would be mutually advantageous for all participants. The idea did not appeal to everyone, however. Communist countries refused to have anything to do with the GATT—or for that matter with the World Bank or the IMF. The conviction that Communist states had found a more assured and somehow more just path to development continued to inspire much political thinking, even in Western countries, for some decades after the Second World War. Social-Democratic parties in Western Europe gradually came to terms with the success of market economies. But as late as the 1970s, there were still powerful constituencies hoping to find collective solutions to basic economic problems.

The outlook championed by Communist countries found a receptive audience in the poorest countries. As European nations granted independence to former colonies in Africa and Asia, these newly independent states emerged as the largest faction in the UN. They presented themselves as a "Third World," distinct from the worlds of advanced Western democracies and Soviet satellites. Third World nations were quite heterogeneous, with different cultural traditions, and differing economic and geopolitical circumstances. What they had in common—perhaps the only significant thing they had in common—was a very low level of per-capita wealth, compared with Western Europe and North America. Poverty could link Latin America with India or China. Anticolonialist rhetoric carried over into anticapitalist conclusions: Poor countries were poor because they were exploited by rich countries—or at least because rich countries did not share their wealth equitably with the poor.

A UN conference supposed to address the grievances of the poor countries emerged in the mid-1960s as a permanent forum for those grievances: the UN Conference on Trade and Development (UNCTAD). By the 1970s, UNCTAD was endorsing claims of "developing countries" (or less-developed countries—LDCs) to expropriate mines and oil wells and other foreign-owned business operations in the name of "economic sovereignty." The General Assembly then voted a series of resolutions affirming the "inalienable right" of all countries—"and in particular developing countries"—"to secure and increase their share in the administration of enterprises which are fully or partly operated by foreign capital."[21]

UN resolutions said little or nothing about compensation to foreign owners. Victims of such expropriations—both the affected "foreign-owned" businesses and their home governments—often sought to retaliate against expropriations, with economic sanctions to enforce compensation. Under a 1974 General Assembly resolution proclaiming a "New International Economic Order," such retaliations were declared contrary to international law. The program assumed that affluent nations would instead commit themselves to assist developing countries in establishing global cartels for the production and distribution of raw materials—so that prices would remain "stable" and developing countries would be assured an "equitable share" of returns from international trade in such materials.[22]

Such visions bore more than a passing resemblance to the internal control schemes adopted in many Western countries during the 1930s. The whole vision has been aptly described as "international social democracy."[23] But majorities in the General Assembly could not force Western countries to subscribe to it in the 1970s. The global schemes envisioned by UNCTAD never moved much beyond rhetoric. What was proposed was not "trade" based on mutual advantage, but global controls—which Western countries did not, at that time, recognize as being to their advantage.

Even Western states, however, were quite ready to endorse the notion that all governments must respect "universal human rights," and that this concept extended to claims for government assistance to ensure universal access to education, housing, health care, and employment. Such claims, already suggested in broad terms in the Universal Declaration of Human Rights (adopted by the General Assembly in 1948), were reemphasized in the International Covenant on Economic and Social Rights, which took effect in 1976. A UN committee charged with monitoring compliance with this treaty subsequently insisted that every state give priority to its provisions and at least take immediate steps toward implementing them, even if full compliance were constrained by limited resources.[24]

Meanwhile, an international convention on sex discrimination, completed in the 1970s, also insisted that men and women must be paid comparable wages for work of "comparable value"—on the assumption that governments could somehow determine the economic value of every job.[25] In the mid-1980s, the European Commission insisted that member states must indeed implement a scheme to ensure that jobs dominated by female workers receive appropriately "comparable" wages in relation to jobs dominated by male workers. The International Labour Organization adopted dozens of new standards, spelling out obligations of employers not only for avoiding discrimination but also for promoting healthful and safe working conditions. The European Court of Justice by the 1980s held that some of these standards, too, might be part of international human rights law, binding as such on European states.[26]

Did this body of law apply to developing countries? Most were not exactly scrupulous in their observance of international human rights standards, in general. They did not do any better in complying with supposed obligations regarding labor or social rights. The International Labour Organization insisted in the 1990s that all member states must comply with what it deemed "core labor standards," even if a state had not subscribed to the particular conventions in which these standards were defined.[27] But the ILO had no direct powers of enforcement.

By then, important constituencies in Western countries were warning that labor and social protections would be eroded if business firms found it easy to circumvent such standards by relocating to countries in which the protections were not in force or not seriously enforced. The European Parliament demanded protections against "social dumping"—that is, selling goods at cheaper prices by producing them in countries where lax regulatory standards allowed for production at lower cost.[28] Developing countries protested that they could only compete, given their other disadvantages, by providing lesser pay and lesser protection for their workers. If affluent nations tried to protect themselves against "social dumping," they would simply be making poor countries less able to compete in world markets.

By the 1990s, however, protests against "social dumping" had gained reinforcement from a new constituency, which had attained considerable political strength in Western countries: environmental advocacy groups. Less-developed countries had not persuaded Western states to endorse production cartels in the 1970s, and Western states could not persuade developing countries to implement Western ideas about social rights. But environmentalists sought to speak for the entire earth, since the world might be threatened by global environmental hazards. As early as 1972, a UN conference in Stockholm proclaimed a global consensus based on abstract acknowledgments of the importance of "development planning" and "rational planning" and "demographic policies," geared to overall "planning, managing or controlling environmental resources." Developing countries could see this as a call for international commitment to "development"—indeed, a call for "accelerated development through the transfer of substantial quantities of financial and technical assistance." Environmentalists, meanwhile, emphasized the Stockholm Declaration's recognition of the need for common action against common threats.[29]

In practice, of course, the concerns of Western advocacy groups took priority in subsequent international forums. In the 1980s, environmentalists publicized the discovery that the ozone layer in the earth's atmosphere was thinning around the polar regions, apparently due to the accumulation in the atmosphere of chlorofluorocarbons (CFCs)—chemical compounds used as refrigerants as well as propellants in aerosol sprays. In a succession of treaties, beginning with the Montreal Protocol in 1985, Western countries agreed to phase out use of the chemical. The thinning ozone layer, it was feared, would allow higher levels of ultraviolet radiation to penetrate the atmosphere, producing sizable increases in skin cancer. But the people most exposed to this threat, scientists acknowledged, were people with fair complexions in countries at the greatest remove from the equator.

Notwithstanding the fact that people in affluent countries were most at risk, developing countries were soon coaxed into committing to the treaty scheme, with promises from the West to finance their transition to new refrigerants—and threats to impose trade penalties if they did not subscribe to the scheme. So developing countries, too, agreed to phase out their use of the CFCs and rely on new compounds for refrigerants. American and European companies happened to hold the patents on these new compounds. The financial assistance actually delivered to LDCs also turned out to be far less than the costs of making the transition to such substitute chemicals. But then a number of developing countries, while accepting such aid, actually increased their production of CFCs—in the cases of India and China, by fivefold and tenfold, respectively.[30]

Environmentalists drew no lessons from this experience. Or, rather, they drew the lesson that differing interests of rich and poor countries could be made to disappear under a cloud of globalist rhetoric. A convention on trade in hazardous substances in the mid-1980s (the so-called "Basel Convention," from the Swiss city in which it was negotiated) restricted shipments of scrap metal and other supposed hazards to developing countries, effectively creating a monopoly on recycling for European countries that had invested in relevant technologies. Affluent nations would monopolize lucrative business—for the benefit of people in poor countries, it was said. Poor countries would be spared the burden of having to decide for themselves how to balance the possible risks and financial rewards in offering secondary uses or disposal sites for such "hazardous" material as scrap iron. The treaty was celebrated by environmental groups, but the United States refused to participate in this cartel pact. Many unwary developing countries did sign, but the main economic consequences followed, in any case, from the commitment of European states to implement the treaty scheme, ensuring that recycling trade would remain within Europe.[31]

In 1992, the UN marked the twentieth anniversary of the Stockholm Summit with a far larger "Earth Summit" in Rio de Janeiro. Officially designated the Conference on Environment and Development, the Rio Summit continually emphasized that rich and poor countries had a common interest in "sustainable development." The phrase was supposed to link environmental concerns of the affluent nations with the economic development priorities of poor nations, but it inevitably raised questions about "development" with its suggestion that some forms of it might not be "sustainable." The conference produced a summary statement of agreed-upon "principles" called the Rio Declaration. A "precautionary principle" asserted that "lack of full scientific certainty shall not be used as a reason for post-poning cost-effective measures to prevent environmental degradation." It is, of course, hard to judge whether a remedy is "cost-effective" if there is no clear understanding of the dangers it is supposed to prevent. Champions of the precautionary principle evidently believe that hypothetical environmental dangers should take priority over more immediate dangers to human well-being—such as the starvation and disease associated with extreme poverty.[32]

The Rio conference launched a treaty structure to safeguard global bio-diversity. It was supposed to provide a general framework for protecting ecosystems around the world. In return for unspecified cooperation, developing countries were promised unspecified forms of royalty payments for biotechnology developed from species in their territories. The promised revenue flow never materialized. Biotechnology did not generate vast profits from adaptations of species found in tropical forests. In fact, many countries that should have provided large markets for bioengineered products turned out to be very hostile to this new technology. European farmers, already heavily subsidized, were fearful of competition from foreign producers experimenting with bioengineered crops. Advocacy groups persuaded European consumers to see bioengineering as a technology that would create terrifying "Frankenfoods." Europeans were still prepared to accept ancient practices such as grafting, hybridization, and selective breeding—as long as they were not contaminated by too much laboratory science.

Along with the precautionary principle, the Biodiversity Treaty then became the legal platform for European negotiators to develop a Biosafety Protocol, to restrict trade in genetically modified crops. Canada, Australia, New Zealand, Argentina, Chile, Uruguay, and the United States—all exporters of agricultural commodities that make use of bioengineering—resisted the proposal. In the end, the EU was largely successful in crafting a treaty to limit trade in such products. A UN panel warned that African countries had the most to lose from technophobic resistance to bioengineering, since African harvests were most vulnerable to pests and weather damage, and new crop strains could be designed to be more pest-resistant and durable. But European resistance to biotechnology turned out to be quite entrenched—and for the moment, at least, African states have gone along.[33]

Meanwhile, the Rio conference had authorized a Framework Convention on Climate Change. Environmental advocacy groups trumpeted evidence that the world was warming and gave full credence to scientific speculation that human activity was the cause. In fact, ice ages have alternated with warming trends over millions of years, without human assistance. Adherents to the theory of anthrogenic warming pointed to the buildup of carbon dioxide and other "greenhouse gases" in the earth's atmosphere which might be trapping heat on the earth's surface, forcing a continual and perhaps accelerating warming trend. The Framework Convention acknowledged in general terms that nations should reduce their emissions of greenhouse gases in order to prevent global warming—but it did not commit nations to any particular level of emissions reductions by any definite date. Carbon dioxide, the primary greenhouse gas, is released by the burning of fossil fuels—oil, coal, natural gas—the lifeblood of modern economies. Over one hundred countries agreed to the Framework Convention's premise that carbon dioxide (CO_2) emissions should be reduced; nonetheless, almost all of them proceeded to increase their consumption of fossil fuel.

An implementing treaty negotiated in Kyoto, Japan in 1997 committed some two dozen advanced nations to specific reductions in CO_2 emissions. For most of these countries, the reductions were in the range of 7 to 8 percent below 1990 levels, to be achieved over the next fifteen years. Given the consequences of continuing increases in fuel use in the interim, reductions of 7 or 8 percent below 1990 levels would mean actual reductions in fuel use on the order of 20 percent—more than any country achieved amid the sharp hike in oil prices (engineered by the OPEC cartel) in the 1970s.

Less-developed countries refused to commit themselves to any overall reductions in their emissions, insisting that they should not bear any responsibility for correcting a problem generated by the industrialized world. But fuel consumption is rising rapidly in populous nations of the developing world. Without curbs in their own emissions, all the promised emission reductions by developed states will be more than offset by the growth in emissions from the less-developed countries.

For poor countries to accept caps on their own emissions, however, they would have to accept a much lower standard of living than that enjoyed in the affluent nations. Even if the United States cut its fuel consumption by 20 percent, for example, and China were allowed to increase its own emissions to the same extent (so that net global emissions would remain the same), per capita fuel use in China would still be barely a quarter of America's.[34] Meanwhile, if global warming does bring serious weather problems in the future, the effects would be most severe for the countries that are most dependent on agriculture (the most weather-dependent economic sector), and more generally, for the poorest countries, those with the least developed transportation infrastructure and therefore the most exposure to public health and safety threats from severe weather. Poor countries would be better off having developed as rapidly as possible in the meanwhile—without regard to their greenhouse gas emissions.[35]

The Kyoto Protocol assumed not only that everyone gave the same priority to its aims, but that every country would be prepared to make sacrifices—even if the impact of such sacrifices on different nations varied enormously. It assumed that formulas could be devised to make sacrifices seem equitable and acceptable to all countries involved. All of this had to be achieved without direct means of coercion. The program laid down in the Kyoto Protocol itself would only be a meaningful response to global warming if it were merely an initial, preparatory stage in a far more ambitious project, which would generate more encompassing and constraining controls on energy use in future decades. Could such vast changes really be accomplished without coercion?

And if coercion did prove necessary, how was it to be exercised, and who would be trusted to exercise it? The obvious alternative was economic coercion, which might be most effectively exercised by trade sanctions. Prior treaties already included some provision for trade restrictions. Human rights advocates had demanded and occasionally won trade sanctions—most notably against South African apartheid in the 1980s. It was not always clear whether trading rules under the GATT were consistent with trade sanctions for issues unrelated to trade. Potential conflicts might be evaded if such restrictions only intruded here and there on the general principles of trade law. The conflict could not be avoided if nontrade agreements were going to tackle challenges as vast as the Kyoto Protocol's goals.

WTO as the Global Balance Wheel

Potential conflicts between the aims of the trading system and the ambitions of the environmental movement were already apparent when the World Trade Organization officially launched in 1994. At a signing ceremony in Marrakesh, Morocco, both Vice President Gore and French President Mitterrand urged that the new organization find ways of reconciling trade rules with new environmental treaties. GATT rules allowed member states to exclude goods if they were found to pose a hazard to health or safety within the importing country. The rules did not make specific provision for imposing trade sanctions to enforce such environmental agreements as the Basel Convention (on trade in waste materials) or the Montreal Protocol (on ozone-depleting substances). Both the American delegation and various European delegations also expressed interest in making some provision to link trading privileges with respect for fundamental labor rights, though the new agreement made no provision for such linkage.

In principle, the WTO had a mechanism for changing the rules between general negotiating rounds. The agreement establishing the WTO provided that amendments to the latest GATT round could be adopted by a vote of three-quarters of the signatory states. Such amendments could then be made obligatory on all signatories if endorsed by seven-eighths of the states in the WTO. In principle, these provisions might raise constitutional doubts regarding American adherence, since they could bind the United States to terms not formally agreed to by Congress, nor even approved by the president. The supermajority requirements, however, were calculated to discourage controversial proposals. In fact, the required majorities proved so high—in an organization which now had such a diverse membership—that this interim "legislative process" proved impossible to implement. No amendment has ever been adopted in this way nor even come close to adoption.

On the issues broached at Marrakesh, the disagreements among WTO members turned out to be very hard to bridge. Developing countries, by now a majority of WTO members, were fiercely opposed to any standard that would constrain their access to the markets of affluent states because they failed to live up to environmental or labor practices favored by the latter. The WTO organized a Committee on Trade and Environment which was supposed to develop suggestions for integrating international environmental treaties with existing trade rules. The committee failed to reach any consensus on this subject and could offer no suggestions for compromise. There was no more agreement on proposals to incorporate labor standards into the WTO. Such proposals were fiercely resisted at the Singapore meeting of trade ministers from member states in 1996 and dwindled to a vague conference declaration expressing sympathy for the aims of the International Labour Organization.

But the WTO had other ways of elaborating its existing rules. There had long been a practice, under the GATT, of referring disputes between specific member states to panels of trade experts. The panels would make findings on the validity of the complaints and offer recommendations for redressing patterns of noncompliance. In principle, panel reports had to be approved by the entire membership of the GATT, however. Any state—including the one complained against—could block approval of a report. So there was always some assured connection between expert interpretations of the GATT rules and a background of diplomatic understandings or political negotiations among the members. The GATT remained a diplomatic forum as much as a legal structure, as its founding members had intended. A proposal floated in 1947 to allow disputes about GATT rules to be submitted to the International Court of Justice was dismissed almost out of hand at the time.[36]

The WTO created a more formal structure for dispute resolution. Disputes could be submitted to panels, as before. Instead of subjecting panel reports to approval of the entire membership, however, the WTO agreement provided that states dissatisfied with panel findings could appeal to a separate, permanent "Appellate Body." And the decision of the Appellate Body (AB) would then be "final." To lend authority to the AB, its members were assigned fixed terms and annual salaries, while the panel members would still be selected on a temporary, ad hoc basis (as they had been under the GATT) from a list of eligible trade experts with outside careers. The AB now had the look of an established tribunal, whose judges could devote themselves to building a consistent body of case law.

As it turned out, the AB took a quite activist approach to its duties. In its very first decision, the AB announced that it would be guided not only by actual trade agreements of the WTO but also by "general principles of international law" and such guides to treaty interpretation as the 1970 Vienna Convention on the Law of Treaties (which, as it happens, has never been ratified by the United States).[37] Where the architects of GATT had rejected the idea of appeals to the International Court of Justice, the Appellate Body now conceived itself as a replacement for it. In fact, the AB would be more than that. The ICJ can only hear a dispute when both parties agree to accept the court's jurisdiction. The AB presides over a system in which appeals can be pursued as a matter of right. And the AB emphasized that all WTO members had incurred a formal obligation to abide by the agreements as a matter of law.

What had once seemed a series of trade bargains was now presented as a set of solemn legal duties, embedded in a wider framework of international law. In short order, the AB cast itself as the grand harmonizer of potential conflicts between trade agreements and all other kinds of international legal commitments. Potential conflicts would not be left for states to sort out in their own diplomacy but definitively settled by the formal judicial rulings of the Appellate Body.

The pattern was displayed in an extended dispute about a U.S. statute that sought to protect endangered sea turtles by excluding from the U.S. market any shrimp caught in nets that might entangle these turtles. In effect, the statute set down regulatory standards for the world and sought to enforce these standards with unilateral sanctions against noncompliant states. In the absence of any trade agreement, the United States could certainly have excluded any product from its markets for any reason whatever. But the founding principle of the GATT was that member states would not discriminate against other member states. States could exclude products they regarded as a direct danger to their own consumers, but they could not exclude a product merely because they objected to the way it had been produced in the exporting state.

Restrictions based on objections of the latter sort were understood to be an endless source of mischief, since they allowed the home state to invoke almost any difference in national practices as a pretext for import restrictions. In its most protectionist phase, in the early twentieth century, American tariff law actually sought to impose "compensatory duties" to assure that goods produced at lower cost in foreign countries would not be sold in U.S. markets at lower rates than their American counterparts.[38] Trade agreements would be pointless if countries remained free to impose "compensatory" tariffs of this sort against foreign competition.

The GATT did authorize some exceptions to the general rule against restricting imports based on objections to the production process in the exporting state.[39] But nothing in the GATT provided for the unilateral imposition of environmental standards of the sort that the U.S. legislation had attempted. An arbitration panel accordingly judged the U.S. law in violation of the WTO agreement.

The 1998 ruling of the Appellate Body took a more accommodating line. The AB faulted American policy for treating some exporting states differently than others, but took pains to emphasize that trade law might well accommodate a more consistent approach. Or, rather, the AB held that trade law should be viewed in more accommodating terms in order to reconcile it with principles proclaimed at the 1992 Rio conference (though not adopted as formal treaties), and with provisions in the Biodiversity Convention and other treaties that had not actually been ratified by the United States. It treated hortatory language in the preamble to the agreement establishing the WTO, with its reference to "sustainable development," as an endorsement of a range of unrelated international initiatives associated with the same cliché of the 1990s.[40] Three years afterward, in a later version of the dispute, the AB endorsed a slightly more flexible version of the U.S. law excluding shrimp not harvested with "turtle-excluding devices." The AB found that the United States had made efforts to persuade other nations to embrace U.S. policy as an international standard. It then concluded that the United States was entitled to apply this standard even to states that did not accept it.[41]

It was surely a Pyrrhic victory. What the United States could do to others, others could do to it. During the 1980s, America had pursued a series of trade disputes with the European Community (before it became the EU) over a different but related issue: European regulators sought to exclude American beef exports on the grounds that cattle treated with growth hormone were not safe for human consumption. The GATT allowed different countries to set different safety standards but required that they be backed by some scientific evidence of actual health or safety risk. Not to have included such a requirement would again offer openings to endless pretexts for protectionism—as with the Japanese policy that excluded American-made skis on the grounds that Japan and the United States had different kinds of snow, so skis manufactured for American snow would be unsafe in Japan.[42]

If an environmental treaty by itself could justify a new trade restriction, however—even a treaty otherwise inconsistent with GATT obligations—then American products could be excluded from European markets whenever they rounded up a few other states to endorse an EU trade nostrum. Perhaps the member states of the EU itself would be sufficient, as the members continue to be individual signatories to international environmental agreements. A long-running dispute over the safety of bioengineered crops could be settled without any reference at all to scientific evidence of any kind, as long as European lawyers could wave a treaty on the subject before the Appellate Body. A U.S. complaint filed in spring 2003 would test the question.

The obvious objection to this approach is that it allows trade agreements to be retroactively amended outside the agreed-upon procedure for amendments. It thus accomplishes in a slightly indirect or concealed way precisely what would raise constitutional objections if pursued directly through the "legislative" method of amending WTO agreements. In effect, it delegates the treaty-power of the United States to an international body.[43] And the objection to this practice is not a mere formalistic quibble. Each new round of agreements takes years of intense bargaining to negotiate among all the GATT members. Now states can pocket concessions they may have received from others in the general bargaining and then remove the obligations they had offered in return by signing a separate, subsequent agreement with a subset of GATT members.

Nonetheless, the Appellate Body seems committed to this path. From its very first decisions, it insisted that trade agreements must be interpreted against the background of wider principles of international law. So in its interpretation of actual trade agreements it cited decisions of the International Court of Justice and other courts never before associated with the GATT. Among other things, this approach served to bolster the notion that trade agreements were not just bargains for mutual advantage, but standards carrying the prestige of law. The obligation to conform to agreements was not, then, simply a way to hold others to the same bargains, but a legal obligation with the moral force of law. Noncompliance would not simply risk retaliation or the loss of trade benefits, but the odium of lawlessness or the stigma of international outlawry.

Meanwhile, opening the WTO to the wider currents of international law meant that it might also be open to new constituencies. If the AB stuck to interpreting actual agreements, the WTO would offend environmental enthusiasts—lots of them. Most viewed the WTO with considerable suspicion and some with outright hostility. To such advocates, the WTO seemed to give a privileged status to commerce, since only commercial disputes could seek direct arbitration and enforcement through it.

In an earlier version of the shrimp-turtle dispute, a GATT panel condemned a U.S. law excluding tuna caught with nets that could snare dolphins. The ruling had energized environmental opposition to the very agreement establishing the WTO. American environmentalists, while often rallying to such ad hoc, unilateral policies, were themselves more enthused about international treaties, however—in part because such treaties could provide new leverage to extend the ambitions of American policy.

American advocacy groups had played prominent roles at the Rio summit and its successors, at the Kyoto conference and its successors, and at dozens of comparable forums. In these forums, they readily made common cause with advocacy groups from Europe and other parts of the developed world. In such settings, environmental advocates were no longer mere interest groups struggling with other interest groups, but the voice of "global civil society," whose demands could be amplified by the publicity and excitement generated by international conferences in famous world capitals. By contrast, bargaining over GATT standards had generally been pursued at closed-door sessions among government trade officials. To advocacy groups, the WTO, unlike UN forums, seemed remote and secretive.

The AB's approach sought to accommodate these disaffected constituencies. It not only acknowledged that the handiwork of environmental enthusiasts had an official place in interpreting trade disputes; it also made room for the NGOs themselves. In the shrimp-turtle dispute, the AB held that amicus briefs from private advocacy groups might be considered along with briefs from member states of the WTO. The new approach did have a certain logic, after all: If the WTO were not simply mediating disputes between parties to a specific trade agreement but ensuring conformity with general principles of international law, then it ought to consider what a range of possible experts had to say about international law.

Perhaps the logic is more apparent if one views the issue in less legalistic terms. If disputes are no longer seen as simply a matter of interpreting a particular bargain between states, it makes sense to incorporate the concerns of other constituencies besides governments. And the whole thrust of NGO advocacy was to insist that NGOs spoke for claims that were wider or deeper or in any event different from those which happened to be endorsed by governments. These claims needed to be heard and considered in international forums. UN-sponsored forums on environmental and human rights issues—and a half-dozen related issues—adopted this premise in the 1990s and generated publicity and prestige for themselves by mobilizing the energy and media skills of NGOs on their behalf.

Groups active in other forums saw the WTO as a point of leverage on recalcitrant states that could be far more decisive than other international organizations. As one WTO official remarked, the trade organization looked like "a sheriff in a world of weaker international institutions." Labor organizations, for instance, frustrated with the limited power of the International Labour Organization, "wanted the WTO sheriff to include core labor standards on its beat."[44] In 1996, the International Confederation of Free Trade Unions (ICTFU) urged the WTO to "integrate" core labor standards into its trade rules in order to maintain the "political authority" of its own organization.[45] But labor advocates in rich countries were not the only ones looking to borrow the leverage afforded by the WTO.

In 1997, the International Commission of Jurists (a UN advisory group), in collaboration with American and European human rights advocates, published a set of guidelines on the legal implications of the Covenant on Economic and Social Rights, called (in echo of a more formal European project) the "Maastricht Guidelines." Among other things, it admonished the WTO and its member states to "ensure" that the rights enumerated in the covenant "are fully taken into account in the [WTO's] development of policies and programs."[46] A number of scholars chimed in with legal analyses showing that the existing GATT framework, inherited by the WTO, already could be interpreted as making room for trade sanctions to enforce compliance with labor standards in other countries.[47] In 2002, Friends of the Earth Europe petitioned the European Commission to impose trade sanctions on the United States for its failure to take steps to reduce its greenhouse gas emissions as required by the Kyoto Protocol and, as the group argued, by general principles of international law embraced by the WTO.[48]

By September 2003, a meeting of trade ministers from WTO member states, held in Cancun, Mexico, had attracted a host of NGO advocacy groups, much like the UN social forums of the 1990s. But governments, bargaining now over genuinely enforceable policies, found it much harder to reach agreement on new trade rules. Three years earlier, President Clinton had proposed that trade rules should allow for sanctions against states failing to comply with core labor standards of the ILO and provoked furious protests from representatives of developing nations. At Cancun, developed and less-developed countries were divided on many other issues, notably on agricultural subsidies in affluent states, which worked to exclude exports from developing countries. But earlier disputes about labor and the environment also remained unresolved when the Cancun talks ended in stalemate.

Given the scale and intensity of the underlying conflicts, the Appellate Body may find it increasingly difficulty to nurture compromise and consensus by creative interpretations of the existing agreements. And it may also feel that the WTO's future stability requires it to break deadlocks when negotiations among governments remain stalemated. If the system is besieged, adjustments may be required to maintain political support. If governments cannot agree on new compromises, the system may require adjustments to keep it from collapsing under the stress of opposing political pressures. And the Appellate Body seems to think it has the task of reconciling these pressures with carefully modulated adjustments, cast as "general principles of international law."

The project may seem wildly ambitious for a mere body of trade-law specialists. But it is, after all, the role the European Court of Justice assumed in the formative decades of the European Community, when it repeatedly broke through diplomatic stalemates among member governments with its own bold initiatives to advance the momentum of European integration.[49] The ECJ cultivated its own political constituencies, as business interests found that appeals to the European Court could force rewarding changes in policy. Over time, the ECJ also nurtured constituencies among a variety of social advocacy groups as it read social issues or human rights claims into the terms of European trade standards. One way it did this was by invoking international treaties, such as ILO conventions, as a basis for its decisions, even though these legal claims had no direct connection with the EU itself or with the ECJ's jurisdiction. Now the AB seems to think that the way to stabilize the WTO is to follow the path already blazed by the ECJ.

A growing literature, mostly of European origin, already extols the WTO as the framework of a "world constitution."[50] It would be the extension of the European project: liberalizing trade in many areas, while simultaneously elaborating new regulatory constraints at the same level. Less-developed states would be coaxed into adopting these new standards in return for market access to more affluent states, and more affluent states would be coaxed into keeping their markets open to others in return for extending their own regulatory priorities to poor states. And the whole world could go forward in harmony, as Europe has, with wise judges sustaining the best ideas of wise bureaucrats and the noblest enthusiasms of globally minded advocacy groups.

Retaining Sovereignty

The AB's vision is probably too ambitious to be sustainable, too presumptuous to gain enduring acceptance. Pressed very far, it is more likely to blow up the WTO than to establish its Appellate Body as the balance wheel of world politics. But it should be taken seriously as a threat to sovereignty.

In form, it is true, the United States retains traditional safeguards of its sovereignty, whatever the rulings of the WTO's Appellate Body. Agreements under the WTO are binding law within the United States because they are enacted by the U.S. Congress. The current procedure requires Congress to enact the whole package of changes negotiated in a new round when it approves the agreement.[51] Legal scholars may claim that decisions of the Appellate Body are binding as a matter of international law, but AB rulings have no direct effect in U.S. law.[52] When a WTO ruling holds some aspect of U.S. law to be in violation of relevant agreements, it remains for Congress (or the president, in directing the specialized tariff-setting agency in the Commerce Department) to change U.S. law. The United States can resist compliance with a ruling of the AB. Other states may be authorized to impose retaliatory tariffs, but they could impose tariffs on American products even if the WTO had never existed. In form, the whole structure rests on consent, since the United States remains free, in principle, to exit the organization if it rejects the trend of AB case law.

Still, it is one thing to agree to submit international obligations to arbitration—something the United States has done on various occasions since the 1790s. It is something else again to allow a major international obligation to be rewritten in activist ways by an international entity pursuing its own policy visions. It is something new—and potentially dangerous—to have that entity nurturing its own constituencies, entangling its policy ventures with a range of different policy priorities, and finally spinning a web of political claims that may prove quite difficult to repudiate. Sovereignty is not simply a matter of formalities maintained for ritual purposes. Formal safeguards have been insisted upon for the more fundamental purpose of safeguarding political independence.

If the forms are now starting to look like mere formalities, one reason is that a more judicialized dispute-settlement process has given the WTO more direct connection with business constituencies. In form, complaints of non-compliance can only be raised by governments. In principle, the United States, like any other state, retains the capacity to handle disputes through diplomatic negotiation. It can decline to initiate a formal complaint before a panel. It can decline to appeal an unfavorable panel report to the Appellate Body. In practice, however, a more judicialized system has encouraged business interests to engage private legal assistance to prepare formal complaints. There was a dramatic increase in complaints once a judicialized system offered the prospect of authoritative determination apart from bargaining.[53] A whole new legal practice has arisen in Washington and elsewhere of specialists in WTO law, prepared to offer up their specialized advice on the compilation of "winning" arguments to present to the AB. With private claimants preparing their own filings, the trade officials of the United States government can come to be little more than ceremonial sponsors of such claims.

To the extent that this approach offers gains to business—or even a more plausible hope of gains—it transfers attention and support from American trade negotiators to WTO judges. This was a central part of the ECJ's political development—that it attracted constituencies to its own policymaking initiatives. National governments found it increasingly difficult to insist on their own power and responsibility to make the basic decisions in the European Community. European jurists have now suggested that WTO rulings ought to enter directly into national law, as rulings of the ECJ do.[54] Even if the United States refused to adopt the same policy, adoption elsewhere would greatly augment the prestige and authority of the AB—and might make it harder to treat its rulings as anything less than supreme law. The "direct effect" approach to international trade law would, in the meantime, allow advocacy groups and the European Court of Justice to seize the initiative in pressing interpretations of trade law ahead of the AB. This approach would likely make it much harder for government negotiators to restrain the extension of WTO law into environmental and social issues in ways that groups like Friends of the Earth or the ICFTU now urge.

Several broader trends may lend momentum to such tendencies. The Uruguay Round, which launched the WTO, not only extended the GATT but also combined it with two new projects. A General Agreement on Trade in Services (GATS) offered protection, for the first time, for providers of specialized services seeking to enter foreign markets. An agreement on Trade-Related International Property Standards (TRIPS) provided protection for copyrights and patents. These agreements extended new protections for commercial activity. They also extended a stake in the WTO to new constituencies, apart from direct exporters and importers of goods.

Meanwhile, as social activists and NGOs become more active in lobbying for and against changes in WTO standards, more traditional business lobbyists seem increasingly willing to cut deals to protect their own priorities. Jagdish Bhagwati, a longtime defender of free trade, now warns that "multinationals are so keen to get markets . . . they're like salivating dogs, they will make concessions on labor rights and the environment, the minimum necessary, just to get you out of the way. They're a bunch of cynical bastards."[55] The more complex and ambiguous the terms of new agreements, the more the system depends on the AB to sort out the actual meaning of the different gestures made to different constituencies.

Another dynamic also seems to be at work, adding more fuel to the ambitions of the Appellate Body. Governments still face pressure from industries hurt by foreign competition. The United States, with other countries, often tries to reassure such constituencies with measures that are known in advance to violate agreed-upon trade rules. As they sometimes do with domestic courts, politicians learn to rely on WTO judges to save them from their own impulses—or to ensure that gestures to particular constituencies can be made at little cost, because they will later be nullified when they impose too much burden on the system. So the Bush administration imposed tariffs on imported steel in 2002, knowing that this interference with standard trade practice was sure to be challenged at the WTO—as it promptly was, by the EU. The Bush administration probably expected the WTO in this case to save it from the consequences of its own political gesture. When the WTO did rule against the steel tariffs, the administration promptly ordered their removal. Having displayed its concern for American steel workers, the Bush administration could now rely on the WTO to save it from an awkward trade dispute with steel-exporting nations (and relieve burdens on U.S. steel importers).

The more governments depend on the system, the more unnerving or intolerable it seems to exit the treaty structure. The alternative to participation is not seen as a new round of negotiations but as frightful chaos— as if a mere treaty system had the same moral claims for continuity and compliance as the legal framework of a sovereign state. That has been the history of the European integration process, which continued to move forward, decade by decade, because governments viewed any serious move to constrain its forward momentum as threatening the whole enterprise—and threatening the whole enterprise had come to seem an intolerable risk.[56]

The history of American federalism teaches its own sobering lessons. Well into the twentieth century, the U.S. Supreme Court tried to enforce limits on federal legislation, so that the congressional power to regulate interstate commerce could not be invoked as a mere pretext for interfering with legal standards within a state. The Court struggled, not always convincingly, to distinguish matters properly relating to interstate commerce from matters properly left to legislative determinations within each state. The Court abandoned most of these limiting doctrines by the end of the 1930s, and, for decades thereafter, federal controls were allowed to reach even the most localized activities, on the ground that even activities not directly related to commerce (let alone interstate commerce) could still have some indirect effect on interstate commerce. The Court has made very modest efforts to revive some boundaries since the mid-1990s.[57] But even modest limitations remain controversial and have done little to constrain the flow of policy initiative from state capitals to Washington, D.C. Any constituency that cannot achieve its aims in a state legislature has obvious incentives to try to attach its proposed policy to federal legislation.

State legislatures may worry that a particularly ambitious or costly policy would place the state at a disadvantage in competing with other states for business investment. A federal policy seems to remove this concern. But business expansion can now move outside the reach of federal regulation in the United States to offshore production sites, from which entry back into the American market is protected by trade agreements. The same pressure to extend federal controls may thus generate demands for international controls to plug what some advocates see as escape hatches from federal regulatory schemes.

The WTO cannot impose its own social regulation in the same direct way the European Commission can. The Appellate Body can only give approval for individual states to impose trade penalties on states that do not subscribe to international treaties setting down preferred social regulation. The United States could accept such penalties rather than subscribe to the standards. But it is easy to imagine advocacy groups citing the threat of such penalties as additional reason for the United States to cooperate in these schemes.

True, even if there were no WTO, other states could still impose trade sanctions to coerce changes in American policy. But without the WTO, the United States would also be free to retaliate in kind against such attempted coercion. Without the WTO, other states might be far more reluctant to venture into such trials of strength, with their risk of degenerating into escalating trade wars. With a compliant WTO, other states may imagine that they can attempt to coerce the United States without jeopardizing their own access to American markets or risking the overall stability of international trade. In practical terms, this means that the European Union can hope to extend its own business standards to the United States, making increasing conformity with European social standards the price for American access to European markets.

The point of sovereignty is to secure the right of each nation to make its own determinations. If treaties can reach into any matter of domestic policy, if trade can be held hostage to any treaty, sovereignty will look increasingly hollow—as it now does for member states of the European Union. If no government can control the rippling effects of international trade on its own, it may seem logical for all states to cooperate in common regulatory ventures that are as global as trade itself. To accept this reasoning, however, one must start with the initial presumption that government is responsible for every social and economic effect that results from private exchanges. Once one views sovereignty in that light, there is no easy way to distinguish government policy from private activity, let alone local or national standards from international aims; sovereignty will gradually melt down into an amorphous structure of "global governance." This may appeal to Europeans who already live with something of the sort, but it is not something that can ever be reconciled with the United States Constitution.

Global governance of this kind is, in fact, at odds with the fundamental logic of trade. Competition from foreign producers may sometimes generate pressure to relax regulatory burdens on domestic production. But as an empirical matter, there is not much evidence for the claim that without common standards, all jurisdictions will be dragged into a "race to the bottom" because the jurisdiction with the least regulatory controls will be the most attractive site for investment.[58] Regulatory constraints (along with taxation and government spending programs) often achieve results that make a particular setting more attractive to investors, because, for example, government policies promote a healthier or more contented workforce or a more pleasant and secure place for managers to operate. Different governments (or the electorates they respond to) may reach different conclusions about the best mix of policies in their circumstances.

One of the great advantages of trade is that it allows different jurisdictions to determine, over time, what mix of policies works well for them, given their purposes and priorities and the various advantages and disadvantages of their situations. Competition among jurisdictions is a way of working out such adjustments, just as competition among firms allows business managers to find their comparative advantage. Just as the logic of trade requires initial ownership rights, the logic of adjustment among jurisdictions requires that each remains free to make its own adaptations. The logic of sovereignty is parallel to the logic of trade.

The danger in the WTO's current trajectory is not that it will gradually generate an unstoppable global tyranny. The danger is that, as Europeans have found, it is very difficult ever to restore constitutional boundaries to a process too amorphous to be confined within demarcated boundaries. The process can go forward, embracing more and more "global" standards. It is hard to hold it to account, to insist on relaxing or removing global standards. Global institutions are not accountable to a global electorate. And the usual question for voters—not what they might prefer in the abstract, but what they prefer given alternatives on offer—is especially hard to frame in global terms. Citizens of any particular state can hope to force changes in the policy of their own government if they elect a new party to office. No one knows how to impose changes on the European Commission or the European Court of Justice. No one will know how to impose changes on the amorphous network of constituencies embracing and sustaining an overreaching WTO.

To safeguard its own constitutional structure—which is what sovereignty requires—the United States must resist this trend. The more the WTO follows the trajectory of the European Union, the more it threatens American sovereignty. The United States must, accordingly, insist that the WTO rest on actual trade agreements between actual governments and not on open-ended aspirations toward international consensus on all aspects of global policy. The United States government must retain responsibility for pursuing disputes to arbitration and resist the notion that WTO agreements confer, in some way, direct rights on private beneficiaries to pursue redress on their own initiative. To drive home this point, it would be useful for the U.S. trade officials to emphasize that the United States will not pursue every case it might be able to win before the WTO, because they regard the WTO as a forum for advancing general policies, not a direct arbiter of rights claimed by any particular private constituency.

The United States can emphasize the same point by resisting quick compliance with unfavorable AB rulings. The United States has a diplomatic obligation to other members of the WTO. It should not acknowledge that it has a direct legal obligation to private beneficiaries of WTO rulings. An AB ruling against an American practice requires that the United States try to satisfy the concerns of the complaining states in subsequent diplomacy. It is dangerous to leave the impression that AB rulings, however ambitious, will flow irresistibly and almost automatically into American domestic law.

But U.S. constituencies will often be eager to invoke AB rulings as pretexts for advancing their own policy agendas. The AB ruled in 2002, for example, that provisions of the U.S. tax code were an improper subsidy to U.S. corporations (because of the way they reduced their tax liability to compensate for taxes already paid to other countries on their foreign sales). The House Ways and Means Committee immediately took this rather dubious ruling as the occasion for a general reform of a variety of tax measures.[59] The tendency to treat rulings of the AB as if they were rulings of our own Supreme Court may often be hard to resist—but that is reason in itself to show that the United States does not feel bound to give immediate and scrupulous adherence to doctrines set out in AB initiatives.

A more fundamental strategic response is to insist that trade agreements stand on their own footing. The United States may have many environmental concerns which require international cooperation and which may be advanced through international treaty structures. But treaties do not constitute an international legal code, all elements of which must be harmonized to ensure their systematic and comprehensive implementation. Different treaties have different aims. Sometimes these aims are in tension. It is one of the challenges for American diplomacy to decide which treaty commitment should receive priority in any particular context. We are not advancing American diplomacy but supplanting it if we delegate this responsibility to an international authority like the WTO's Appellate Body. Such delegation is particularly perverse when the AB has the avowed aim not merely of harmonizing obligations entailed in actual U.S. treaties, but of reconciling obligations entailed in various international treaties, including a number which the United States itself has not embraced.

Most developing countries have strong reasons to welcome the separation of trade agreements from other projects of international coordination. In fact, they have been quite emphatic in their opposition to "linkage" or "integration" of labor and environmental standards with trade rules. It might be feasible to negotiate, in the current round of trade negotiations, a set of basic rules protecting WTO agreements from such intrusions by clarifying, for example, when and to what extent the AB may consider outside treaties in judging trade disputes. Meanwhile, the United States can insist in other forums that trade issues should not be held hostage to environmental or human rights standards—at least not routinely. It makes little sense to allow the World Bank to build up programs supposed to facilitate compliance with environmental treaties when the United States remains undecided about such treaties on the merits. That is, however, what the World Bank has been doing—pursuing policies which prominent political analysts interpret as a sign that the bank has been "captured by environmental NGOs."[60]

But all other efforts to constrain the WTO depend, in the last analysis, on a plausible threat to exit the organization if it does develop along unacceptable lines. When Congress did approve American participation in the new organization, even many advocates wanted to reassure doubters with the promise that the United States could withdraw if the organization proved to be something different than expected. Senator Robert Dole, the majority leader at the time, offered legislation which would have established a commission of jurists to review every AB ruling affecting the United States. If the commission found fault with three different rulings, Congress would automatically be required to vote on whether the United States should remain in the organization.[61] The proposal was never enacted, and perhaps such a mechanical scheme could not really have provided the assurances its sponsors had imagined for it, in any case.

Politically, the threat to withdraw depends on the prospect of alternatives. Most countries, in fact, are eager to retain access to American markets and would not be less eager for such access even if they had to negotiate for it outside the WTO. The European Union is no exception, since the United States is also Europe's largest single trade partner. Successive GATT rounds of bargaining have started with bilateral negotiations between the United States and the EU as the two largest participants. The United States could still bargain with the EU even if the bargaining were not connected with a global trade agreement.

But it is easier to contemplate trade negotiations without the WTO if alternatives are already in place. The North American Free Trade Agreement is the most important alternative at present. It was created in 1993 by expanding the 1989 Canada-U.S. Free Trade Agreement to incorporate Mexico. The success of the NAFTA negotiations is widely credited with providing leverage to complete the Uruguay Round negotiations that led to creation of the WTO the following year: the launching of NAFTA reminded European negotiators that the United States had alternatives to a new global agreement.[62]

Even before the NAFTA negotiations were completed, American officials began to talk about a larger project—a Free Trade Agreement of the Americas, ultimately stretching from Canada to Argentina. Leaders from almost every nation in the Western Hemisphere agreed on the framework for negotiating this grand project in the fall of 2003. Meanwhile, separate agreements have already been concluded between Chile and each of the NAFTA partners, making this dynamic South American economy a forerunner of a larger scheme of trade liberalization. The United States has also concluded parallel free trade agreements with Singapore, Jordan, and Israel. A looser program for gradual dismantling of trade barriers among nations on the Pacific Rim—the so-called Asian-Pacific Economic Conference (APEC)—aims at mutual understandings among China and other Asian economies with Australia and New Zealand, along with Chile and the NAFTA partners.

Each of these alternatives poses certain risks of its own, and all regional agreements pose some risk of diverting trade into regional blocs. NAFTA raises a particular constitutional difficulty by purporting to make a specialized set of arbitration rulings (on countervailing tariffs against below-cost "dumping") immediately binding in U.S. law. As a number of legal scholars have contended, this provision is probably unconstitutional.[63] But it applies only to a small section of NAFTA and could almost certainly be renegotiated if the U.S. Supreme Court did someday find it so. Meanwhile, NAFTA and several of the later agreements include provisions that pledge each party to refrain from reducing its own environmental or labor standards to gain advantage in trade with the others. By design, these provisions make very limited demands on U.S. domestic policy and are very difficult to enforce. But they may set precedents that could prove awkward if extended in the future.[64]

Still, the virtue of all these alternative trade agreements is that the law they establish is almost entirely that set down in the agreements themselves, which are very long and detailed in consequence. And they do not create permanent courts with the incentive and capacity to build up an activist case law. The still more informal approach of APEC may be so unconstraining to members that it is not very effective. Even APEC, however, remains a forum or foundation that may be developed more intensively in future negotiations.

It may be that global standards offer more advantage, in purely economic terms, than regional agreements that divert trade into regional centers simply because regional agreements are easier to sustain. But global trade standards will only improve global economic outcomes if they do not themselves become diverted into schemes for controlling rather than liberating trade. Participation in regional understandings can be a powerful tool to keep global trade agreements in reasonable bounds by preserving realistic alternatives. Most developing countries have even less reason to accept global controls on trade than does the United States. Here, as elsewhere, the United States can protect more than its own sovereignty by insisting that trade agreements stick to trade issues and leave parties to trade agreements to decide where and when and to what extent they want to cooperate on other matters. A world where trade agreements are kept within reasonable bounds will be a more open world in economic as well as political terms. Preserving openness in the world was always the central appeal in making sovereignty the underlying principle of international order.

6

American Aims
in a Diverse World

The United States finds itself with a degree of military preponderance that is unique in modern history, perhaps in all history. It is the power-house of world trade, the leader in most fields of science and technology, and the creator and exporter of popular culture viewed and heard throughout the world. Yet the United States still faces a world with many independent states, some of which are hostile, many of which are suspicious or resentful, few of which are prepared to conduct themselves in all ways as Americans might wish.

The situation is both dizzying and perplexing. Some argue that the United States needs to harness its great power to the building of international institutions that can start to organize the world as we might hope to see it organized a century from now, after American power has begun to ebb. Others argue that the United States should admit that its preeminence makes it an imperial power and reorder the world according to American ideas—for the world's own good. Neither project is likely to have broad appeal to the majority of Americans. Both defy our own political and constitutional traditions. Both assume that America can only protect itself by taking responsibility for the world at large. But that would imply that there is no distinct American claim, that there is only a global argument about what is good for the world at large. Americans have always assumed that the United States had a distinctive contribution to make to the world—which requires, of course, that it remain a distinct nation. The best light in our current perplexities might be found in our beginning, when the United States asserted its own independence as its first claim on the outside world.

Constitutional Government at Home

The Declaration of Independence begins by acknowledging the obligation to display "a decent respect to the opinions of mankind." It is not "decent" to make arbitrary assertions. But mankind has more than one opinion. And one can "respect" a different opinion without embracing it for oneself. Nations with different opinions might live together in peace, without agreeing in all of their opinions. That is one basis for the claim in the Declaration that each independent nation is entitled to a "separate and equal station" in the world.

There are, of course, differences of opinion among individuals within the same nation, too. The Declaration proclaims that "all men are created equal" and "endowed by their Creator with unalienable rights," from which it follows that no one is naturally entitled to rule another. Governments instead derive "their just powers from the consent of the governed." But this does not eliminate the need for government: "[T]o secure these rights, governments are instituted among men." Even God-given rights would not be secure, it seems, without a government to protect them. It is therefore among the "dictates" of "prudence" not to let a "long established" government be "changed for light and transient causes."

Perhaps this is not everyone's opinion. In any case, "prudence" may mean different things to different people. But the Declaration does not disguise the underlying problem. "Just powers" of government are still powers; government is still about coercion. What if the government abuses its powers? What if it coerces people excessively or improperly? The Declaration insists that people always retain the right to "alter or abolish" the existing government—to make a revolution. It insists that when government abuses its proper purposes, it is not only the "right" of the people to change it, but "it is their duty to throw off such government." Government need not actually degenerate into "absolute despotism" before this duty comes into play, for by then it may be too late to make a successful revolution. There is a duty to act even if there is only a "train of abuses" that "evince a Design" to impose such tyranny later on. The Declaration advocates preemptive action.

This is a very disturbing challenge. What if existing "abuses" are simple mistakes that can be corrected under the existing "form" of government?

Might it not be more consistent with "prudence" to wait for confirmation of people's worst suspicions? But people who wait too long may find they have lost their chance to organize a successful rebellion. The body of the Declaration provides an implicit answer to this challenge, in setting out American grievances against British authority. Few of the complaints deal directly with individual rights. Certainly, the Declaration does not argue that injuries to this or that fellow American must be righted by revolution. The argument is less moralistic than that. It is a political argument, resting on an assessment of what the pattern implies about British political intentions.[1] The Declaration protests the deployment of troops without proper political control, the imposition of taxation without representation, constraints on the ability of local legislatures to enact new laws, and recourse to criminal trials outside the normal system of due process. A government that resorts to such practices is a government that cannot be trusted.

The Declaration itself points to a political answer to the political problem it raises. When is it reasonable to resist government? The Declaration answers: when government transgresses fundamental constitutional constraints. In conformity with this theory, every one of the new American states adopted a formal, written constitution to fix the proper form and limits of their new governments. They did so even while the Revolutionary War placed extraordinary demands on those new states.[2] But it was not unreasonable for the states to give such priority to establishing new constitutions; constitutions were their ground for claiming support when they most needed it from their distracted, impassioned, and divided citizens.

A decade later, the underlying arguments were extended by those who wanted to replace the original confederation of the states with a proper national government. If people in the confederated states sought a "common defense," they would need to establish a national government with powers adequate to this object. The argument, as *The Federalist* remarked, relies on "one of those truths which . . . carries its own evidence along with it" and "cannot be made plainer by argument or reasoning."[3] The truth of the argument is, in other words, as "self-evident" as the Declaration's claim that individuals are "endowed with unalienable rights," and that "to secure these rights, governments are instituted." *The Federalist* then sought to show that the constitutional structure of the new national government would make it worthy of trust.

The underlying issue is not just a matter of legal provisions or formal constitutional arrangements, however. To trust a government is to trust the individuals who exercise power through it. To trust a democratic or republican government, citizens must have some level of trust in each other. Over time, a successful and effective government can nurture more such trust among the people who live together in freedom and security under it. The Constitution, in effect, constitutes a people as well as a government. The Declaration of Independence takes for granted that it is only political unity of this kind—a willingness to act together or be represented in common—that constitutes a people: "[O]ur British brethren" had disregarded "the ties of our common kindred," so Americans had to hold the British no differently than "we hold the rest of mankind."

In the first part of the nineteenth century, secessionists in the American South insisted that the states had retained their fundamental sovereignty, even while delegating supreme governmental functions and authority to the Union. The "people" as a political community were the people of each state, who could leave the Union at will if they did not accept the results of a national election. This theory was put to rest by the outcome of the Civil War. Most Americans, having come to rely upon federal authority, did not imagine that the Union was something that could be dissolved by individual members, any more than individual citizens could disavow their obligation to obey a law that they regarded as objectionable. No one has seriously contested, since the Civil War, that ultimate sovereignty remains with the federal government.

It is not that Americans now have only one loyalty. In a free country, people are bound to have numerous and conflicting loyalties. Today's Americans come from many different lands, adhere to many different faiths, pursue many different ways of earning their livelihoods. They are bound to acknowledge differing claims on their consciences, feel differing sympathies, recognize differing interests. Such impulses may often link Americans of different backgrounds with communities of shared belief or shared interest, stretching to many parts of the world. It is part of the strength of America that its society draws on the energy and understanding of so many different people.

What makes it possible for all these people to work together in the United States is that they all accept a common political structure.

Americans belong to many different communities. It matters which community can make paramount political claims. The Constitution provides that the federal government has the last word, within the limits laid down for it. That is what sovereignty means. Sovereignty matters, not because such claims must be beyond question, but precisely because they may be open to question. A constitution is a way of clarifying these questions so they do not need to be regularly reopened—or put to the ultimate test, by resort to force. A lot is at stake, therefore, in whether the U.S. Constitution remains the "supreme law" for Americans.

As a matter of legal logic, it follows that no international commitment or treaty can take precedence over the system of governance set out in the Constitution. Certainly the Supreme Court has always endorsed this view, as (until recently) did the most prominent legal commentators. A treaty in conflict with the Constitution is void. Such a treaty cannot supply validity for legislation that would otherwise be unconstitutional. Treaties cannot override guarantees in the Bill of Rights. Nor can they rearrange the architecture of government set down in the Constitution. Accordingly, the treaty power cannot be delegated to supranational institutions. If it could be, international obligations could be imposed on the United States, not by the consent of the president and Senate, nor even by the executive authority of the president, but by the act of an international body. An international body could then claim to act on behalf of the American people without any of the constitutional accountability to the American people which the Constitution demands.

Constitutional integrity also precludes the president from delegating his responsibilities as commander in chief to an international authority. So, too, the judicial power of the United States cannot be delegated to international tribunals. The United States can participate in international arbitrations to settle its obligations to other states under international law. But "the judicial power of the United States" established by the Constitution—the authority to determine the law within the United States, as enforced by American courts on private individuals—cannot be settled by international bodies, operating outside the constitutional structure of the American legal system.

These conclusions follow from the logic of constitutional government: We have acknowledged the authority of our government because it is bound by our Constitution. The government can't retain this claim on the loyalty of citizens unless it adheres to the Constitution.

Beyond such abstract logic, however, is a more immediate political point. If major policies affecting private citizens are made in international forums, the attention and engagement of citizens—with their advocates and lobbyists and lawyers—will increasingly focus on those forums instead of our own institutions of government. Whether the U.S. government can resist or repudiate an international policy will then become a question of whether the most active constituencies have more to gain from the international policy than from the American policy. And which should take priority, even as a matter of law, may be entangled in the interested calculations—or passionate enthusiasms—of particular constituencies. Business firms may think this way, along with environmental advocates and "rights" advocates for particular ethnic or ideological constituencies.

Our Constitution tries to safeguard the political integrity of the government it constitutes. The Constitution makes it unnecessary to debate whether government would do well to provide assistance to any particular church. It makes it unnecessary, in the same way, to debate whether an international forum has more authority—for Americans—than the government that is accountable to the American people. The Constitution is designed to remove some issues from ordinary political contention. Just as it places limits on the delegation of governmental authority to any particular religious institution, it places limits on the delegation of American governmental authority to international institutions—and for much the same reasons.[4]

The United States needs to safeguard its sovereignty in order to safeguard its own form of government. It is not simply a matter of legal technicalities. It is about preserving a structure under which Americans— in all their diversity, with all their rights, and all their differences of opinion—can live together in confidence and mutual respect, as fellow citizens of the same solid republic. Preserving American sovereignty cannot be a debating point in our diplomacy. In fact, American presidents have been quite careful not to commit the United States to international structures that might compromise American sovereignty.[5] Holding to that standard must remain the aim of American diplomacy.

We should certainly want to shape the outside world in ways that make the United States more secure—but that means making the United

States, under its own Constitution, more secure. Might we be more secure under a North American federation or a Euro-Atlantic federation or a world federation? Some people may think so, and they are certainly free to argue and expound their views. But the government is not free to experiment with such devices until the Constitution is changed. The Constitution is a safeguard against such experiments with the personal rights and political heritage of the American people.

The Constitution commands great reverence, because it has endured for over two centuries as a framework for government that is removed from the partisan passions of any particular era. The Constitution has achieved this status because it is, by design, very hard to amend. On a few points—like the equal representation of states in the Senate—the Constitution is not, by its own terms, open to amendment at all.[6] As a matter of principle, the American people might retain their original right "to alter or abolish" our "long-established" system of government. But we have a Constitution to guard against the temptations of making unnecessary revolutions. The Constitution cannot function as this kind of safeguard if it can be twisted into entirely new forms by gradual, accumulating distortions. The first duty of the government is to protect the Constitution. That is why all government officials are required, by the Constitution itself, to take an oath to "support" the Constitution.

None of this means that the United States cannot make treaties. Of course it can, as the Constitution itself provides. The United States can even participate in international organizations founded on treaties. But treaties must be consistent with the Constitution. Treaties cannot have higher authority than the Constitution. No organization founded on a treaty can have higher authority—at least for the United States—than the government constituted by the U.S. Constitution. European states have founded supranational structures on treaties, and the EU sought in 2003 to cement these structures in what was called a "constitutional treaty."[7] The United States cannot follow this example—not, at least, while it adheres to its own Constitution.

The Constitution does not allow Congress to enact a law and then prohibit future repeal of it. No Congress has the power to change the powers granted to a future Congress in the Constitution itself. So, too, the Constitution does not permit the United States government to make a treaty that our own government is—as a matter of American law—unable to renounce or repudiate. The power to make treaties is granted in the Constitution and necessarily includes the power to renounce them. The government cannot revise or limit the treaty power by a mere treaty, as it cannot amend the Constitution by a mere treaty. Our Constitution remains fundamental, even if Europeans regard their own national constitutions as mere provisional standards readily overridden by treaty structures.

The American view takes the constitutional doctrine of separation of powers to its logical extension in international affairs: Our power is separate from the power of other nations. No treaty can take the place of a constitution in forcing different nations to adhere to the same political structure. Any international structure that could legally override the authority of our own government would be challenging our own constitutional arrangements. Our Constitution cannot be subordinate to a world constitution. It presupposes a world in which no institution is legally or constitutionally superior to our own system of government.

Holding to this doctrine is the first obligation of American government. If forced to choose between the risk of undermining the Constitution on one side and the danger of undermining some international treaty structure on the other, Americans cannot hesitate. And it is the first duty of American officials not to hesitate in this choice. Their paramount duty is to safeguard the Constitution. No treaty, no international authority, can give them a license to betray their oath to support the Constitution.

Looking Out

These American opinions are not accepted everywhere. That has always been so. The Founders proclaimed their faith in the "self-evident truths" of human equality and individual rights, but they were quite aware that most rulers in Europe—not to mention elsewhere—did not subscribe to this doctrine. The Founders were prepared to act on their beliefs within their own country, and to settle for constitutional liberty in "one country," if it came to that.[8] The central purpose of the federal government—literally, the aim which appears in the center of those aims listed in the Constitution's

Preamble—is to "provide for the common defense." Other peoples may have different views, but the central duty of the United States government is to prevent others from interfering with the way America organizes its own government, in conformity with its own principles.

Countries that do not share American principles may present no threat to American security. Countries that do not respect liberty or equality or democracy may still respect sovereignty and allow others, including the United States, to live by their own, differing principles. The United States long relied on the Monroe Doctrine—and Britain's Royal Navy—to keep hostile powers from extending their conquests anywhere near its borders. In the twentieth century, the United States fought two world wars and the long Cold War (encompassing many smaller wars) to destroy or contain hostile regimes. Fascism and Communism were detestable forms of government. But what made the regimes that embraced these demented ideologies dangerous to America was that they were bent on imposing their evil creeds on other lands, whether through covert subversion or open aggression. In a way, the most immediate problem was that Fascist and Communist regimes preached—and practiced—a doctrine at odds with the principle of national sovereignty.

There are still crusading faiths in the world that dream of imposing their visions by force. The most immediately dangerous is the Islamist creed of terror organizations like al Qaeda. They envision a world in which all states that happen to have a majority of Muslims will be united in one great Islamic community which can, in turn, reorganize world affairs as an endless struggle between Dar al-Islam and the infidels outside it. Terrorists cannot hope to conquer the United States. After September 11, however, the United States cannot ignore the security threat that Islamist networks pose even to American citizens going about their daily lives on American soil. Terrorists pose even more threat to smaller nations, especially those with substantial Muslim populations, where people can be incited to participate in violent activity or provide social camouflage for those who do. It is important to keep other states from being intimidated by terror forces. It will often be necessary to assist them in battling a common menace.

But other states may not always agree on what should be done, particularly when it comes to dealing with actual governments that provide assistance to terror groups. Other nations did not agree, for example, on how to respond to Saddam Hussein's government in Iraq. Such disagreements present many challenges for American strategy and diplomacy.

These challenges cannot be resolved—at least not in general—by falling back on international organizations. Many people in Europe and in other countries believe that international organization is the only reliable way of reconciling conflicting security concerns. That was, of course, the argument of many critics of the Anglo-American war against Iraq in the spring of 2003. It is not an answer the United States can embrace. To say that the United States can only exercise force with the approval of the Security Council or NATO or some other outside body is to say that American force no longer answers to the government of the United States. In committing itself to such limitations, the United States would be forfeiting its own sovereignty. It would be ceding to international authorities a kind of superintending providence that American policy—and American law—has never previously granted them.

What makes this approach seem plausible to many people, particularly in Europe, is that Europeans already live under a system in which, as is commonly said, "sovereignty is pooled." Why should Americans fuss over their sovereignty when the largest states in Europe do not? After all, Europeans have learned to delegate authority to a supranational bureaucracy that claims supremacy over their own national parliaments and a supranational court that claims supremacy over their own constitutional courts. Haven't Europeans survived quite well under these arrangements?

The European system has had echoes or extensions in global institutions. Increasingly ambitious global environmental treaties envision international institutions empowered to assign regulatory obligations to particular states. The World Trade Organization threatens to mutate into a system for integrating trade rules with a complex of social standards, at the direction of a supranational court, akin to the European Court of Justice. Meanwhile, global conferences, coached and inspired by nongovernmental advocacy groups, have spun out an endless series of "declarations" and "agendas" which their sponsors expect to become binding as customary international law. And an International Criminal Court will cap the whole scheme by punishing those who disregard basic human rights or fight wars in improper ways.

The whole package has great appeal to many people in Europe. Like European institutions, the instruments of "global governance" seek to appeal over the heads of governments to the people within each nation. Advocates insist that global institutions of this sort will provide "security" in a wider sense than armies and fleets and missiles. Why shouldn't it finally fold these more old-fashioned security concerns within its gambit?

Even if there were no immediate security challenge, Americans would have great difficulty accepting these arrangements. They challenge basic constitutional limitations and the basic political premises of the American constitutional scheme. Why suppose that people will go along with whatever is generated by international institutions? One must believe either that people are very docile—that they will accept anything that is presented as "law" or "justice" or "conclusions of experts"—or else one must suppose that NGOs have generated such an inspiring and compelling vision that people around the world will all embrace these new orthodoxies in the same way and with the same level of enthusiasm. On either premise, we would not need to have our own Constitution, let alone our own sovereignty.

But we have no reason at all to believe this scheme would actually provide security, even if we were prepared to yield our constitutional boundaries to this vision. Europeans have indeed accepted the subordination of their national governments and national constitutions to supranational management, but with all of this subordination, they have not trusted the EU to mobilize or deploy military force on their behalf. On these supreme concerns, they have relied on amorphous provisions for "coordinating" a "common policy." And faced with the challenge of public dispute about Iraq, the whole structure of "coordination" collapsed, as Britain and other governments went one way and France and Germany went another.

The premise of the European scheme is that you can delegate extensive powers to a larger structure even if you aren't prepared to entrust it with the exercise of force, so different peoples can enter into a governing structure with many others, even when they don't trust the others to provide for their own underlying security. The British do not have great trust in countries that crumbled under German assault in 1940. The Dutch and the Danes and the Italians do not have great trust in Germany—or in France, Germany's collaborator for most of the Second World War, which now seeks to become the new center of a new European order. Perhaps apart from their different historical memories, these peoples, who speak different languages and retain different customs, simply don't like each other all that much.

Europeans could trade with each other without admiring or trusting each other, as they have done for centuries, and as they still do with China. But they have wanted to have trade managed and its effects managed and other things managed, so they have submitted to elaborate schemes of collective management, with their fingers crossed behind their backs: they still retain their own troops. If this scheme of governance could really work, it might seem to be one that all the world could join. Extensive powers could be delegated to supranational authorities, while each nation or people somehow retained its own essential sovereignty.

Except it doesn't work. It is hard to sustain a common policy with people you don't trust on fundamental matters merely because you want to cooperate with them in all sorts of lesser projects. It is hard to find security in a structure you don't really trust to provide security. But Europeans naturally find it painful to contemplate the real choices involved—and rude to speak about them too openly with their "partners." "Of course, I would do anything for you," says the Frenchman to his mistress, "but the château must remain with my wife, and you know that I can't divorce her." Perhaps it is not, after all, the best approach to security, even if it speaks to *l'esprit d'amour*.

America, which starts with the premise that individuals have rights and are bound to disagree, also recognizes that nations have rights and are bound to disagree, at least on some points and at some times, about what those rights are or how they can be exercised in a world of other states. We have a whole structure of government to nurture trust among ourselves. The Europeans and the advocates of global governance have international institutions—like the UN Commission on Human Rights, chaired by Libya; like the Security Council, in which China gets a veto on American action, along with Russia and France. Which offers more assurance?

Placing great hopes in international structures is foolish. It can also be dangerous. It is certainly dangerous for Americans to think that international structures can supplant their own constitutional structure. We can't insist that others withdraw. But we can insist on our own terms for participating in international institutions. And we will have many tacit allies, at least, in drawing lines against overreaching by international institutions. Outside of Europe, the largest states—Russia, China, Japan, India, Pakistan—actually share American reservations about global governance. None has agreed to embrace the ICC. All, in different ways, have expressed reservations about environmental commitments. America is bound to find partners, at least on many particular issues, in many particular settings.

We must take account of basic facts. One is that in the debate over Iraq, the Security Council was used, quite openly, as a forum for mobilizing opposition to American policy—even when the United States was seeking to enforce resolutions of the Security Council itself. If the United States antagonized many nations, we should also recognize that the UN itself lost much prestige. It was supposed to constrain the United States from making war against Iraq, and it failed to do so. It is not in American interest to see the prestige of the United Nations restored, unless we mean to go forward by giving China a veto on American policy. Or Russia. Or France.

NATO also suffered a fatal blow. When Turkey asked for the assistance of NATO members to guard against possible dangers in the event of war with Iraq, France, Belgium, and Germany opposed any such assistance, on the grounds that providing it would seem to endorse an attack on Iraq. The fundamental principle of the alliance—that members must stand by each other—proved less important to France and Germany than registering their opposition to American policy. The episode eliminated any remaining doubt about the status of NATO as an actual defense alliance: There cannot be an alliance when member states do not feel bound to it, even to the extent of heeding pleas to assist in the defense of other members in their own territory.

The fact of American military predominance may make engagement with outside structures seem merely a matter of symbolism or imagery. But for the sake of retaining our constitutional culture, we should be careful even of imagery that encourages unreasonable expectations. Global organizations, like the United Nations or the World Trade Organization, seek to inflate their authority by pretending to universality. To insist that the United States cooperate with these organizations or at least remain within them is to offer immense leverage to nations that interpret the requirements of membership or the powers of such organizations in ways the United States does not endorse.

The question is not whether the United States will always get its way. It will often be necessary to compromise on some aims in order to secure more vital objectives. That is the heart of diplomacy. But the ultimate American claim—the claim to reject particular resolutions when necessary or withdraw from an international organization altogether—is one the United States can never surrender. Universalist rhetoric should not be allowed to conceal this ultimate claim to independence. It is vital to the constitutional integrity of American government, and it is not a small part of American bargaining strength in international negotiations. It may not be diplomatic to flaunt this ultimate claim in every negotiation. Still, it may help others to respect our conditions for participation if we make clear that we are prepared to exit an international organization or international agreement altogether rather than give up our fundamental commitments.

The same principle must apply to smaller and seemingly more congenial organizations, such as North Atlantic security forums. There was much talk, in the months before the onset of the war in Iraq, about the importance of preserving harmony in "the Western alliance" or "the Atlantic community." During the Cold War, such talk served to mobilize support for a common defense strategy to keep Soviet armies from rolling into Western Europe. It also served to cover the awkward truth that, prior to 1945, many of the countries in the subsequent NATO alliance were not partners of the United States at all but partners of Nazi Germany. Once the Soviet menace vanished, older European resentments toward the United States were bound to reassert themselves—as they have.

NATO was designed to mobilize European defenses for a threat that no longer exists. It may have other uses. NATO helped organize security in Afghanistan, for example, after the successful American war against the Taliban in 2001. But continuing turmoil in Afghanistan is a reminder that European forces, even operating under a NATO command structure, have no unique capacity for coping with today's challenges—and no claim at all to insist on being involved in American policy. The treaty establishing NATO does not, in fact, require members to coordinate their activities in all parts of the world. Even in legal terms, the United States is not obligated by the NATO pact to defer to its European partners when it contemplates military action outside Europe. The mere fact that NATO is a multilateral organization gives it no more legal standing to "authorize" disputable military actions than any sovereign state has on its own: Sovereign states gain no additional authority in international law merely because they call themselves an "alliance."

Here, too, there is more at stake than abstract principle. The United States, as a very great power, can certainly afford to be generous and forgiving with fretful or constrained partners. But in general, the disproportion in resources makes it more dangerous for the United States to invest too much authority or prestige in multilateral institutions. For the United States, the obvious alternative is independent action—the exercise of its own sovereign rights. This is a hard perspective, in some ways, for small states. They cannot so easily imagine hardy independence. They are easily cajoled into going along with others. They feel they must be inside the tent and not out in the cold. Almost all small states of Europe, despite misgivings about surrendering their own independence, feel they must join the European Union. Even Switzerland, after decades on the outside, finally decided it had to be inside the United Nations. But the seeming insecurity of small states cuts both ways when it comes to international commitments. Smaller states often seek the benefits of international organization and then assume that others will bear the burden of cost or responsibility required to sustain a shared objective.

In a world in which the United States has such great military preponderance, almost all states may be inclined to think in this manner. Canada, in some ways America's closest partner, is a good example. In the Second World War, Canada built up the world's third-largest navy to assist in guarding transatlantic convoys and contributed significant military forces to the war in Europe. By the 1970s, Canada had allowed its military resources to dwindle into utter insignificance so that, in practice, it had almost no forces to contribute to common defense efforts. Canada denounced the American war in Vietnam while pursuing improved relations with Castro's Cuba and an assortment of nasty tyrannies in the Third World. Canada could indulge itself in such an uncooperative policy, in the serene confidence that the United States would not allow its northern neighbor to succumb to any serious foreign threat.

In a similar way, almost every country in Western Europe has come to assume that, if ultimately needed, American protection would be there—so there is no need to cooperate with the United States, and there may be much advantage in posturing as a critic. Every country in Western Europe faces a threat from Islamist terrorism at least as great as that faced by the United States. In some ways, Europeans face a more serious threat, since, given European policies and attitudes, immigrants from Islamic countries have been much less well assimilated into European societies than their counterparts in the United States. Almost every country in Western Europe has a sizable number of seething, resentful immigrants drawn to terror. The actual 9/11 terrorists organized their operations in Europe. Rather than cooperate in a common defense strategy, however, major European governments have found it more appealing to leave the actual effort to the United States and posture as critics of American "overreaction" or American "unilateralism" (translation: "Don't blame us!").

This is, in a way, the international counterpart to the politics of class demagoguery, which is so much stronger in Europe than in the United States. Demagogues insist that employees can always be rewarded at the expense of stockholders and investors, on the pleasant assumption that investment will always remain and jobs will always continue. A constitutional system of checks and balances provides some safeguard against class politics of this kind within a nation. Still more helpful is the presence of people in a variety of different economic circumstances—self-employed professionals, small businessmen, and many others with crosscutting interests and perspectives—who may resist policies that threaten to drag down an entire economic structure simply to placate particular, vociferous constituencies. There are no constitutional safeguards in international politics. Nor is there, at present, a large variety of states on a continuum of power. On the largest strategic issues, there is, in effect, one great stockholder with many small beneficiaries.

The main problem is not simply free-riding, in the sense that others fail to pay their share of security costs. The underlying problem is that there is an inherent asymmetry in every American partnership. The United States has military capacities that no country and no combination of countries can now match. That means, in turn, that the United States figures, at least potentially, in almost any conflict in the world. For that reason, a military setback for the United States has potential ramifications in every part of the world. No international organization can compensate for this problem, but international organizations can certainly complicate it.

It did not matter, for example, that American intervention in Somalia was undertaken pursuant to a UN resolution. When U.S. forces were attacked and American bodies dragged through the streets of Mogadishu, the American withdrawal was not a terrible loss for the United Nations. But it did send a signal to Osama bin Laden that the United States could be rattled into withdrawal by some well-placed attacks. Much horror that followed may have been encouraged by this episode.

In 1995, Dutch troops abandoned Bosnian civilians to slaughter in Srebrenica, after promising that the town would be defended as a safe haven for refugees. Afterwards, the Dutch professed to be regretful. But no one has relied on Dutch steadfastness since the seventeenth century.[9] It may matter a great deal if American commitments are shrugged off. Whatever Europeans may say about the essential legitimacy provided by the United Nations, it is the deterrent capability of the United States that matters. No one has ever been saved by a UN resolution, and no one is likely to be deterred by one. To the contrary, in the debate over war in Iraq, enthusiasm for the UN's "essential role" was strongest among those governments most anxious to preserve the Saddam regime—precisely because the UN was understood to be incapable of enforcing its own resolutions.

When the United States does provide a strategic guarantee, it loses credibility in dangerous ways if it appears to back off it. After fifty years of pledging to protect Taiwan, the United States cannot easily shrug off Chinese threats to the island—not if it wants its word to be heeded any-where else. The United States may pressure Israel in the interests of a future peace agreement, but American demands for one-sided conces-sions by Israel would be seen—as proponents intend such concessions to be seen—as a gesture of appeasement to terrorism.[10] Whatever is done, it is important not to send signals of weakness.

But we do a disservice to smaller states if we do not indicate the lim-its on our obligation to international organization. NATO may seem to guarantee small states a voice in U.S. policy. For that reason, it is more valuable to European states than to the United States. To mislead them about the importance of NATO is to mislead them about the extent to which the United States actually feels bound to heed their views. It is not in the American interest nor that of other states to leave the impression that the United States will be there when others need assistance, even if they ignore American aims or work to frustrate American policy in the meanwhile. Conversely, the United States developed a special relationship with Poland when the Poles provided small but specialized and visible assistance in the Iraq war and then took responsibility for organizing an occupation zone in Iraq. Poland gains less from membership in a ceremonial organization like NATO than it does from a direct and active partnership with the United States.

In practice, NATO seems to have operated as a unilateral security guarantee from the United States to the other members. America is not allowed to make any particular claims on any member. It does allow every member to be Canada—which sat out the 2003 Gulf War even though Britain and Australia joined the United States. The United States is not likely to take counsel from countries that contribute nothing but counsel. It is in the interest of potential partners themselves for the United States to make clear that partnership is not a ceremonial role—or cannot be more than that if the partner does not treat it as more than that. American policy should provide incentives for other countries to develop separate and distinctive cooperative relations with the United States, and discourage any notion that an international organization can allow states to place their diplomacy in a blind trust.

If this creates divisions within Europe, the United States can emphasize that it was the European Union that initiated them. In the mid-1990s, EU membership was extended to countries that had pledged themselves to remain outside of NATO (Sweden, Austria, and Finland). Yet the EU was already committed to the development of a "common foreign and security policy," which all its member states would help to shape. The structure of the EU already places EU concerns above NATO concerns. Meanwhile, in its own internal operations, the EU claims that it can secure an "ever-closer union" while allowing some members to opt out of its common currency, some to opt out of its agreement suspending border controls, some to opt out of its "Social Charter" on labor protections, and so on, and so forth. While U.S. states are prohibited by the Constitution from conducting their own military and foreign policy, EU member states still retain many attributes of sovereignty. As long as EU member states claim to negotiate their own treaties, control their own military forces, and occupy their own seats at the UN, the United States should not accept the suggestion that it has no right to bargain separately with nations in the EU.

An independent American policy is one that looks to independent partners. States disabled from pursuing an independent policy should not be allowed to present themselves as independent states. At least, they cannot expect to be taken seriously by American diplomacy.

Like Minds

Too often, debates about American foreign policy are framed as contests between "realists" who care only about power and "idealists" who care about higher aims. It is, for the most part, a childish way of conceiving the issues at stake. Winston Churchill, after recording a particularly exasperating encounter with idealistic American arguments, put the point succinctly: "The human race cannot make progress without idealism, but idealism at other people's expense and without regard to the consequences of ruin and slaughter . . . cannot be considered as its highest or noblest form."[11] Our foreign policy cannot be separated from American ideals, but we cannot pursue our ideals in abstraction from consequences. Precisely because the United States now has such immense power, it must use its power cautiously.

When it comes to the challenges of diplomacy, a literal reliance on the Declaration of Independence is apt to mislead us. Having asserted American independence, the Declaration describes the American stance in these stark terms: As we had to with the British, so "we hold the rest of mankind, Enemies in War, in Peace, Friends." This stark choice follows in a way from the Declaration's embrace of sovereignty: Nations that do not challenge American sovereign rights are, in principle, countries with which the United States can maintain friendly relations. But even Jefferson, when conducting American foreign policy, knew that this formula was no guide to diplomacy.[12] Apart from actual enemies, there are countries we must recognize as potential enemies. Apart from all those with which we maintain "friendly relations," there are countries we would hope to retain as special friends.

At the most general level, there are certainly good reasons to think that dictatorships are potential enemies, in ways that democratic governments will not be. Dictatorships are not restrained by public opinion in the same way as democracies. They often equip themselves to mobilize intense feelings of hatred and grievance directed at outsiders. So, too, countries with successful economies are less inclined to risk military confrontations and only market economies can sustain long-term economic development. Dictatorships rarely permit reliable legal protections for property rights and contracts, and without such protections, they cannot sustain healthy markets or long-term economic development. We have good reasons to think that a world where democracy and liberal institutions are more prevalent will be one in which peace is more secure.

But it does not follow that the United States can impose democracy or market reforms throughout the world. It does not follow that we have the strength or the understanding to dictate policies of reform to China—or Burma or Belarus or Syria. The United States does have carrots and sticks that are not inconsiderable. We can offer—or withhold—special trade concessions, loans and grants, security cooperation, and technical assistance. Leverage of this kind was exercised in the 1980s to pressure military dictators in Latin America to make transitions to democracy. It makes sense for the United States to encourage reforms in countries still struggling under repressive or corrupt regimes.

There are limits to what we can expect to achieve, however. Latin American countries had long traditions of support for democracy, at least in their official rhetoric. They also had considerable experience with democratic institutions, even if it was often unhappy or unsatisfying experience. Not all countries provide such promising foundations for democratic reforms. Meanwhile, the United States has competing concerns which must sometimes take priority—for example, securing cooperation in efforts to halt the spread of weapons of mass destruction or disrupt terror networks. And we must expect that pressure which is too direct or heavy-handed will be viewed as American domination, and often resisted and resented as such.

When the United States tries to pressure or threaten a dictatorial regime, it can be quite helpful to have partners or allies in the venture. Acting with a coalition can help blunt the charge that America is acting in a purely self-serving manner. Such assistance can reassure the American people that some of the financial burdens will be shared and that other states also recognize the need to act, even when action seems risky or burdensome. It was reassuring—and not surprising—that in the war on Iraq, the United States found itself, as so often before, in the company of Britain and Australia. These friends are heirs to many of the same political and constitutional traditions as the United States. They share many background assumptions about how the world actually works, and how it can be coaxed to work better in the future.

But Britain and Australia, along with many other friends or potential friends, feel much more sympathy for international organizations than the United States does. That is one good reason for the United States to continue participating in international forums. Even countries that have particularly close ties with the United States do not want to appear as "lap dogs" or "poodles" or "vassals" to a purely American policy. Policies affirmed by international organizations have, in the eyes of many countries, more prestige or "legitimacy" than ones simply advanced by the United States on its own. Nations with no special relationship with the United States nor any strong disposition to accommodate its policy aims may still be influenced by policies associated with international organizations. These are all good reasons to hope that international organizations can make some contribution to American policy aims.

If this is to be the case, however, it is the interest of the United States to have more such multilateral forums. If we seek coalitions of the willing, we should want forums of convenience in which to organize them. Of course, "forum shopping" can breed cynicism, among American policymakers as among others. But there is nothing inherently cynical about this approach. The same person often belongs to several different organizations or travels in several different social circles. People often have friends with whom they feel free to discuss business matters and friends with whom they would never do so, friends in whom they confide family or health problems and friends they would never entrust—or burden—with such intimate confidences. It is a common enough experience, though, that a friend of one sort turns out, in a moment of special need, to be a friend in a deeper way—but only for that one moment of crisis. It is bad to have only one international forum, even as it is bad to have only one friendship to fall back on. Those who prefer more tough-minded metaphors can say that it is reckless to put all your eggs in one basket, to place all your investments in one company, to entrust all your hopes to one lawyer or one political leader.

It is, at any rate, a common experience that organizations founded for one purpose often have proved more adaptable for others. The Economic Organization of West African States (ECOWAS), for example, turned out to have more to contribute as a forum for organizing peacekeeping missions in West Africa (sponsoring Nigerian troops in Sierra Leone and then in Liberia) than it ever contributed to actual commercial development in the region.

What is true in strategic and security matters is also true in regard to international cooperation on trade, the environment, and other matters. We are better off seeking alternatives than relying exclusively on global forums. NAFTA provided useful leverage in negotiations with the EU on the WTO agreements.[13] APEC may provide useful leverage against Chinese- or Japanese-dominated regional trade agreements. Of course, there is a danger of descent into trade blocs. But there are dangers as well in overreliance on the WTO. These dangers can be reduced by developing alternatives—insurance against the day when it may be necessary to depart the WTO, and reminders that threats to do so are not idle talk.

Most environmental agreements have been negotiated in stages, staking out more ambitious goals and recruiting more adherents over time, in a process that aims for ever-more-encompassing global "regimes." There is no reason such diplomacy must always move in this direction. On many issues, it may be easier to establish local or regional cooperation if there is no expectation that each agreement must lead to another, larger agreement. Some of the most intractable issues, like conservation of fisheries or even the threat of global warming, might prove much easier to address if states prepared to take action in common did not insist on awaiting or pressing for a global consensus.[14]

On security initiatives, our partners may be particularly drawn to the legitimacy the United Nations or NATO is supposed to provide. We should try to wean them away from the notion that diplomatic blessings are only available from one pulpit. We should try to discourage rigid collectivist thinking and encourage respect for initiative and pluralism, in diplomacy as in business and in politics.

The idea of assembling some organization of genuine democracies has much appeal as an alternative to other bodies that are supposed to promote democracy and human rights. The United Nations cannot contribute anything of value in this area. Aiming to be universal, it embraces the world's most tyrannical regimes and regularly elevates them to positions of honor and influence in its so-called human rights forums. The United Nations is now so large and unwieldy, and so sunk in the politics of bloc voting, that it is a cesspool of political corruption. An organization restricted to genuine democracies might do better. A start was made at a conference in Warsaw in 2000. It might be worthwhile to pursue this initiative.

But we ought not to have exaggerated expectations for what such a forum can accomplish. A new organization cannot expect to attain the prestige of older ones built on long-established affinities. The British Commonwealth of Nations, which seemed to have so much common ground, has had almost no success in fostering democratic institutions among its members. Zimbabwe, which was practically a creation of Commonwealth diplomacy, has been allowed to sink into murderous despotism. Canada shrugged off Commonwealth solidarity when it rejected the policy of Britain and Australia on Iraq. The Organization of American States, which could draw upon long traditions of hemispheric solidarity, has had little success in mobilizing members to resist tyranny in their region—to mobilize pressure, for example, against the Castro dictatorship in Cuba.

A new organization—or, more reasonably, a new forum—will labor under many of the same constraints as existing ones. The Council of Europe was organized for the very purpose of building solidarity among the European democracies. After the collapse of Communism, the council welcomed new democracies in Eastern Europe—or states it hoped would soon become democracies. It ended up embracing Albania and Ukraine and a number of other authoritarian states on the premise that calling them democracies would encourage them to live up to the name. It has not been a highly effective tactic, in part because it required the council to start by discarding its main source of leverage: the denial of admission unless an applicant could satisfy certain standards of democratic government. Any new organization will face similar temptations and problems.

A new organization will also face other problems. The United States will not be able to submit to binding determinations from such an organization and cannot escape the charge of hypocrisy if it encourages others to submit to supranational controls it will not accept for itself. Nor is it really in the American interest—if the United States is determined to retain its sovereignty—to encourage the idea that supranational authorities can be trusted with wide regulatory powers. The United States should seek to encourage democracy in other nations, but that means, precisely, encouraging other nations to decide for themselves. The aim should be to dispel the illusion that the world can be run by some central, higher authority. It is not an aim that can be readily reconciled with a powerful new organization, authorized to certify which states do or do not conform to proper policies for democracies—as the European Union or the Council of Europe might define them.

Any forum of genuine democracies might still contribute something as a rallying ground for common stances toward the most threatening and illiberal regimes in other parts of the world. But members are bound to have different views—some of the sharpest disputes over Iraq were between democracies. Member states of the EU, since they no longer enjoy full constitutional independence (and for that reason, no longer operate under genuine constitutional government), may often have a very different view of "democracy" than the United States, and very different ideas about how to advance constitutional government in other nations.

Even when there is more common thinking, often there will be much reluctance to commit to common policies. Almost all the members of the Organization of American States are democracies. Nonetheless, Latin states voted Cuba a seat on the Human Rights Commission in 2003, even while the Castro government was tightening the screws of repression on its tormented people. If the United States is often distracted by other concerns, that is not less true of other nations—and may not be less true in any new forum of democratic nations.

The most urgent moral challenges will remain among the most difficult. Faced with mass murder, the United Nations has always been paralyzed. Nations that denounced American action in Iraq urged the United States to send troops to Liberia only a few months later. Humanitarian interventions may be condemned without some form of international approval, but waiting for it may mean waiting too long, as in Rwanda. Sending international forces not genuinely prepared to put down perpetrators of atrocities may be a recipe for continuing violence, as in Bosnia in the mid-1990s and Sierra Leone later in the decade. The United States may often be able to assist in organizing timely interventions. It has better prospects of doing so if it is not tied down to particular formulas about when and how they must be approved. We may not be able to improve on the classical view that humanitarian interventions should be seen as commendable in particular circumstances but not generally recognized as a lawful action under international law.

Expectations

There will always be severe limits on what diplomatic initiatives, with or without international organizations, can accomplish. The United States does not own the world. It cannot be responsible for everything that happens in the world. But we cannot ignore the fact that the very preponderance of American power gives the United States choices—and, therewith, responsibilities—that no other nation faces.

It is a burden, in some ways, as much as an opportunity. It also means we have more opportunity to live up to our own best traditions. Our best traditions should be a source of satisfaction. The United States has not emerged as the world's greatest power because North America happens to have a uniquely favorable climate or uniquely advantageous mineral deposits. American success reflects, in the main, the result of well-constructed political institutions, wisely maintained by a people that has not let itself be overly distracted by the opinions of outsiders.

The United States has no choice about responding to security challenges. It may hope to achieve more than deterring or suppressing immediate threats. But it also makes a very important contribution by remaining what it is. The United States can still show the world, as in centuries past, what an independent nation may accomplish. It is a lesson from which the world at large can still benefit.

Independence requires a degree of moral discipline. Americans can take pride in maintaining it. A central cord of American discipline is the commitment to live by rules—not any rules, not necessarily the rules endorsed by others, but the basic political rules laid down in our own national Constitution. That can be an especially good example to a world in which people in so many nations still expect outside powers to fix their problems, because they cannot learn to rely on their fellow citizens. The United States may still provide the greatest service to the world by the power of its example.

Notes

Preface

1. The survey was conducted by Eurobarometer for the European Commission. "Iraq and Peace in the World," Flash EB No. 151 (October 10–16, 2003), available at http://europa.eu.int/comm/public_opinion/flash/fl151_iraq_full_report.pdf. Asked about fourteen countries, whether each "presents or not a threat to peace in the world," respondents were most likely to name Israel (59 percent), with the United States in second place (53 percent). In the EU aggregation, North Korea and Iran were tied with the United States, while many fewer respondents saw much threat from other countries: Syria (37 percent), Saudi Arabia (36 percent), China (30 percent), Russia (21 percent). Country-by-country responses differed considerably, from a high of 88 percent of Greeks holding the United States as a "threat to peace" to a low of 43 percent of Italians. In only four of the fifteen EU countries surveyed (Denmark, Germany, Luxembourg, Portugal) did respondents rank both Iran and North Korea as greater threats to peace than the United States. Only in three countries (Italy, Ireland, and Portugal) did respondents rank Iran or North Korea as more of a threat to peace than Israel. Respondents in almost all countries saw the EU as the least threatening to peace (with only 8 percent of respondents overall identifying the EU as a threat to peace, though 14 percent in Greece and 9 percent in Spain thought the EU might be a threat, which was more in these countries that identified Somalia as a threat).

2. Kim Willsher, "Jews Attacked in French Anti-War Protests," *Sunday Telegraph* (London), April 6, 2003.

3. Robert O. Paxton, *Vichy France: Old Guard and New Order* (New York: Knopf, 1972), 289.

4. For a survey of collaborationist trends in Western Europe in 1940–41, see Mark Mazower, *Dark Continent: Europe's Twentieth Century* (New York: Vintage, 2000), 138–50.

5. Jürgen Habermas, "Nach dem Krieg: Die Wiedergeburt Europas" ["After the War: A Reborn Europe"], *Frankfurter Allgemeine Zeitung*, May 31, 2003. An English translation by Ludwig von Tranzivan was posted on the website,

Aldiborontiphoscophornio.blogspot.com, on its archive for the week of June 1, 2003.

6. Examples of both responses among Europeans—expressions of sympathy for Islamist terror and exasperation at America's refusal to accommodate it—are surveyed in Jean-Francois Revel, *Anti-Americanism* (San Francisco: Encounter Books, 2003), 126–41.

Chapter 1: Sovereignty in Principle

1. For a staunch defense of the security stakes in fighting the war at the time, by a centrist British journalist, see William Shawcross, *Allies: The U.S., Britain, Europe, and the War in Iraq* (New York: Public Affairs, 2004), which also offers extensive summaries and analysis of antiwar arguments from European critics.

2. The Human Rights Committee, monitoring compliance with the Covenant on Civil and Political Rights, seemed to think it was engaged in a constructive dialogue with the regime of Saddam Hussein. In 1998, for example, the committee's review of Iraq's compliance noted under "positive aspects" the report from the Iraqi government of "Revolutionary Command Council Decree No. 91, which repeal[ed] the application of the death penalty and amputation in certain cases"—which the committee acknowledged as a change that it "welcome[d]." On the other hand, it expressed "grave concern" over "reports from many sources concerning the high incidence of summary executions, arbitrary arrests and detentions, torture and ill-treatment by members of security and military forces." The committee expressed "regret at the lack of transparency on the part of the Government in responding to these concerns." Apparently assuming that "summary executions" and "torture" had been committed without the Saddam government's approval, it concluded: "The Committee recommends that all allegations mentioned above be fully, publicly and impartially investigated, that the results of such investigations be published and that the perpetrators of those acts be brought to justice." "Consideration of Reports Submitted by States Parties under Article 40 of the Covenant," *22nd Annual Report*, UN Doc. A/53/40, September 15, 1998, par. 94, 97. The Anglo-American invasion in 2003 prevented the Saddam regime from continuing such "dialogue." It remained, to the end, a party to the Covenant on Civil and Political Rights.

3. Jan Aart Scholte, *Globalization: A Critical Introduction* (London: Palgrave, 2000), 139.

4. Article 12 provides that the ICC may have jurisdiction when a crime is committed by a national of a ratifying state or on the territory of a ratifying state, even if the accused perpetrator does not belong to a ratifying state. By itself, this arrangement would allow a state to seek prosecution of enemy nationals only if prepared to submit its own nationals to prosecution. But Article 12 goes on to offer a loophole to states afraid to submit their own nationals to the ICC's

jurisdiction. Paragraph 3 also allows a state not party to the treaty—which therefore does not accept ICC jurisdiction over its own nationals—to provide the court with jurisdiction over particular crimes committed on its territory "by declaration lodged with the Registrar" (an administrative official of the court). The court's jurisdiction will then be limited "to the crime in question." If the United States should undertake an air strike against, for example, Iran, the Iranian government could secure ICC jurisdiction to investigate this action as a "crime" without subjecting Iranian officials to comparable liability. Such one-sided obligations, with no element of reciprocity, have almost no precedent in international law, apart from the "one-sided" treaties imposed on backward countries by imperial powers in the nineteenth century.

5. Statute of the International Criminal Court, art. 8, par. 2(b) (iv), (making it a crime to cause "damage to civilian objects" that is "excessive").

6. Following the massacre of Israeli athletes at the Munich Olympics in 1972, for example, the German government arrested some of the perpetrators and then released them, ostensibly to secure the release of German hostages—but the hostage seizure was itself arranged with the complicity of the German government: "Germany made secret agreements with Palestinian and other international terrorist groups in a desperate bid to keep them away from German borders." Simon Reeve, *One Day in September* (New York: Arcade, 2000), 157–58. France followed the same policy, "bribing terrorist groups to persuade them to avoid France during their attacks" (209).

7. Economist William Nordhaus calculated that full implementation of the Kyoto standards would have cost the United States $2.2 trillion, while aggregate compliance costs for EU states would have been less than one quarter of that amount. Nordhaus, "The Costs of Kyoto," *Science*, November 9, 2001. See also Eugene Trisko, "What Climate Change Policy Means for American Workers," and Brian Fisher, "International Impacts: An Australian View," in *The Costs of Kyoto*, ed. Jonathan Adler (Washington, D.C.: Competitive Enterprise Institute, 1997).

8. See, e.g., Ronald Asmus, "Rebuilding the Atlantic Alliance," *Foreign Affairs* 82, no. 5 (September/October 2003).

9. Louis Henkin, "Notes from the President," *Newsletter*, American Society of International Law, March 1993. Among the most sustained postmodernist critiques of "sovereignty" is Jens Bartelson, *A Genealogy of Sovereignty* (New York: Cambridge University Press, 1995). Among the most concise summaries of the claim that "sovereignty" is an inherently "contested" and unstable concept is Richard Falk's entry on "Sovereignty" in the *Oxford Companion to the Politics of the World* (New York: Oxford University Press, 2001), 789–91.

10. James Madison, for example, described Grotius as "not unjustly considered . . . the father of the modern code of nations" in "Examination of the British Doctrine which Subjects to Capture A Neutral Trade not Open in Time of Peace," *Writings of James Madison* (Philadelphia: J. B. Lippincott, 1867), 2:234. Patrick

Henry spoke of Grotius and his immediate disciples among treatise-writers as "kind instructors of human errors and frailties . . . benevolent spirits who held up the torch of science to a benighted world." Quoted in Henry Wheaton, preface to 3rd ed., *Elements of International Law*, 6th ed. (Boston: Little, Brown, 1857), cxc.

11. Hugo Grotius, *De Jure Belli ac Pacis* (On the Law of War and Peace), trans. Francis W. Kelsey (Washington, D.C.: Carnegie Institution, 1925), bk. 1, chap. 3, sec. 7, p. 102.

12. Ibid., bk. 1, chap. 3, sec. 13, pp. 119–30; bk. 2, chap. 14, sec. 12, pp. 387–89 (on internal constitutional limitations on sovereignty); bk. 2, chap. 20, sec. 40, pp. 504–6 (on permissible punishments directed at other states for violating the law of nature).

13. Ibid., bk. 1, chap. 2, sec. 8, pp. 70–81. The full discussion of whether it is proper for Christians to endorse war extends over the last four subsections of bk. 1, chap. 2, totaling some thirty pages (61–90) in the Carnegie edition.

14. For a lucid exposition of the controlling premise of the Grotian argument for freedom of the seas, see Richard Tuck, *The Rights of War and Peace* (Oxford: Oxford University Press, 1999), 107–8. The argument is by no means obsolete, even in an age when few powers compete with American naval strength. See, e.g., William Langewiesche, "Anarchy at Sea," *The Atlantic Monthly*, September 2003. Even if it had the resources to do so, the United States would not feel the same compulsion to impose order on the high seas as it does in its own territory, among other reasons, because its claims on the high seas would encounter more resistance.

15. At the Virginia ratifying convention, a Federalist delegate dismissed the idea that treaties could be "paramount to the Constitution itself and the laws of Congress": "It is as clear as that two and two make four that the treaties made are to be binding on the States only." This "rational" interpretation was endorsed by no less an authority than James Madison, who also emphasized the limited significance of the "supremacy clause" in relation to treaties. John Kaminski and Gaspare Saladino, eds., *Documentary History of the Ratification of the Constitution* (Madison: State Historical Society of Wisconsin, 1993), 10:1392 (speech of Francis Corbin, June 19, 1788), 1395 (speech of James Madison, same day). The Supreme Court affirmed the validity of legislation in conflict with treaty obligations in *Whitney v. Robinson*, 124 U.S. 190 (1888): "[I]f the two [a statute and a treaty] are inconsistent, the one last in date will control the other" (194). To the same effect: *Chae Chan Ping v. U.S.*, 130 U.S. 581 (1887).

16. Carl Becker, *The Declaration of Independence: A Study in the History of Political Ideas* (1922; repr., New York: Vintage, 1970), 142. The substitution of "self-evident" seems to have been the inspiration of Benjamin Franklin.

17. Modern historians estimate that the population of the Holy Roman Empire (essentially, present-day Germany and the Czech Republic) fell by some 20 percent over the course of the Thirty Years War, so "the loss of people was proportionately

greater than in World War II." Geoffrey Park, *The Thirty Years War* (London: Routledge & Kegan Paul, 1984), 211, 215. Archaeological evidence indicates a still greater level of carnage in prehistoric tribal warfare, where one-quarter of all men may have lost their lives in battle, according to Steven A. LeBlanc, *Constant Battles* (New York: St. Martin's, 2003), 97, 123.

18. Edward Luttwak, "Give War a Chance," *Foreign Affairs* 78, no. 4 (July/August 1999): 36–44.

19. One of the prime state sponsors of terrorism, for example, is the government of Syria. The idea that the United Nations could take effective action against Syrian terror policy is, to put it mildly, improbable. Syria was elected in 2001 to the UN Security Council. In 2003, it served on the UN's "Counter-Terrorism Committee," where it argued that support for groups launching suicide bombings against civilians in Israel did not constitute support for terrorism but for a "legitimate struggle against foreign occupation." Ruth Wedgwood, "Self-Defense Sans Frontieres," *Wall Street Journal*, October 8, 2003, A24.

20. See, e.g., Wheaton, *Elements of International Law*, 6th ed. (Boston: Little, Brown, 1857), the first full-length treatise on international law by an American commentator, originally published in London and Philadelphia in 1836 and republished in successive editions over the next two decades (culminating in a sixth edition in 1857). More than half the treatise deals with restraints in war, rights of neutrality, and diplomatic usages regarding ambassadors. Apart from abstract expositions regarding the general theory of international law, the rest covers technical claims regarding criminal jurisdiction and navigation rights. The spirit of the work, which follows closely from the exposition in Vattel's *Droit des Gens* ("The Law of Nations") (1757), is well captured in this exposition of the "absolute rights of nations": "Of the absolute rights of States, one of the most essential and important, and that which lies at the foundation of all the rest, is the right of self-preservation. It is not only a right with respect to other States, but a duty with respect to its own members and the most solemn and important which a State owes to them. This right necessarily involves all incidental rights which are essential as means to give effect to the principal end." Wheaton, *Elements of International Law*, part II, chap. 1, sec.2, pp. 85–86.

21. Samuel Huntington, *The Clash of Civilizations and the Remaking of World Order* (New York: Simon and Schuster, 1996).

22. Huntington notes that talk of "the West" began to replace talk of "the Free World" in the early 1990s, after the end of the Cold War and the collapse of the Soviet Union. He does not notice that talk of "the West" actually gained momentum only in the early period of the Cold War. American statesmen in the nineteenth century emphasized not America's place in "the West"—Americans would have been baffled by the suggestion of some special affinity with the Hapsburg Empire or Prussia or the Papal States of Italy—but rather "the New World." As late as 1918, a survey of American diplomatic practice by one of the chief legal

advisors to the State Department noted that "the established rule of policy" in "the popular as well as the official mind" was that "the political arrangements of Europe [were to be] treated as belonging to what was called the European system, while those of the independent nations of America were jealously guarded as belonging to the 'American system.'" John Bassett Moore, *The Principles of American Diplomacy*, rev. ed. (New York: Harper, 1918), 444–45.

23. Paul Hirst and Grahame Thompson, *Globalization in Question* (Cambridge, UK: Polity Press, 1996), 49: "[T]he level of integration, interdependence, openness or however one wishes to describe it, of national economies in the present era is not unprecedented. Indeed, the level of autonomy under the Gold Standard [in the last decades before the First World War] was much less for the advanced economies than it is today." Among other things, as the authors note, modern economies are less exposed to the effects of trade because governmental programs, which are so much larger than in earlier times, do not rely on imports or exports.

24. Few states actually subscribe to the "monist" doctrine that international law and domestic law are all part of the same, integrated legal system. As Mark Janis has written, "Most states and most courts, including those of the United States, presumptively view national and international legal systems as discrete entities"—so that international law does not automatically enter into the domestic legal system. Mark Janis, *Introduction to International Law*, 3rd ed. (New York: Aspen, 1994), 86, with a survey of complexities in applying treaties to domestic law in various countries, 97–101. Ian Brownlie, *Principles of Public International Law*, 4th ed. (New York: Oxford University Press, 1990) provides another useful survey, 52–55.

25. For book-length versions appearing before the war against Iraq, see Joseph Nye, *Paradox of American Power* (New York: Oxford University Press, 2001); Clyde Prestowitz, *Rogue Nation* (New York: Basic Books, 2003); and John Ikenberry, *After Victory* (Princeton: Princeton University Press, 2001).

26. Theodore Roosevelt's justification for intervening in Santo Domingo, to collect debts owed to European powers so that European powers would not be tempted to intervene themselves, appears, with relevant citations, in John Bassett Moore, *International Law Digest* (Washington, D.C.: Government Printing Office, 1906), 6:518–29. See the approving (or at least complacent) account in T. J. Lawrence, *Principles of International Law*, 7th ed. (London: Macmillan, 1923), 260–61. Samuel Flagg Bemis, *The Latin American Policy of the United States* (1943; repr., New York: W. W. Norton, 1971), describes Franklin Roosevelt's new policy after 1933 as "absolute non-intervention" (chap. 16, 276–94).

27. John Locke, *Second Treatise of Government*, par. 4, 6.

28. Ibid., par. 14.

29. Thomas Jefferson, "Opinion on the French Treaties," April 28, 1791, in *Thomas Jefferson: Writings*, ed. Merrill Peterson (New York: Library of America, 1984), 423.

30. Ibid. Emmerich de Vattel's *Droit des Gens* (The Law of Nations), first published in 1757 and much relied upon by the American Founders, offers the same

analysis: "Nations . . . may be regarded as so many free persons living together in a state of nature. . . . Since nations are free and independent of one another as men are by nature, the . . . general law of their society is that each Nation should be left to the peaceable enjoyment of that liberty which belongs to it by nature. . . . In consequence of that liberty and independence it follows that it is for each Nation to decide what its conscience demands of it and what it can or can not do; what it thinks well or does not think well to do; and therefore it is for each Nation to consider and determine what duties it can fulfill towards others without failing in its duty toward itself." Vattel, introduction to *Droit des Gens*, trans. Charles Fenwick, sec. 12, 15, 16 (Washington, D.C.: Carnegie Institution, 1916), 6–7.

31. Locke, *Second Treatise*, par. 217. Locke does not say that revolution is justified when the "foreign power" abuses the rights of citizens. The transfer of legislative authority to foreign power, even if authorized by the existing legislature, constitutes in itself a "dissolution" of the existing social contract, justifying rebellion: "For the end why People entered into Society, being to be preserved one intire, free, independent Society, to be governed by their own Laws; this is lost, whenever they are given up to the Power of another."

32. For a review of "populist" complaints, see Robert O'Brien, Anne Marie Goetz, Jan Aart Scholte, and Marc Williams, *Contesting Global Governance: Multilateral Institutions and Global Social Movements* (New York: Cambridge University Press, 2000), ch. 5. For market-oriented criticisms, see John Micklethwait and Adrian Wooldridge, *A Future Perfect, The Challenge and Hidden Promise of Globalization* (New York: Crown Business, 2000), 175–80, reviewing studies suggesting that the IMF has done more harm than good in policies it has pursued with less-developed countries.

33. See, e.g., Robert Whelan, Joseph Kirwan, and Paul Haffner, *The Cross and the Rain Forest: A Critique of Radical Green Spirituality* (Grand Rapids, Mich.: Eerdmans, 1996).

34. "Human rights is misunderstood . . . if it is seen as a 'secular religion.' . . . To make it so is a species of idolatry." Michael Ignatieff, *Human Rights as Politics and Idolatry* (Princeton: Princeton University Press, 2001), 53.

35. Rowan Williams, "When Politics is Value-free, Religious Belief Can Fill the Gap," *Daily Telegraph* (UK), December 20, 2002, based on "Archbishop of Canterbury Delivers Richard Dimbleby Lecture 2002," December 19, 2002, available at http://www.archbishopofcanterbury.org/sermons_speeches/021219.html, last visited March 12, 2004.

36. ". . . [L]aw properly defined . . . in its essence lies in leaving to another that which belongs to him or in fulfilling our obligations to him." Grotius, *De Jure Belli ac Pacis*, prolegomena, sec. 9, p. 13; "[A] right becomes a moral quality of a person, making it possible to have or to do something lawfully" which is "a legal right properly or strictly so called," bk. 1, chap. 1, sec. 4–5, 35. On the claim that Grotius originated the modern conception of rights, see Knud Haakonssen,

"Hugo Grotius and the History of Political Thought," *Political Theory* 13 (May 1985): 239–65.

37. Shashi Tharoor, "Why America Still Needs the United Nations," *Foreign Affairs* 82, no. 5 (September/October 2003): 68. Commentators without official status have been even less inhibited in celebrating UN authority as a kind of planetary providence: "Traditionally a 'state' was held to be sovereign when there was no authority which had precedence over it. . . . But theorists such as Bodin [in the sixteenth century] held that there was indeed a superior authority—God. . . . [T]here was after the end of the Cold War an expression in more utilitarian and secular terms of the ancient qualification of sovereignty as an absolute: there was a stronger form of the international community which was a modern equivalent of the divine order." Paul Taylor, "The United Nations in the 1990s: Proactive Cosmopolitanism and the Issue of Sovereignty," in *Sovereignty at the Millennium*, ed. Robert Jackson (Oxford: Blackwell, 1999), 117.

38. Charles Cheney Hyde, *International Law, Chiefly as Interpreted and Applied by the United States,* 2nd ed. (Boston: Little, Brown, 1945), 1582–1608. Even while expressing skepticism, Hyde reviews the traditional practice that insisted on excluding from arbitration disputes that involve "vital interest" or "independence," or disputes "of a political nature"—even in arbitration schemes designed to ensure peaceful resolution of conflicts such as the Kellogg-Briand Pact and the Locarno Pact. The "Statute" of the International Court of Justice, adopted along with the UN Charter, evaded the problem by allowing states to decide, on a case-by-case basis, whether they would agree to submit cases to the court.

39. *Federalist 63, The Federalist Papers*, ed. Charles Kesler (New York: New American Library, 1999), 351.

40. Barely a year after the ending of the war in Iraq, reports surfaced that UN officials and their cronies (including the son of Secretary-General Kofi Annan) had taken kickbacks from Saddam Hussein in return for allowing the dictator to violate the terms of the UN's "oil for food" program. For an early account, see Charles Laurence, "UN Caves in on Inquiry into Its Iraq Oil-for-Food Scandal," *Sunday Telegraph*, March 14, 2004. But there is a long history of complaints about corruption in UN programs. Vernon Walters, U.S. ambassador to the UN in the late 1980s, complained that UNESCO, which was supposed to encourage "educational, scientific and cultural" activity around the world, actually expended nearly 80 percent of its budget on its own officials at its headquarters in Paris— and such corruption alone would have justified the U.S. decision to withdraw from this specialized UN agency in 1984. For a recent review, see Jay Nordlinger, "An Impolitic Assessment," *National Review*, October 1, 2002. Nor was the UNESCO case exceptional. In the late 1990s, for example, the UN agency responsible for assisting children in poor countries, UNICEF, which had solicited charitable contributions from private citizens in affluent countries for decades, was found to be spending almost half of its budget on "overhead"—that is, on its

own bureaucrats. For one version of the resulting protest, see David Frum, "UNICEF is No Sweet Charity," *Toronto Sun*, October 31, 1998.

41. "To many Iraqis, the UN is not a benign and impartial bystander. It legitimised ten years of bombing and economic sanctions. . . . Under sanctions Saddam Hussein became one of the richest men in the world. The UN's oil-for-food programme dumped cheap food on 40 percent of the country and in so doing devastated Iraq's farm sector, forcing people into Baath-dominated towns. It was mad. Iraqis may be glad Saddam is gone, but they seem disinclined to say thank you to the UN." Simon Jenkins, "Ten Reasons Why the UN Should Stay Out of Iraq," *The Times* (London), September 10, 2003.

42. "Annual Message to Congress," December 1, 1862, in Abraham Lincoln, *Abraham Lincoln: Speeches and Writings, 1859–65*, ed. Don E. Fehrenbacher (New York: Library of America, 1989), 415.

43. "Special Message to Congress," July 4, 1861, ibid., 256.

Chapter 2: Sovereignty Despite Atlantic Community

1. *Mighell v. Sultan of Johore*, 1 Q.B. 149 (1894), dismissing a breach of promise suit by a jilted lover against the Sultan, on advice from the Colonial Office that Johore was a "sovereign" enjoying exclusive British "protection" based on treaty.

2. The legal significance of the empire was hardly a matter of ceremonial form, even in the early twentieth century. When Britain declared war on Germany in 1914, the dominions were automatically at war, too—and by the end of the war, Australia had suffered more combat casualties, proportionate to its small population, than Britain itself. Following the 1931 Statute of Westminster, each of the dominions had to decide for itself whether to join Britain's declaration of war in 1939, and national parliaments in South Africa and Australia deliberated for several days before agreeing to commit to war.

3. The Senate Foreign Relations Committee acknowledged that the "self-governing dominions . . . are most properly members of the League." It protested that India, which was not self-governing but "merely a part of the Empire," had been admitted to a vote in the League's Assembly merely "because Great Britain desired it" and also protested that "Great Britain also will control the votes of the Kingdom of Hejaz [today's Saudi Arabia] and of Persia." The committee did not insist on changing this pattern: "If other countries like the present arrangement, that is not our affair, but the Committee failed to see why the United States should have but one vote in the assembly of the league when the British Empire has six." Accordingly, the committee urged an amendment to the Covenant of the League according six votes to the United States. The Foreign Relations Committee's comments on this proposed amendment are reprinted in Henry Cabot Lodge, *The Senate and the League of Nations* (New York: Scribner's, 1925), 170–71.

4. See, e.g., Moore, *Principles of American Diplomacy*, 371–76, on resistance to U.S. participation in conferences of newly independent Latin nations, on grounds that such conferences might try to establish some sort of supranational legislative authority.

5. See, e.g., "Convention for the Protection of Migratory Birds in the United States and Canada," signed in Washington, August 16, 1916, entered into force December 7, 1916, reprinted in Charles Bevans, ed., *Treaties and Other International Acts of the United States, 1776–1949* (Washington, D.C.: Government Printing Office, 1968), 12:375. The treaty was between the United States and Great Britain, though entirely concerned with birds migrating from Canada to the United States. Discussed in *Missouri v. Holland*, 252 U.S. 416 (1920), without any acknowledgment of this oddity.

6. See the opinion of the International Court of Justice (especially the opinion of the Soviet Judge, S. Krylov) in "Conditions of Admission of a State to Membership in the United Nations," 1948 I.C.J. Rep. 57, on the arguments for refusing to admit the Communist governments of Bulgaria, Romania, and Hungary (to which the Soviet Union responded by rejecting membership for former Axis states Italy and Finland and neutrals Ireland and Portugal, held to be insufficiently devoted to peace by the Soviets because they had refrained from participation in the war). The United States never formally recognized the Soviet annexation of the Baltic states (Lithuania, Latvia, Estonia) in 1940. Accordingly, American negotiators agreed in 1945 that the USSR could send "separate" UN delegations from Ukraine and Belarus (to compensate Stalin for the supposed American influence on states in Latin America), but they would not agree to have Soviet-controlled delegations from the Baltic states seated at the UN. Representatives from the Baltic states were seated at the UN only in the early 1990s, when these countries regained full sovereignty. Ironically, Ukraine and Belarus also achieved independence from Moscow shortly thereafter, making good (in a quite unexpected way) on the 1945 bargain.

7. At the Philadelphia Convention, James Wilson, subsequently a justice of the U.S. Supreme Court, insisted that the colonies had achieved independence "not Individually but Unitedly," and under the Articles of Confederation they remained "wholly incompetent to the exercise of any of the great and distinguishing acts of Sovereignty" [given Confederation control over war and peace and foreign affairs] so "the states are now [even before adopting a new constitution] subordinate corporations or Societies and not Sovereigns." Max Farrand, *Records of the Federal Convention of 1787* (1937; repr., New Haven: Yale University Press, 1966), 1:331. Alexander Hamilton (1:323) argued in much the same terms, as did Rufus King (1:328).

8. Charles Pinckney of South Carolina, another delegate to the convention, argued in a subsequent pamphlet that any notion that each member state of the United States remained "a sovereign State must be given up; for it is absurd to

suppose there can be more than one sovereignty within a Government." Ibid., 3:112. *The Federalist*, while conceding reserved powers to the states, mocked critics of the Constitution for trying to embrace "repugnant and irreconcilable" claims, by trying to combine "sovereignty in the Union and complete independence in the members." *Federalist* 15, p. 86.

9. Letter to Wilson Cary Nicholas, September 7, 1803, in Jefferson, *Writings*, 1140.

10. "A treaty to change the organization of the Government, to annihilate its sovereignty, to change its republican form, or to deprive it of its constitutional powers, would be void." Joseph Story, *Commentaries on the Constitution*, vol. 3, sec. 1502 (1833; repr., New York: DeCapo Press, 1970), 355–56.

11. "The treaty power, as expressed in the Constitution, is in terms unlimited except by those restraints which are found in that instrument against the action of the government or its departments, and those arising from the nature of the government and that of the States. It would not be contended that it extends so far as to authorize what the Constitution forbids or a change in the character of the government or in that of one of the States. . . ." *Geofroy v. Riggs*, 133 U.S. 258 (1890), 267. Earlier rulings had endorsed the same doctrine: *Holden v. Joy*, 84 U.S. 211 (1872); *The Cherokee Tobacco*, 78 U.S. 616 (1870); *Doe ex dem. Clark v. Braden*, 57 U.S. 635 (1853); *New Orleans v. United States*, 35 U.S. 662 (1836).

12. Text of Senate's "Reservations, Understandings and Declarations" to the ICCPR at 138 Cong. Rec. S4781-01 (1992). For evaluations by legal scholars, see "Symposium: Ratification of the International Covenant on Civil and Political Rights," *DePaul Law Review* 42 (1993): 1167.

13. 354 U.S. 1 (1957), passage quoted in text at 16.

14. Lee Casey, "The Case Against the International Criminal Court," *Fordham International Law Journal* 25 (2002): 840, reviews U.S. constitutional objections to the ICC Statute.

15. Quincy Wright, *The Control of American Foreign Relations* (New York: Macmillan, 1928), 95–126.

16. Pitman B. Potter, "Inhibitions upon the Treaty-Making Power of the United States," *American Journal of International Law* 28 (1934): 456.

17. "Statement on U.S. Actions Concerning the Conference on the Law of the Sea," July 12, 1982, *Public Papers of the Presidents, Ronald Reagan*, 1982, 2:911–12.

18. "Final Kyoto Protocol to the U.N. Framework Convention on Climate Change, Approved December 11, 1997," reprinted in *International Environment Reporter*, January 7, 1998, 33. Article 12 establishes a "clean development mechanism" which will supervise trading in emission rights between signatory and nonsignatory states and certification of "projects" qualifying for assistance or recognition under the treaty, all "subject to the authority and guidance" of the signatory states but "supervised by an executive board of the clean development mechanism." (par. 4) The initial Framework Convention of 1992 also established a

freestanding "Subsidiary Body for Implementation" (art. 10) and a "Subsidiary Body for Scientific and Technological Advice" (art. 9), with vaguely defined powers.

19. Reservation 2 stipulated that "The United States declines to assume . . . any obligation . . . to interfere in controversies between other nations, members of the league or not, or to employ the military or naval forces of the United States in such controversies. . . ." The Senate Foreign Relations Committee, in justifying this proposed reservation, commented that it was "intended to meet the most vital objection to the league covenant as it stands. Under no circumstances must there be any legal or moral obligation upon the United States to enter into war or to send its Army and Navy abroad. . . . Under the Constitution of the United States the Congress alone has the power to declare war. . . ." Reprinted in Lodge, *The Senate and the League*, 173.

20. Sec. 8(a): "Authority to introduce United States Armed Forces into hostilities or into situations wherein involvement in hostilities is clearly indicated by the circumstances shall not be inferred . . . from any treaty heretofore or hereafter ratified unless such treaty is implemented by legislation specifically authorizing the introduction of United States Forces into hostilities. . . ." 87 Stat. 555 (1973), 50 U.S.C. sec. 1548.

21. See Louis Fisher, *Presidential War Power* (Lawrence, Kan.: University of Kansas Press, 1995), 114–33.

22. Laurence Tribe, *American Constitutional Law*, 3rd ed. (New York: Foundation Press, 2000), 660: "Even if a treaty is, in a sense, an inchoate declaration of war [in pledging military action in the event that certain stipulated conditions come to pass], it is one formulated by the treaty makers—that is, the President and the *Senate*—not by *Congress*, as the Constitution demands" [original emphasis]. As Tribe notes, before the NATO treaty was ratified by the Senate, the secretary of state assured senators that the treaty would not supersede the constitutional requirement for congressional declaration of war, and subsequent mutual defense treaties made this explicit.

23. *Printz v. United States*, 521 U.S. 898 (1997).

24. John Keegan, *The First World War* (New York: Alfred Knopf, 1999), 374–75, offers useful background on the tactical considerations that motivated British and French commanders to urge that American troops be integrated into existing Allied units in France—urgings which the United States adamantly rejected on "point of principle." A quarter-century later, when the British urged American reinforcement for Commonwealth troops fighting in Egypt, the United States again refused, citing "the difficulty of mixing our troops with the British in Egypt"—a "mixing" accepted in the subsequent campaigns in Morocco, Algeria, and Tunisia, where joint forces operated under American command. The British government agreed not only to place British troops under American command but also—in order to placate French hostility—to place them temporarily in American uniform; but the United States would only allow

full-strength divisions to operate temporarily under British command two years later in Northwest Europe. B. H. Liddell Hart, *History of the Second World War* (New York: G. P. Putnam's Sons, 1970), 312, 316. In organizing North American Air Defense (NorAD) with Canada in the 1950s, the United States again took care to ensure that no American air force units would operate under Canadian command.

25. For a relatively cautious version, see *Restatement of Foreign Relations Law*, 3rd, sec. 702 (New York: American Law Institute, 1987), 152–83. A more ambitious version is Richard Lillich, "The Growing Importance of Contemporary International Human Rights Law," *Georgia Journal of International and Comparative Law* 25 (1995–96): 1.

26. Curtis A. Bradley and Jack L. Goldsmith, "Customary International Law as Federal Common Law," *Harvard Law Review* 110 (February 1997): 815, offers extensive documentation of how widely established this view has become—and how questionable it is, viewed from a traditional constitutional perspective.

27. The classic account of the ECJ's success in "constitutionalizing" the European treaties is J. H. H. Weiler, "The Transformation of Europe," *Yale Law Journal* 100 (1999).

28. See Alec Stone Sweet, *Governing With Judges: Constitutional Politics in Europe* (New York: Oxford University Press, 2000), 170–74.

29. See, e.g., *Federalist* 69, pp. 386–87, where Blackstone's authority is invoked to counter arguments advanced by anti-Federalists, and in *Federalist* 84, p. 480, where "the judicious Blackstone" is quoted at length to establish the importance of the writ of habeas corpus.

30. *Federalist* 47, p. 269.

31. Bodin's treatise, *Six Livres de la République*, first published in French in 1576, was subsequently published in a Latin version (by the author), and in an English translation in 1606. The English edition ran to over 800 portfolio pages, which gives some idea of the extent of interest the work aroused in England. The treatise of Grotius on the laws of war and peace, a work of comparable size, was not fully translated into English until the early twentieth century. One of the earliest English pamphlets advocating the principle of parliamentary sovereignty, published at the outset of the seventeenth century, seems to have drawn its arguments from Bodin's treatise. Frederick Pollock, *Introduction to the History of the Science of Politics* (Boston: Beacon Press, 1960, reprinting 1911 revised edition by Macmillan), 57.

32. Jean Bodin, *Six Livres de la République*, bk. 1, chap. 10 (Paris: Fayard, 1986) sets out nine "marks" (*marques*) of sovereignty: 1) power to make laws; 2) power to declare war and conclude peace; 3) power to appoint judges and higher magistrates; 4) power to hear last appeals; 5) power to grant pardons; 6) power to demand ultimate or primary fealty of feudal lords; 7) power to coin money; 8) power to regulate weights and measures; 9) preemptive right of taxation. Art. 1,

sec. 8 of the Constitution grants all these powers to Congress, apart from the pardon power (accorded to the president), the appointing power (shared between the president and the Senate), and the appellate power (granted to the Supreme Court). Even the seemingly anachronistic feudal claim is echoed in art. 1, sec. 9, where conferral of "title of any kind whatever, from any King, Prince or foreign State," is made conditional upon "the consent of the Congress."

33. On the sovereign's obligations to respect "the law of nature and of God" and the magistrates' obligation never to transgress "laws of God and nature, " see Bodin, *Six Livres*, bk. 3, chap. 4, 97, 105. And see the reference to "Nature's God" ("dieu de nature") in bk. 4, chap. 2 (72). "Jefferson as a Reader of Bodin," in J. P. Mayer, *Fundamental Studies on Jean Bodin* (New York: Arno Press, 1979), reproduces a few pages from Jefferson's personal copy of Bodin (now in the Library of Congress), showing Jefferson's markings in the margin, including his highlighting of a passage on the binding authority of the law of God and nature (25).

34. *Federalist* 19, p. 98.

35. *Federalist* 19, p. 97; *Federalist* 17, p. 89.

36. *Federalist*. 43, pp. 247–48.

37. *Federalist* 16, p. 84.

38. *Federalist* 10, p. 46.

39. *Federalist* 43, p. 248.

40. 8 U.S.C. sec. 1448: The prescribed oath goes on to require new citizens to swear "to bear true faith and allegiance" to the Constitution and laws and "to bear arms on behalf of the United States when required by law."

41. U.S. Constitution, art. 3, sec. 3.

42. *Federalist* 11, p. 55.

43. James D. Richardson, *Compilation of the Messages and Papers of the Presidents, 1789–1897* (Washington, D.C.: Government Printing Office, 1899), 1:222.

44. David Brion Davis, "Some Themes of Counter-Subversion: An Analysis of Anti-Masonic, Anti-Catholic and Anti-Mormon Literature," *Mississippi Valley Historical Review* 47 (September 1960): 205; Harvey Klehr, *The Heyday of American Communism* (New York: Basic Books, 1984), 409, 415 (on the Communist Party's difficulty retaining support among Americans when its domination by Moscow became irrefutable).

45. Letter to Lafayette, October 6, 1789, in Alexander Hamilton, *Alexander Hamilton: Writings*, ed. Joanne B. Freeman (New York: Library of America, 2001), 52.

46. The French National Assembly voted, by the overwhelming margin of 569 to 80, to scrap the existing constitution and authorize the preparation of a new system under Marshal Pétain. The armistice with Germany did not require France to change its government in the unoccupied zone. There was "massive assent to the idea of building a new regime at once"—though this was understood to mean

abandoning past republican models. Robert O. Paxton, *Vichy France: Old Guard and New Order* (New York: Knopf, 1972), 32. The new government proved quite willing to collaborate with Germany, and even to participate in genocide. France was the only country in Europe to volunteer assistance in the roundup of Jews in its territory without being occupied by German forces. Michael Marrus and Robert Paxton, *Vichy France and the Jews* (New York: Schocken, 1983), 363.

47. On the initial appeal of the German new order in Western Europe, especially to Belgian, Dutch, and French politicians, see Mark Mazower, *Dark Continent: Europe's Twentieth Century* (New York: Vintage Books, Random House, 2000), 140–43. For a more probing account, see Helen Fein, *Accounting for Genocide* (New York: Free Press, 1979), 267–89. Fein reports that in the Netherlands, the prime minister at the time of the German invasion departed to London, but then resigned from the government in exile there and returned to the Netherlands. There he published a pamphlet urging his countrymen to collaborate with the new order in Europe. Dutch civil servants and police proved so ready to collaborate that more Jews (almost 80 percent) were rounded up and "deported" from the Netherlands than from any other country in Western Europe. A German Foreign Office official reported in July 1942 that Dutch authorities "approved deportation of Jews without official protest" (284). The following year, when Germany began to conscript non-Jews for labor service in the Reich, a nationwide "social defense organization" emerged which proved quite effective in hiding Dutch "Aryans." There was no organized effort to shield Dutch Jews (286–87). Even protests were limited to Communist and Roman Catholic leaders—those with strong enough loyalties to resist German appeals for collaboration. The Dutch Reformed Church abandoned a planned protest against the deportation of Jews when German authorities promised not to interfere with the church itself (270, 285).

48. Joint Declaration by the President and Prime Minister, August 12, 1941 (which came to be known as "The Atlantic Charter"), par. 3, text in Winston S. Churchill, *The Grand Alliance* (Boston: Houghton-Mifflin, 1951), 443.

49. The "prevailing view" in Vichy France, even after German occupation of its territory in November 1942, was that "German occupation might be bad, but liberation by force would be worse." Paxton, *Vichy France,* 287. Pierre Laval, a leading Vichy official, told the U.S. ambassador in 1941 that he "hoped" for a German victory, so that "Britain [would] pay the bill [for resisting Germany] and not France" (85).

50. Daniel Philpott, *Revolutions in Sovereignty* (Princeton, N.J.: Princeton University Press, 2001), 261–62, argues that Christian-Democratic parties in postwar Europe embraced a traditional Catholic distrust of sovereignty; the treatise of Grotius, he notes, had remained on the Vatican Index of banned books until the end of the nineteenth century, and classical international law was denounced by Church officials as a "Protestant science."

51. Quoted in John Laughland, *The Tainted Source: The Undemocratic Origins of the European Idea* (London: Little, Brown, 1997), 52.

52. Ibid., 38–39.

53. Ibid., 69. During the 1930s, Spaak belonged to the Belgian Worker's Party and helped to secure the party leadership for Henri de Man, the most prominent collaborationist during the German occupation (70). Robert Schumann, author of the Schumann Plan which launched the Coal and Steel Community that was the forerunner to the Common Market, served in the Vichy government of Marshal Pétain, voted in the National Assembly to invest that government with dictatorial powers, and was charged with collaboration at the end of the war—though he was ultimately rescued by the intervention of Charles de Gaulle (76–78).

54. *Federalist* 2, pp. 6–7.

55. Eisenhower's speech to the North Atlantic Council in Rome, November 26, 1951, reprinted in David Weigall and Peter Stirk, *The Origins and Development of the European Community* (London: Leicester University Press, 1992), spoke more diplomatically of the need for a European defense policy "gaining German strength without creating a menace to any others" (79). The editors summarize the underlying policy as reflecting "the view that German rearmament could only be palatable to the French if it meant rearming Germans without rearming Germany" (72). Edouard Herriot, president of France's National Assembly, spoke for the majority in the assembly, however, when he protested that the EDC treaty "aims at restoring Germany's sovereignty but represents a backward step for France with regard to her sovereignty" (speech to the assembly, 86).

56. Not one of the major opinion magazines of that era—*The New Statesman, The Spectator, The Tattler, The Listener*—bothered to carry any comment or analysis regarding British adherence to the ECHR at the time it was ratified by Parliament. See A. W. Brian Simpson, *Human Rights and the End of Empire, Britain and the Genesis of the European Convention* (New York: Oxford University Press, 2001) for an account emphasizing British initiative in the project, which, for all its exhaustive research, has almost nothing to report about public debate in Britain at the time. Simpson devotes over one hundred pages to the actual drafting and ratification process (649–753) without describing any serious public opposition or expressions of concern.

57. Alan Milward, *The European Rescue of the Nation State* (New York: Routledge, 1999).

58. Fritz Machlup, *A History of Thought on Economic Integration* (New York: Columbia University Press, 1977), 11, notes that the term seems to have been coined by the American administrator of Marshall Plan assistance to European states in the late 1940s.

59. The process began with *van Gend en Loos v. Nederlandse Administratie der Belastingen*, 1963 E.C.R. 1, which held that many provisions of the Treaty of

Rome must be given direct effect in national law, and citizens could sue their own governments for failing to conform to ECJ interpretations of these provisions. In *Costa v. ENEL*, 1964 E.C.R. 585, the court held that such treaty provisions would nullify even subsequent enactments of national parliaments. Sweet, *Governing With Judges,* describes the overall pattern in a separate chapter on the ECJ.

60. *Internationale Handelsgesellschaft mgH v. Einfuhr- und Vorratsstelle für Getreide und Futtermittle,* 1970 E.C.R. 1125, held that a regulation issued by the European Commission would take precedence over a constitutional ruling of a national constitutional court, but claimed that it would hold the commission to common traditions of rights protections of the member states. In *Hauer v. Land Rheinland Pfalz,* 1979 E.C.R. 2717, the ECJ held that the European Convention on Human Rights could provide guidance, though other cases have looked to such disparate sources as conventions of the International Labour Organization and the "Social Charter" adopted by the Council of Europe in 1961 (and never submitted to monitoring or interpretation by the Court of Human Rights).

61. The Human Rights Court rendered only 10 judgments in the 1960s; 26 in the 1970s, 169 in the 1980s, and 818 between 1990 and 1998. Though Britain had the oldest and seemingly best-established traditions of legal protections for individual liberty of any signatory to the Human Rights Convention, easily a third of the court's cases in its formative decade (between 1975 and 1987) involved challenges to British practices. Among the notable rulings in the 1990s: *Hartley v. United Kingdom,* 13 E.H.R.R. 157 (1993) (condemning detention for questioning of terror suspects in Northern Ireland, when not authorized by a magistrate, even for suspects previously convicted of terror crimes); *Brannigan v. United Kingdom,* 17 E.H.R.R. 594 (1993) (condemning British reliance on a "public emergency" exception to the Human Rights Convention, on the grounds that terror attacks in Northern Ireland did not qualify as an "emergency"); *Open Door Counseling and Dublin Women v. Ireland,* 15 E.H.R.R. 243 (1992) (condemning an Irish law restricting advertisement of abortion services in neighboring Britain); *Lustig-Prean & Beckett v. United Kingdom* (1999), Butterworths Human Rights Cases 7 (1999): 65 (condemning the exclusion of homosexuals from British armed forces); *Sutherland v. United Kingdom,* 22 E.H.R.R. 22 (1996) (condemning a law making eighteen years the age of consent for homosexual relations).

62. Simon Hix, "Executive Selection in the European Union," in *European Integration After Amsterdam,* eds. Karlheinz Neunreither and Antje Wiener (Oxford: Oxford Press, 2000), 104–5, attributes low turnouts to the fact that campaigns for the European Parliament (EP) are not conducted on European issues but as referenda on national governments within each state—though this pattern may, in turn, reflect assumptions of candidates that voters will not care what they say about European issues, given the EP's lack of power. Neunreither, "Political Representation in the European Union," in the same volume, argues that parties do not bother to assert or defend European issues when fielding candidates for

the EP (129–49). Roger Scully, "Democracy, Legitimacy and the European Parliament," in *The State of the European Union*, eds. M. G. Cowles and Michael Smith (Oxford: Oxford University Press, 2000), 5:240–41, reports survey findings at the end of the 1990s that less than half of EU "citizens" claimed to have heard anything at all about the EP, and less than half wanted the Parliament to have more power—a proportion that declined over the course of the 1990s.

63. The directorate of the European Commission that was assigned special responsibility for environmental issues grew from 55 staff persons in 1986 to 450 by 1992. Justin Greenwood, *Representing Interests in the European Union* (London: Macmillan, 1997), 181. Chapter 2 of John McCormick, *Environmental Policy in the European Union* (London: Palgrave, 2001), provides a useful overview indicating the extent to which mushrooming activity in the environmental field coincided with the European Commission's new authority to dismantle trade barriers, following approval of the "Single Europe Act" in 1987. On efforts of the European Commission and the European Court of Justice to initiate ambitious regulations to ensure comparable-worth pay standards for women, see Mark Pollock, "Reregulating Europe," in *The Engines of European Integration* (New York: Oxford University Press, 2003), 350–72.

64. In Bernard Connolly, *The Rotten Heart of Europe* (London: Faber and Faber, 1995), the author, a British economist employed at the European Commission, depicts its priorities as reflecting French and German concerns for "preserving regulatory state power" from "inroads . . . made by the world (that is, 'Anglo-Saxon') market" (379).

65. James A. Caparaso, "The European Union and Forms of State: Westphalian, Regulatory or Postmodern?" *Journal of Common Market Studies* 34 (March 1996): 29–52, argued for the last alternative in the subtitle. A serious effort to connect this characterization to "postmodern" concepts in literary theory and social philosophy was offered by Ian Ward, "The European Union and Postmodernism," in *New Legal Dynamics of the European Union*, eds. Jo Shaw and Gillian More (Oxford: Clarendon Press, 1995), 15–28.

66. The proposed new constitution for the European Union will address this problem with a characteristic compromise. On the one hand, the president of the European Commission will be elected by the European Parliament, which is supposed to provide more authority for the holder of that position. On the other hand, member states, whose prime ministers had previously taken turns chairing meetings of top ministers for six-month terms, will now elect their own "president" for a two-year term. To deal with the problems arising from the lack of a strong political executive, then, the new constitution proposes to create two presidents, one representing "Europe" and the other representing the member states.

67. By 1996, the EU was channeling 9.25 percent of its budget to direct payments to nongovernmental organizations. Not all of this funding went to advocacy groups, but the EU does not provide direct social services itself, so

qualifying recipients were hardly a cross-section of nonprofit organizations in Europe. A. M. Agraa, *The European Union: History, Institutions, Economics and Policies* (London: Prentice Hall Europe, 1998), 319. An analysis of EU funding for outside research found that of roughly $12 billion expended, 8.3 percent was devoted to "environmental issues," and 6.8 percent to studying "cooperation with non-EU countries." B. Harvey, *Networking in Europe: A Guide to European Voluntary Organizations*, 2nd ed., ch. 3 (London: NCVO Publications and Community Development Foundation, 1995).

68. Yasemin Nuhoglu Soysal, *Limits of Citizenship: Migrants and Postnational Membership in Europe* (Chicago: University of Chicago Press, 1994).

69. "In condemning the bombing [Prime Minister Raymond] Barre noted that three of the victims were 'innocent.' He meant non-Jewish." "A Guilty Conscience 40 Years Old," *The Economist*, October 25, 1980, 41, noted that concerns about echoes of the Vichy era prompted protests all over France in the wake of the bombing and the prime minister's remark. By spring 2003, French opinion had become quite complacent about the bombings of synagogues, and President Chirac warned that it was "dangerous" to accuse France of anti-semitism—though he did not make clear how his government would retaliate against those making such charges. Where two decades before there had been talk of a "guilty conscience," Chirac now insisted that France had never been antisemitic, even in the past—evidently regarding the Vichy government's collaboration in genocide as mere policy, unrelated to the essence of French "culture." Beatrice Gurrey, "Jacques Chirac réassure les organisations juives américaines," *Le Monde*, September 24, 2003 ("La France pays antisémite? Un jugement inexact, injuste et même dangereux, selon l'Élysée. . . . La France n'est pas un pays antisémite, ne l'a jamais été dans sa culture . . . a répété avec force M. Chirac"). Two months later, when such denials were followed by continuing arson and violence directed at Jewish institutions in France, President Chirac reversed course and announced that he would demand that cabinet ministers mobilize adequate protection for French Jews. Hugh Schofield, "Chirac to Chair Anti-Semitism Cabinet after School Burning," *Agence France-Presse*, November 16, 2003. Not everyone was reassured. Two days later, the chief rabbi of France advised French Jews to make themselves less conspicuous in public places in order to avoid attack. Angela Doland, "France's Chief Rabbi Warns Jews That Wearing Skullcaps Could Make Them Targets," *Associated Press*, November 19, 2003. Finally, it became a joke. In December, a government-controlled television network in France broadcast a "sketch" by a "comedian" who, dressed in Hassidic garb, responded to the sight of a Muslim boy by shouting, "Where is the French army? Where is Sarkozy [minister of the interior]? . . . The presence of this boy is an insupportable provocation, an act of anti-Semitism. . . . Convert yourself, as I have, to the American-Zionist axis." The "comedian" closed by giving a Nazi salute and shouting "IsraHeil!" For a description of the episode, see

Eve Bonnivard, "L'Affaire Dieudonne," in *L'Arche*, no. 551–52 (January/February 2004): 124–27.

70. Charlemagne, "Snoring While an EU Superstate Emerges?" *The Economist*, May 10, 2003.

71. Jack Rakove, "Europe's Floundering Fathers," *Foreign Policy* (September/October 2003): 28, notes that, in contrast to the U.S. Constitution of 1787, the EU model "remains, in essence, a negotiation among nation-states and their governments, with a formal requirement for unanimity which places the entire project in jeopardy" (33). The article offers a useful bibliographic survey of the first wave of comment in Europe (38).

72. See, for example, the November 2003 European Commission poll, http://europa.eu.int/comm/public_opinion/flash/fl151_iraq_full_report.pdf.

73. For a detached account in English, see Alan Riding, "What drives Jacques Chirac?" *The Gazette* (Montreal), February 25, 2003.

74. Larry Siedentop, *Democracy in Europe* (New York: Columbia University Press, 2001), 221.

75. Ambrose Evans Pritchard, "'Asiatic' Turkey is Threat to EU, Warns Giscard," *Daily Telegraph* (London), November 9, 2002; Yasmin Alibhai-brown, "Do Muslims Not Belong in this Christian Europe?" *The Independent* (London), December 16, 2002; Mark Mazower, "Beyond the Christian Club of Europe," *The Financial Times* (London), December 12, 2002.

76. Christopher Patten, "Let's Get Emotional," *The Spectator* (London), May 18, 2002: "A healthy European democracy will develop only when people begin to feel an emotional commitment to their European identity. It is hard to develop such attachment. People are not drawn to international society by sentiment or tradition. But it will happen. You can already feel the stirrings perhaps in shared indignation at US steel protectionism."

77. Kim Willsher, "Jews Attacked in French Anti-War Protests," *Sunday Telegraph* (London), April 6, 2003. A Socialist member of the French National Assembly complained to foreign journalists that "the phrase 'Anglo-Americans' thrown around in the [French] media and in political circles to describe the coalition in Iraq—sometimes linked with 'supported by the Jews'—echoes the rhetoric of Vichy France." But he was described as "one of a handful in parliament as a whole" to protest the tone of official rhetoric. "France's Realists, Continued," editorial, *Wall Street Journal*, April 9, 2003.

78. *Federalist* 11, pp. 58–59.

Chapter 3: Sovereignty and Security

1. The main theme of *Federalist* 3, pp. 9–13.

2. See Madison's long, learned pamphlet, "Examination of the British Doctrine which Subjects to Capture a Neutral Trade not Open in Time of Peace,"

in *Writings of James Madison*, 2:230–391, which he published anonymously while serving as secretary of state under Jefferson. Jefferson had already advanced similar appeals while serving as secretary of state under Washington.

3. *Federalist* 3, p. 13.

4. *Federalist* 15, p. 77.

5. *Federalist* 43, p. 248.

6. Richardson, *Messages and Papers of the Presidents*, 1:222.

7. See Max Boot, *The Savage Wars of Peace: Small Wars and the Rise of American Power* (New York: Basic Books, 2002).

8. Michael Morrison, *Slavery and the American West* (Chapel Hill: UNC Press, 1997), 13–38, reports that the effective argument for advocates of annexation was that the Republic of Texas would otherwise fall under British influence, and the United States was not willing to share a protective influence in Texas any more than in the Oregon territory.

9. Bemis, *Latin American Policy*, 152–66.

10. At American insistence, a provision was added to the Covenant of the League of Nations, disclaiming any effect of the covenant on "the validity of international engagements, such as treaties of arbitration or regional understandings like the Monroe Doctrine. . . ." (art. 21). But as a British legal commentary was quick to point out, this provision "does not define the doctrine; much less does it incorporate it as a rule of International Law. In fact, the Monroe Doctrine is nothing more than a time-honored expression of American foreign policy. . . ." Lawrence, *Principles of International Law*, 259.

11. The official compilation of U.S. State Department pronouncements in the late nineteenth century covers policy toward Liberia as an annex to the Monroe Doctrine: "Liberia, although not a colony of the United States, began its independent career as an off-shoot of this country . . . which relationship authorizes the United States to interpose its good offices in any contest between Liberia and a foreign state" (citing statement of Secretary Blaine in 1881). But Secretary Evarts warned that the United States had no legal obligation to "interpose" its "naval forces to preserve order or to compel obedience to law in Liberia." And he subsequently added: "Nor should the United States minister in Liberia interfere with the government thereof by obtruding political advice." Francis Wharton, *Digest of International Law of the United States*, sec. 66 (Washington, D.C.: Government Printing Office, 1886), 445.

12. Bemis, *Latin American Policy*, celebrates this achievement in chap. 22.

13. Ibid., chap. 13–14, on efforts to codify "International Law of the Americas." Moore, *Principles of American Diplomacy*, devotes an entire chapter to "pan-American" policy (365–419). From the outset, he notes, Congress resisted any commitment that might imply legislative powers in a pan-American international organization. The United States agreed to arbitration of disputes in the hemisphere, with the stipulation that no nation would be required to submit for arbitration a dispute threatening its "independence" (371–76).

14. Calvin DeArmond Davis, *The United States and the First Hague Peace Conference* (Ithaca, N.Y.: Cornell University Press, 1962), 29–35.

15. See, e.g., Wright, *Control of Foreign Relations*, arguing that the League posed no threat because it could not compel action by members apart from their own constitutional processes for committing troops or changing trade relations or expending funds.

16. UN Charter, art. 45.

17. UN Charter, art. 107.

18. UN Charter, art. 27, par. 3. When plans for the charter were first published, a distinguished American legal scholar noted that the scheme looked less like the League of Nations than like earlier schemes for securing peace in Europe: "The relation among the Big Five, since they alone can effectively employ major force—though exposing smaller members to the dangers of enlistment in their enterprise—is really that of a military Alliance, on the order of the Holy Alliance and Quadruple Alliance of Napoleon's day." Edwin Borchard, "On Dumbarton Oaks Proposals for New World Organization," *American Journal of International Law* 39 (1945): 97–100.

19. For a recent version of the call to combine reform of the UN with renewed U.S. commitment to the world organization, see Michael Ignatieff, "Why Are We in Iraq?" *New York Times* (Sunday magazine), September 7, 2003.

20. See, e.g., Ingvar Carlson, "The UN at 50: Time to Reform," *Foreign Policy*, no. 100 (Fall 1995): 3.

21. For a sympathetic account, see Ronald J. Rychlak, *Hitler, The War and the Pope* (Huntington, Ind.: Our Sunday Visitor, 2000), 182. ("Perhaps the most valid criticism of Pius XII would be that he was too willing to compromise in order to achieve peace") and further discussion (269).

22. "Pope Says War Against Iraq 'Threatens Fate of Mankind,'" *BBC International Reports*, March 24, 2003; Michael Novak, "Civilian Casualties and Turmoil," *National Review*, February 18, 2003; Richard Owen, "Pope Takes Issue with America's 'Just War,'" *The Times* (London), February 10, 2003. A survey of Iraqi hospitals, undertaken by the Associated Press after the war, was able to document 3,240 civilian casualties between March 20 and April 20, 2003 (the period of most direct fighting). "Iraq Halts Its Count of Civilian Deaths," *Los Angeles Times*, December 11, 2003.

23. S.C. Res. 487, reprinted with commentary in *American Journal of International Law* 75 (1981): 724.

24. The United Nations made no comment on the slaughter of some two million civilians by the Khmer Rouge government in Cambodia. But when that regime was overthrown by a Vietnamese invasion at the end of 1978 and the Vietnamese installed a successor regime (which did, at least, stop the mass slaughter), the UN General Assembly voted, by a two-to-one margin, to allow the deposed, genocidal regime to retain its seat at the UN rather than recognize the

propriety of the Vietnamese intervention. The episode is described, with suitable disgust, in Samantha Power, *A Problem from Hell* (New York: Basic Books, 2002), 149–54.

25. Tony Judt, "Anti-Americans Abroad," *New York Review of Books*, May 1, 2003, on the founder of *Le Monde* in June 1944.

26. Text in David Eisenhower, *Eisenhower at War 1943–45* (New York: Vintage Books, 1987), 256. A small number of French commandos were also involved—though armed, equipped, trained, and commanded by Anglo-American forces.

27. Dutch troops failed to alert UN headquarters in Bosnia, it seems, because fifty-five of their number had been taken hostage by Serb militia forces at the outset of the attack on civilians in Srbrenica, and their fellow soldiers did not want to jeopardize their safety. So Dutch forces looked to their own safety rather than that of the civilians they were supposed to guard. Roy Gutman, "Bosnia: Negotiation and Retreat," in *Soldiers for Peace*, ed. Barbara Benton (New York: Facts on File, 1996), 202–4.

28. General Assembly Resolution 38/7 (1983), adopted by a vote of 108 to 9, with twenty-seven abstentions.

29. Hart, *History of the Second World War*, 313 (on fear of French obstruction or betrayal), 333 (on reliance on Spanish neutrality).

30. Ibid., 333.

31. Robert E. Conot, *Justice at Nuremberg* (New York: Carol and Graf, 1983), 316–17, reports the evasion of Hitler's directives for the execution of Allied prisoners in retaliation for Allied bombing of Germany, and an ultimate policy paper by the German General Staff that explained why this would be counterproductive as a war tactic. German generals assumed British and American authorities would retaliate in kind for the execution of Allied prisoners.

32. Frits Karlshoven, *Belligerent Reprisals* (Leyden, Netherlands: Sijthoff, 1971), 107.

33. For example, French commanders gave advance warning of impending attacks to British pickets and sentries at forward "outposts" so they could avoid being killed for no purpose, and the British reciprocated this "civilized" courtesy of war. See Michael Glover, *The Peninsular War, 1807–1814* (Hamden, Conn.: Archon Books, 1974) 303. Between the French forces and the guerrillas, the war degenerated into a literal battle for survival, centering on the seizure of food supplies and the killing of anyone who interfered with the forced requisition of food (29).

34. The initial article of all four 1949 conventions proclaims the obligation of the "High Contracting Parties" to observe the codified standards "in all circumstances." Common Article 2 elaborates—and qualifies—the meaning of this obligation, however, by stipulating that where a war involves a nonsignatory state, states that are parties to each of these conventions (and engaged in the same war) "shall remain bound" to the convention "in their mutual relations" and "shall be

bound by the Convention in relation to the said Power [that is, the nonsignatory] *if the latter accepts and applies the provisions thereof*" [emphasis added]. The same stipulations regarding eligibility for protection—that combatants fight with identifying insignia, under command discipline, and in conformity to the rules of war—then appear in Article 4 of each of the three conventions: Convention I ("Amelioration of the Condition of the Wounded and Sick in Armed Forces in the Field"), 6 U.S.T. 3114, 75 U.N.T.S. 31; Convention II ("Amelioration of the Wounded, Sick and Shipwrecked Members of Armed Forces at Sea"), 6 U.S.T. 3217, 75 U.N.T.S. 85; Convention III ("Relative to Prisoners of War"), 6 U.S.T 3316, 75 U.N.T.S. 135.

35. "Order of Retaliation," July 30, 1863, in Abraham Lincoln, *Speeches and Writings,* 484.

36. During the war, the U.S. State Department originally considered an approach to a postwar peace organization which would have required that all international disputes be submitted to formal arbitration. The idea was quickly abandoned as unsuitable to American policy. Ruth B. Russell, *History of the United Nations Charter*, chap. 9 (Washington, D.C.: Brookings Institution, 1958), 205–26.

37. International Military Tribunal, *Nazi Conspiracy and Aggression* (Washington, D.C.: U.S. Government Printing Office, 1947), 1:171. A member of the American planning staff suggested, before the start of the trials, that the proceedings should be designated as prosecutions brought by "The People of the United Nations ex rel. the U.S.S.R., the U.S.A., UK, France," but this suggestion was rejected without much discussion and the cases were actually styled as prosecutions in the name of the four occupying governments, with no mention of outsiders. Jeremy Rabkin, "Nuremberg Misremembered," *SAIS Review* 19, no. 2 (Summer–Fall 1999): 87.

38. Robert Wolfe, who served with the American prosecution staff and subsequently organized all the trial records for the National Archives, commented, "Protection for the domestic minority groups against atrocities perpetrated by their own governments does not derive from Nuremberg, where both IMT [International Military Tribunal] and [subsequent] American tribunals rejected prosecution attempts to establish a precedent. . . ." Other American participants in the Nuremberg prosecutions also endorsed this view, according to "Symposium: Critical Perspectives on the Nuremberg Trials and State Accountability," *New York Law School Journal of Human Rights* 12 (1995): 488 (also, 537 and 538 for confirmations by other participants). For a more general discussion, see Rabkin, "Nuremberg Misremembered," 82–86.

39. See Danna Frank Fleming, *The United States and the World Court*, rev. ed. (New York: Russell & Russell, 1968), 195 (for an account of the Senate's determination to resist encroachments by the court in 1945 and its rejection of proposals to cooperate with the predecessor institution under the League of Nations), 117–37

(on rejection of efforts by Secretary of State Hughes in the 1920s), 52–67 (on rejection of subsequent efforts by President Roosevelt in 1934).

40. Art. 6 directs that those charged with genocide "shall be tried by a competent tribunal of the State in the territory of which the act was committed, or by such international penal tribunal as may have jurisdiction with respect to those Contracting Parties which shall have accepted its jurisdiction"—the last clause indicating that even the drafters of a convention on the punishment of genocide did not envision an international tribunal whose jurisdiction could be imposed without consent.

41. American officials continued to negotiate with Serb militia leaders even after their indictment by the International Criminal Tribunal for the former Yugoslavia (ICTY). Even subsequently, when a peace agreement provided more security for NATO forces in Bosnia, commanders remained quite reluctant to risk their own troops by going after indicted war criminals. Gary Bass, *Stay the Hand of Vengeance: The Politics of War Crimes Tribunals* (Princeton, N.J.: Princeton University Press, 2000), 230–41, 248–60.

42. By April 1998, Rwandan courts had tried 346 people, sentencing one-third of them to the death penalty and one-third to life imprisonment (and acquitting 26). In the same four-year period, the UN tribunal did not complete even a single trial, and a year later it ordered the release of a Hutu leader because he had been detained too long: "No one should have expected the Rwandans to be as unconcerned about the punishment of the genocide as the UN was." Bass, *Stay the Hand*, 307–8.

43. By 1963, trials conducted by American authorities in their occupation zone had secured convictions of 1,184 Germans (of whom 450 were sentenced to death), while 10,000 Germans were convicted in the Soviet zone—a contrast which is all the more remarkable, since higher-level officials made every effort to flee to the western occupation zones at the end of the war. Justice administered by British authorities in their occupation zone was broadly similar to the American pattern: 1,085 convictions and 240 capital sentences by 1963. Eugene Davidson, *Trial of the Germans* (New York: Macmillan, 1966), 30.

44. Among the earliest cases pursued by the UN tribunal were ones charging sexual humiliation of women—as by undressing a female student and requiring her to perform "gymnastics" before a crowd of onlookers. If this was a bid for mention in casebooks, it succeeded; see Henry Steiner and Philip Alston, *International Human Rights in Context*, 2nd ed. (New York: Oxford University Press, 2000), 1187–88, on cases designed to establish that "sexual violence" may "include acts which do not involve . . . physical contact," and that "coercive circumstances need not be evidenced by a show of physical force." These were entirely plausible claims for a domestic legal system but not, one might think, of highest priority for prosecutors faced with an actual pattern of mass murder that had taken the lives of nearly a million people. Meanwhile, the tribunal offered such handsome fees for defending accused practitioners of genocide that lawyers

offered to split the fees with accused mass murderers to gain their consent to become clients—so the UN ended up providing financial rewards to perpetrators of genocide (or their families). House Committee on International Relations, *The U.N. Criminal Tribunals for Yugoslavia and Rwanda: International Justice or Show of Justice: Hearing before the Committee on International Relations*, 107th Cong., 2d sess., February 28, 2002 (response of Pierre-Richard Prosper, Ambassador-at-Large for War Crimes Issues, to questioning from Representative Jo Ann Davis). The same hearing also included discussion of procedural irregularities (such as prosecutors withholding exculpatory evidence), assembled by former Justice Department attorney Larry A. Hammond.

45. Bass, *Stay the Hand*, 232–39, on earlier negotiation with Milosevic. At the time of the NATO bombing campaign, on behalf of Kosovo, NATO officials speculated that as many as 100,000 Albanians may have been slaughtered by Serb forces. The indictment by The Hague tribunal, handed down while the war was still ongoing, seemed to endorse the notion of murder on this horrific scale. The Serb capitulation allowed The Hague tribunal to undertake onsite inspections, which discovered only 2,108 bodies. Stepven Erlanger and Christopher Wren, "Early Count Hints at Fewer Kosovo Dead," *The New York Times*, November 11, 1999.

46. In July 1914, Serbia expressed willingness to satisfy many provisions in the ultimatum delivered by Austria-Hungary following the assassination of Archduke Franz Ferdinand in Sarajevo. It refused, however, to agree to the Austrian demand to extradite Serb suspects for trial in Austria. The same constitutional obstacle to extradition was invoked by the Serbian Supreme Court in rejecting demands for the extradition of Milosevic to The Hague in 2001. Under pressure inspired, in fact, by the U.S. Congress (which refused to approve desperately needed aid for Serbia unless Milosevic were extradited), the Serb prime minister arranged for the extradition—in defiance of judgments by the Serbian Supreme Court and the elected president of Serbia (a former law professor) that the extradition would be unlawful. Satisfying international pressures took precedence over the rule of law in Serbia. Bass, *Stay the Hand*, 315–21, provides some details.

47. Grotius, *De Jure Belli ac Pacis*, bk. 3, chap. 11–14, pp. 722–69, recounts in some detail restraints in war accepted by European nations of the day, even though (as earlier chapters demonstrate) ancient writings on war approved utter devastation of enemy lands, enemy civilians, and enemy prisoners.

48. There were, in fact, two distinct conventions drafted at the Geneva Conference of 1975–76, conveniently known as Additional Protocol I and Additional Protocol II. Protocol I set out protections for victims of "international armed conflicts." Protocol II set out protections for victims of "non-international conflicts." One can see at a glance the priorities of conference participants from the relative size of the two instruments: Protocol I (on international conflicts) contains 105 articles, with an appendix containing an additional 15 articles, while Protocol II contains only 28 articles. In *Human Rights—A Compilation of*

International Instruments, published by the United Nations in 1994, Protocol I runs to sixty-seven pages and Protocol II runs to nine pages. Participants at the conference were not much concerned about establishing international standards to protect victims of internal conflicts. By far the worst bloodletting has taken place in internal conflicts in recent decades, but such conflicts have occurred in third-world countries (as they were earlier known), and neither the governments of such countries nor outside states were greatly concerned about such bloodletting. International conflicts have aroused much more interest, since they might be fought by first-world countries against third-world countries, as in the recently ended conflict in Vietnam. At the drafting conference, many governments insisted that Protocol II was merely an expression of good intentions and established no new legal standard that would authorize international control of a domestic conflict. See David Forsythe, "Legal Management of Internal War," *American Journal of International Law* 72 (1978): 287, 289. For a concise statement of the Reagan administration's reasons for opposing Protocol I, see Douglas Feith, "Law in the Service of Terror: The Strange Case of the Additional Protocol," *The National Interest*, no. 1 (Fall 1985): 36. Still the most comprehensive analysis of potential American problems with Protocol I is W. Hays Parks, "Air War and the Law of War," *Air Force Law Review* 1 (1990): 1. David B. Rivkin and Lee Casey, "Leashing the Dogs of War," *The National Interest*, no. 73 (Fall 2003): 57–69, updates the story.

49. As late as 1988, only Belgium, the Netherlands, Norway, and Italy had ratified Additional Protocol I. Over the next three years, which coincided with the ending of the Cold War, Germany, Spain, and Canada also ratified. Britain ratified only in 1998, and France in 2001.

50. "Gegen Völkermord und Diktatur," *Berliner Zeitung*, April 12, 2002.

51. Reeve, *One Day in September*, 157–58 (on Germany), 209 (on France).

52. The medieval view was, in a way, more coherent: theologians regarded war itself as a fit punishment for "crimes" and assumed that civilians deserved to suffer, along with their rulers, since the civilians had allowed their rulers to pursue evil policies. The modern view assumes, to the contrary, that civilians have no connection with the practices of their government, which may be more liberal but is not obviously more realistic. There was some truth, after all, in President Roosevelt's complaint against the view "that the German people as a whole are not responsible for what has taken place—that only a few Nazi leaders are responsible. That unfortunately is not based on fact. The German people as a whole . . . has been engaged in a lawless conspiracy against the decencies of modern civilization." Statement to Secretary of War Henry Stimson, August 26, 1944, in Henry Morgenthau, *The White House Diaries of Henry Morgenthau*, vol. 1, microfilm, 444, quoted in Bass, *Stay the Hand*, 154.

53. The first effort to persuade the ICC to indict Blair and other UK Cabinet ministers was launched as early as July by the Athens Bar Association. Kerin

Hope and Nikki Tait, "Greeks Try to Indict Blair for Iraq War," *Financial Times* (London), July 29, 2003. The effort was then endorsed by professors in Britain, Ireland, France, and Canada: Severin Carrell, "Blair Faces New War Crimes Accusation," *The Independent on Sunday* (London), January 18, 2004. Then public interest lawyers in London launched their own effort. Sandra Laville, "Iraqi Familes to Sue Britain Over Deaths," *Daily Telegraph* (London), March 1, 2004.

54. Res. 2002/8 of the Human Rights Commission affirmed "the legitimate rights of the Palestinian people to resist Israeli occupation" and, in support of this affirmation, invoked a 1982 UN General Assembly resolution on "the legitimacy of the struggle of peoples against foreign occupation" which endorsed "all means of armed struggle." Since there was no word of condemnation against suicide bombings of civilians—and virtually all the bombings had been directed at civilians—the inevitable implication was that the commission endorsed suicide bombings of Israeli civilians. Both Germany and the United Kingdom, noting this implication, refused to endorse the resolution, though France, Belgium, Portugal, and Austria joined in the enthusiasm of the commission for "armed struggle" by means of such bombings against civilians. One advantage of the ICC, from the standpoint of squeamish governments, is that the ICC prosecutor can proceed with a troubling prosecution without requiring any government to take a direct position on the case.

55. Since Israel has declined to ratify the ICC Statute and Palestine cannot do so (as it is not yet an independent state), there might be jurisdictional difficulties in prosecuting Israeli officials for actions taken in Palestinian territory. This is not likely to cause any great problems for the ICC, if it does decide to follow the path marked by other international institutions. Jordan is among the states that have ratified the ICC Statute, and since countless UN resolutions denounce Israel for "occupying" the West Bank, it might be inferred that Jordan—which controlled the territory between 1948 and 1967—is entitled to supply ICC jurisdiction. It is true that Jordanian sovereignty over this territory was never recognized by most nations, and Jordan itself has, since then, renounced any claim to this territory. But UNESCO's World Heritage Committee felt justified in the 1980s in condemning Israel's protection of the Old City of Jerusalem—even though Israel was not, at the time, a party to the relevant treaty (the so-called "World Heritage Convention"). Jordanian participation in the treaty was regarded as a sufficient basis for allowing UNESCO to interfere in territory claimed by Israel. It would not be difficult to construct legal formulas for the ICC to assert jurisdiction over Israel, if the prosecutor and the court are so inclined. And it is not easy to imagine why European sponsors of the court, who were comfortable in endorsing suicide bombing of Israelis, would hesitate to launch a legal action against Israeli officials. Belgian legislators were unwilling to block an attempted prosecution of Israeli Prime Minister Sharon even while he was serving in office. Resentment toward Israel—which pursues so many policies that Europeans have eschewed—seems to be a strong current in European thinking: See Josef Joffe, "Europe's Axis of Envy," *Foreign Policy* (September/October 2002): 68,

which notes that resentment of the United States and resentment of Israel have been merged in European thinking—or, he might have said, have been merged again, as they were in 1941–45.

56. Speaking to a lobby for Germans who had been expelled from Polish and Czech lands in 1945, Rau also compared the expulsion policy to the wartime polices that had earlier "deprived the Jews of their rights." He insisted that all the suffering in that era "can only really be understood in its entire context," in which Germans as well as others were caught up in a "pan-European catastrophe." Peter Conradi, "Germany says Britain shares in WWII guilt," *Sunday Times* (London), September 28, 2003. The speech was condemned in Britain. See Max Hastings, "Germany's President Said Allies Should Share the Nazis' War Guilt," *Daily Mail* (UK), October 4, 2003. It seems to have aroused no notice in Germany, where the government plans to erect a monument in Berlin to honor the memory of Germans victimized by Eastern European nations, as a counterpart to the planned memorial for murdered Jews. Jürgen Habermas, Germany's most prominent moral philosopher, states the demand for equivalence in a positive form: Noting that the United States "became the driving force . . . in carrying out the Nuremberg tribunals," he asks how "this same nation [can] now brush aside the civilizing achievement of legally domesticating the state of nature among belligerent nations." "Letter to America," *The Nation,* December 16, 2002. Other Germans take a somewhat different view: A study by the Allensbach Institute, Germany's leading public opinion research organization, found that while a solid majority of Americans agreed with the claim that "there are absolute benchmarks of good and evil," fewer than a third of Germans agreed: "Most Germans find such unconditional morality incomprehensible." Thomas Petersen, "Issues Endanger Trans-Atlantic Friendship," *Frankfurter Allgemeine Zeitung* (Weekly English edition), March 21, 2003.

57. Bass, *Stay the Hand*, 245, documents that the South African chief prosecutor for the International Criminal Court for Yugoslavia was in touch with American officials during the negotiation of peace efforts in Bosnia, and apparently was not indifferent to American signals. Richard Holbrooke, *To End a War*, rev. ed. (New York: Modern Library, Random House, 1999), also reports communications between Holbrooke, the chief U.S. emissary in the Balkans, and the ICTY prosecutor. These included Holbrooke's pressing for a particular indictment of a Bosnian Serb militia leader who was subsequently indicted (190), and his protesting of particular arrests on ICTY warrants of two Serb military officers subsequently released (332–33). A subsequent prosecutor decided that the right moment to indict Milosevic was just when NATO forces were in the second month of a bombing campaign against Serbia, to force him to accept a NATO autonomy plan for Kosovo. The prosecutor was rather quick thereafter to dismiss charges that NATO bombing patterns had, in themselves, violated laws of war. The point is not that the ICTY was simply a pawn in the hands of Western governments, but that it certainly seemed attentive to the priorities of the governments that created and funded it. There is every reason to

assume the ICC will respond with similar attentiveness to the priorities of its chief creators and funders—though these governments will not need to take responsibility for anything the ICC prosecutor does.

Chapter 4: Holy Empire of Human Rights

1. See, e.g., Louis Henkin, Gerald Neuman, Diane Orentlicher, and David Leebron, *Human Rights* (New York: Foundation Press, 1999), which treats American constitutional traditions as following in the same currents as contemporary international human rights law. The first American court ruling to associate international human rights standards with the "law of nations" was *Filartiga v. Pena-Irala*, discussed below.

2. William Blackstone, *Commentaries on the Laws of England*, facsimile of 1769 edition, bk. 4, chap. 5 (Chicago: University of Chicago Press, 1979), in which the need to punish such "offenses" with "becoming severity" was explained as arising from the hope that, in this way, "the peace of the world may be maintained," since by failing to punish, "the sovereign then avows himself an accomplice or abetter of his subject's crime and draws upon his community the calamities of foreign war." (bk. 4, 68).

3. Bentham explained, "[W]ere it not for the force of custom, [the term] law of nations . . . would seem rather to refer to internal jurisprudence," whereas the new coinage would eliminate such ambiguity. See "Introduction to the Principles of Morals and Legislation," in *A Fragment of Government and Introduction to the Principles*, ed. Wilfred Harrison (Oxford: Basil Blackwell, 1960), 426.

4. Wheaton, *Elements of International Law*, defining "international law" as "rules of conduct . . . among independent nations" and emphasizing that the new term ("international law") gained currency as a way of distinguishing such law from that obtaining within states (pt. 1, sec. 12, 14), 20, 23.

5. A European commentator captures the point by describing the implications of international human rights law and comparable projects in "international social justice" as a "Copernican revolution in the fundamental outlook of international law." Otto Kimminich, "History of the Law of Nations Since World War II," in *Encyclopedia of Public International Law* (Amsterdam: Elsevier, 1995), 2:850–51.

6. It thus remained a disputed question whether international arbitration commissions should calculate awards with an eye to adequate compensation for the injured individuals (to "make them whole," in the way a domestic court might seek to do) or instead to calibrate awards to the level of offense given to the home state. The question seems to have arisen in a number of cases in the 1920s, in which claims commissions tried to determine awards to the United States for the death of American citizens which resulted from negligence rather than deliberate malice by Mexican authorities. Commission awards seem to have

shied away from making the Mexican government liable for full "damages" in such cases. See Clyde Eagleton, "Measure of Damages in International Law," *Yale Law Journal* 39 (1929): 52–75.

7. UN Charter, art. 13, par. 1(b) ("General Assembly shall initiate studies and make recommendations for the purpose of . . . assisting in the realization of human rights and fundamental freedoms"); art. 55, par. 3 ("United Nations shall promote . . . universal respect for, and observance of, human rights and fundamental freedoms"); art. 62, par. 2 ("Economic and Social Council may make recommendations for the purpose of promoting respect for, and observance of, human rights and fundamental freedoms.")

8. A number of communist governments accordingly voted for the Declaration, while the Soviet Union abstained in the final vote. Only South Africa and Saudi Arabia found any provisions of the declaration sufficiently disturbing to cast negative votes in the final balloting in the General Assembly.

9. Jane Connors, "Analysis of the System of State Reporting," in *The UN Human Rights Treaty System in the 21st Century*, ed. Anne F. Bayefsky (The Hague: Kluwer Law International, 2000), 8–9, noting that two-thirds of states failed to meet reporting obligations in 1999 and many reports that were submitted were too cursory to be useful.

10. *Federalist* 64, p. 362: "A treaty is only another name for a bargain. . . ."; *Federalist* 75, p. 418: "The power of making treaties . . . relates neither to the execution of subsisting laws nor to the enaction of new ones. . . . Its objects are CONTRACTS [original emphasis] with foreign nations. . . ."

11. Jefferson's *Manual of Parliamentary Practice* (1801; repr., Washington, D.C.: Government Printing Office, 1993), 97, stipulates that treaties must "concern the foreign nation, party to the contract" and embrace "only those objects which are usually regulated by treaty." This restriction of the treaty power was repeatedly acknowledged by decisions of the Supreme Court. In deference to such authorities, Lawrence H. Tribe acknowledges in *American Constitutional Law*, 646, n. 16, that treaties are "legitimate only for international agreements related genuinely and not just pretextually to foreign relations. . . . The President and Senate could not, for example, circumvent the House of Representatives by creating a fully operating national health care system in the United States by 'treaty' with Canada—although establishment of a joint, binational health care system by a treaty followed by implementing legislation would presumably be possible." If both houses of Congress approved such implementing legislation, under the normal legislative process, it might not seem to matter whether such a background treaty were in itself constitutional. But as Tribe recognizes, there remains a question whether the existence of a treaty could give Congress broader legislative powers than those enumerated in art. 1, sec. 8 of the Constitution: "If, as the Supreme Court has held, the Commerce Clause does not empower Congress to criminalize all gun possession near schools, it is at least arguable that such power

could not suddenly arise from a U.S.-Mexico treaty imposing on each of the signatory nations a free-standing duty to make every possible effort to eliminate guns from the vicinity of schools—at least absent findings, for example, about the relationship between guns near schools and cross border drug traffic." Tribe immediately notices the implications of this line of reasoning for human rights conventions and promptly continues with this disclaimer: "In contrast, human rights treaties imposing on all signatory nations a duty to adhere to specified norms of freedom, equality and decent treatment seem closely enough linked to the effective and humane operation of the international order—for example, by establishing norms of sovereign conduct likely to guarantee humane treatment of persons traveling in foreign lands and thereby to foster international travel, commerce and cooperation—that there would seem to be no comparable danger that the treaty power might be used in this context as a pretext to swell Congress's authority beyond the realm of foreign affairs." This analysis hardly answers the challenge. Human rights treaties do not protect foreign travelers in particular. They purport to protect everyone. If it is encouraging to foreign travelers to know that there will be full human rights protection for every citizen in countries to which they travel, it might just as easily encourage foreign travelers to know that guns will be removed from the vicinity of schools in the countries to which they travel. To put the objection more directly: Is it more likely that advocates for U.S. ratification of CEDAW are concerned about establishing feminist policy preferences—such as government-sponsored day care facilities—in Saudi Arabia or in the United States? Contrary to Tribe's disclaimer, it seems entirely reasonable to worry about the "danger" that so-called "treaties" regarding "human rights" will "be used as a pretext to swell Congress's authority beyond the realm of foreign affairs."

12. Oona A. Hathaway, "Do Human Rights Treaties Make a Difference?" *Yale Law Journal* 111 (June 2002): 1935–2043.

13. Vienna Convention on the Law of Treaties, art. 19(c). This provision sought to codify the compromise offered by the International Court of Justice in its "Advisory Opinion on Reservations to the Convention on the Prevention and Punishment of the Crime of Genocide," 1951 I.C.J. 15 (1951). The ICJ recognized there that the usual practice, requiring the consent of all parties to reservations made by any one party, was "inspired by the notion of contract and is of undisputed value as a principle." But the majority opinion urged a more flexible approach in relation to human rights conventions since "in a convention of this type, one cannot speak of individual advantages or disadvantages to States or of the maintenance of a perfect contractual balance between rights and duties. The high ideals which inspired the Convention provide . . . the foundation and measure of all its provisions. The object and purpose of the Genocide Convention imply that it was the intention of the General Assembly and of the States which adopted it that as many States as possible should participate. The complete

exclusion from the Convention of one or more States would not only restrict the scope of its application but would detract from the authority of the moral and humanitarian principles which are its basis." Dissenting justices protested this logic at the time. The majority sought to balance its concern for "inclusiveness" against dangers of fraudulent ratification by insisting that ratification with unilateral reservations should be accepted as bona fide if the reservations were not inconsistent with the "object and purpose" of the convention.

14. Belinda Clark, "The Vienna Convention Reservations Regime and the Convention on Sex Discrimination," *American Journal of International Law* 85 (1991): 281.

15. At the meeting of the monitoring committee for the Convention Against Torture, held on May 23, 2002, the Saudi delegate, Mr. Al-Madi, protested the committee's criticism of "the imposition of corporal punishments such as flogging and amputation of limbs by Saudi Arabia's judicial and administrative authorities. The Committee thereby presumed to impugn the 1,400-year-old beliefs of Saudi Arabia. It is not within the Committee's mandate to do so." Committee on Torture, "Summary Record," (Geneva, May 23, 2002), par. 8. The matter was left as a standoff. See Committee against Torture, Concluding Observations (Saudi Arabia, December 6, 2002).

16. The episode is reported in some detail in Steiner and Alston, *International Human Rights in Context,* 634–40.

17. This "most unparalleled and astonishing transaction" is recounted, with much indignation, in Blackstone, *Commentaries,* bk. 4, ch. 8, 107: "[P]ope Innocent III had at length the effrontery to demand, and king John had the meanness to consent to, a resignation of his crown to the pope, whereby England was to become for ever St Peter's patrimony; and the dastardly monarch reaccepted his sceptre from the hands of the papal legate, to hold as the vassal of the holy see, at the annual rent of a thousand marks."

18. Leland M. Goodrich, Edward Hambro, and Anne Patricia Simons, *Charter of the United Nations* (New York: Columbia University Press, 1969), 443–46.

19. William Korey, *NGOs and the Universal Declaration of Human Rights,* chap. 2 (New York: St. Martin's Press, 1998).

20. Declaration on the Establishment of a New International Economic Order (adopted by the General Assembly on May 1, 1974) and Resolution 3202, Programme of Action on the Establishment of a New International Economic Order, reprinted at I.L.M. 13 (1974): 715, 720.

21. Myres McDougall, Harold Lasswell, and Lung-Chu Chen, *Human Rights and World Public Order* (New Haven, Conn.: Yale University Press, 1980), 272–75, claiming (with extensive citations to scholarly literature on the point) that resolutions of the General Assembly could be regarded as "instantaneous customary law" and "quasi-legislation."

22. *Filartiga v. Pena-Irala,* 630 F.2d 876 (1980).

23. *Restatement of Foreign Relations Law*, 3rd, sec. 702, comment a., 161–67. Elsewhere, *Restatement* notes that 28 U.S.C. sec. 1331 gives U.S. district courts original jurisdiction "of all civil actions arising under the Constitution, laws and treaties of the United States." The *Restatement* then observes that claims "arising under customary international law also arise under the 'laws of the United States,' since international law is 'part of our law'" (sec. 111, n. 4, 50–53).

24. *Kadic v. Karadzic*, 70 F.3d 232 (2d Cir. 1995) [on Bosnia]; *Beanal v. Freeport-McMoRan, Inc.*, 969 F. Supp. 362 (E.D. La. 1997) [on Indonesia]; *Doe v. Unicol*, 963 F. Supp. 880 (C.D. Cal. 1997) [on Burma]; *Aguinda v. Texaco*, 850 F. Supp. 282 (S.D.N.Y. 1994) [on Ecuador].

25. Louis Sohn, "Sources of International Law," *Georgia Journal of International and Comparative Law* 2 (1995–96): 399.

26. Boutros Boutros-Ghali, "Foreword," in *NGOs, The UN and Global Governance*, eds. Thomas Weiss and Leon Gordenker (Boulder, Colo.: Lynne Riemer, 1996), 11.

27. Kofi Annan, "Full Implementation and Enforcement of International Law Rooted in Shared Global Values," Speech of February 11, 2000, http://www.un.org/News/Press/docs/2000/20000211.sgsm7299.doc.html.

28. Original decision: *Regina v. Bow Street Magistrate*, 3 W.L.R. 1456 (1998); subsequent decision: *Regina v. Bow Street Magistrate*, 2 W.L.R. 827 (1999). Where the subsequent decision relied solely on the Convention Against Torture and then only for the brief period after both Chile and the United Kingdom had ratified, the earlier decision invoked "international law" principles that had "by the time of the 1973 coup and certainly ever since . . . condemned genocide, torture, hostage taking and crimes against humanity . . . as international crimes deserving of punishment" (opinion of Lord Steyn, 1506).

29. The scheme adopted for the ICC allows victims or their representatives to share some of the prosecutor's authority to help move the Court toward decisions to prosecute. Article 15 authorizes the prosecutor, when deciding to investigate possible crimes, to seek "additional information" from "non-governmental organizations or other reliable sources" (par. 2), and then authorizes "victims" to "make representations to the Pre-Trial Chamber" (par. 3), which approves decisions to prosecute. If there is a challenge to the exercise of the Court's jurisdiction in a particular case, Article 19 authorizes "victims" to "submit observations to the Court" (par. 3) regarding the issues in dispute—in addition to the arguments submitted by the prosecutor. Most tellingly, if the prosecutor decides not to proceed to a prosecution in a particular case, this decision must be confirmed by the Pre-Trial Chamber (art. 53, par. 3b). Under the subsequently adopted Rules of Procedure, outside advocacy groups are assured the opportunity to challenge the prosecutor's decision not to prosecute in a particular case. Rule 50 instructs the prosecutor to "give notice" to "victims" or "their legal representatives" before seeking the Pre-Trial Chamber's "authorization to initiate an investigation" (par. 1);

"victims" are then authorized to make their own "representations in writing" to the Chamber (par. 3), and the Chamber may then "request additional information from any of the victims" who have filed such submissions (par. 4). If the prosecutor decides not to pursue the case, Rule 92 then requires victims to be notified "in order to allow victims to apply for participation" in subsequent "proceedings" before the Chamber on whether to approve the decision not to prosecute. The ICC's Rules of Procedure and Evidence are posted on its website: www.icc-cpi.int/library/basicdocs.

30. See Stephen Macedo, ed., *Princeton Principles on Universal Jurisdiction* (Princeton University, Project on Universal Jurisdiction, 2001), 49, n. 20, reporting the partial dissent of Lord Browne-Wilkinson from the consensus of other international legal scholars, who endorsed this broad argument for asserting the jurisdiction of all states to arrest and try anyone, from any state, who might be guilty of extreme human rights abuses. Lord Browne-Wilkinson cautioned that such assertions of universal jurisdiction should only be attempted "with the prior consent" of the home state of the accused. Without this limitation, he warned, "zealots in Western states might launch prosecutions against, for example, Islamic extremists for their terrorist activities. It is naive to think that, in such cases, the national state of the accused would stand by and watch the trial proceed: resort to force would be more probable." Browne-Wilkinson was one of the judges in the House of Lords who endorsed the arrest and extradition of Chilean President Pinochet—on the grounds that Chile, without knowing it, had agreed to such a prosecution when it ratified (under Pinochet's government) the UN Convention Against Torture. As notable as his refusal to extend the precedent to "Islamic extremists" is his characterization of those who might seek to prosecute their "terrorist activities" as "zealots." The *Princeton Principles* have been posted on the website of the Urban Morgan Institute for Human Rights, at www.law.uc.edu/morgan/newdir/univjuris.html.

31. Glenn Frankel, "Belgian War Crimes Law Undone by Global Reach," *Washington Post*, September 30, 2003, A01.

32. American Serviceman's Protection Act, S. Amdt. 2336 (to H.R. 3338), 107th Cong., 1st sess., approved 78 to 21 in the Senate on December 7, 2001.

33. Among the proponents of this amendment were leaders of the American Bar Association and leading scholars of international law. See George Finch, "The Need to Restrain the Treaty Making Power of the United States within Constitutional Limits," *American Journal of International Law* 48 (1954): 57. Finch was a former editor of the *AJIL*. See also Frank Holman, *The Story of the Bricker Amendment* (New York: Committee for Constitutional Government, 1954), warning against proposals to "use the United Nations and the treaty process as a lawmaking process to change the domestic laws and even the Government of the United States . . . along socialist lines." Holman was a past president of the ABA and a former law school dean.

34. U.S. Reservations, Understandings, and Declarations to the ICCPR: I. (1), reprinted at 138 Cong. Rec. S 4781-01 (1992).

35. Gerald Neuman, "The Global Dimensions of RFRA," *Constitutional Commentaries* 14 (1997): 33, arguing, after the Supreme Court's rejection of a federal statute imposing new demands on state and local governments in the name of religious freedom, that the statute could still be sustained if regarded as necessary to implement U.S. obligations under the Covenant on Civil and Political Rights. See also Jordan Paust, "Rereading the First Amendment in Light of Treaties Proscribing Incitement to Racial Discrimination or Hostility," *Rutgers Law Review* 43 (1991): 565.

36. UN Human Rights Committee, General Comment No. 24 of Human Rights Committee, CCPR/C/21/Rev.1/ Add. 6, November 2, 1994, reprinted (in relevant part) in Steiner and Alston, *Human Rights in Context*, 1044–47. The U.S. response (rejecting the claim) is reprinted in *Human Rights Law Journal* 16 (1995): 422.

37. Robert H. Bork, *Coercing Virtue: The Worldwide Rule of Judges* (Washington, D.C.: AEI Press, 2003), 137.

38. See *Atkins v. Virginia*, 536 U.S. 304 at 316-17, n. 21, citing "brief for European Union as *amicus curiae*" for the proposition that "within the world community, the imposition of the death penalty for crimes committed by mentally retarded offenders is overwhelmingly disapproved."

39. *Atkins v. Virginia*, 536 U.S. 304 (2002); *Lawrence v. Texas*, 123 S. Ct. 2472 (2003).

40. *Atkins v. Virginia*, 348. In an earlier case, in which the Supreme Court cited a survey by Amnesty International on policies toward capital punishment in other countries, Scalia admonished: "We must never forget that it is a Constitution for the United States of America that we are expounding. . . . When there is not first a settled consensus among our own people, the views of other nations, however enlightened the justices of this Court may think them to be, cannot be imposed upon Americans through the Constitution." *Thompson v. Oklahoma*, 487 U.S. 815 (1988), 868–69.

41. " . . . the United States is out of step with other democracies . . . and in this aspect 'undemocratic.'" "Death is not Justice," Report by the Council of Europe (Strasbourg, June 2001).

42. On the origins and development of the European regulations in this area, see Steven Rhoads, *Incomparable Worth: Pay Equity Meets the Market* (New York: Cambridge University Press, 1993), 130–47.

43. For example, CEDAW Committee, "Concluding Observations—Belarus," January 31, 2000, par. 361, complaining about perpetuation of stereotyping through such practices as the celebration of Mother's Day. Other observers have noted somewhat more pressing human rights abuses in Belarus.

44. For a review of the resulting controversy, see Dave Kopel, "U.N. Out of North America," *National Review*, August 9, 2001.

45. Emmerich de Vattel, in the mid-eighteenth century, insisted that "no foreign State may inquire into the manner in which a sovereign rules, nor set itself up as a judge of his conduct, nor force him to make any change in his administration. If he burdens his subjects with taxes or treats them with severity it is for the Nation [that is, the subjects of the abusive government] to take action; no foreign State is called on to amend his conduct and to force him to follow a wiser and juster course." But he conceded that "if a prince . . . by his insupportable tyranny, . . . brings on a national revolt against him, any foreign power may rightfully give assistance to an oppressed people who ask for its aid." *Droit des Gens*, bk. 2, chap. 4, sec. 55–56, 131. By the early twentieth century, a leading British scholar insisted that humanitarian interventions by outside powers were clearly contrary to accepted rule of international law, even if they "may laudably be ignored once or twice in a generation. . . . An intervention to put a stop to barbarous and abominable cruelty is a question rather of policy than of law. It is above and beyond the domain of law. It is destitute of technical legality, but it may be morally right and even praiseworthy to a high degree." Lawrence, *Principles of International Law*, sec. 66, 127–28. Even those who argued, after the NATO intervention in Kosovo, that international law should give recognition to humanitarian intervention in some cases, acknowledged that this was not yet the accepted understanding of international law; see, e.g., Antonio Cassese, "Is International Legitimation of Forcible Humanitarian Countermeasures Taking Shape in the World Community?" *European Journal of International Law* 10 (1999): 22–30, which begins with a demonstration that armed intervention for humanitarian ends was "contrary to current international law" as of the time of the Kosovo intervention (25).

46. A massacre of over 100,000 Rwandans—this time, Tutsis killing Hutus—in the early 1970s sparked no interest at all from the United Nations. For an account of the episode, see Stanley Meisler, *The United Nations: The First Fifty Years* (New York: Atlantic Monthly Press, 1995), 210.

47. Korey, *NGOs and the Universal Declaration of Human Rights*, 169, also noting that AI, founded in 1961, did not issue a long report on political prisoners in the Soviet Union until 1975, and that the organization's "non-involvement" in human rights advocacy for Soviet victims during the 1970s and 1980s "was striking."

48. "Council of Europe Urges U.S., Japan to End Death Penalty," *Agence France-Press*, June 5, 2001.

49. Michael BeDan, "Amnesty International Seeks Support on the Mall," *Rocky Mountain News*, October 26, 2002 (reporting on a three-day annual conference of Amnesty International USA in Denver, "kicked off" by a public rally on behalf of U.S. ratification of CEDAW).

50. Ronald Inglehart and Pippa Norris, "The True Clash of Civilizations," *Foreign Policy* (March/April 2003): 62, report survey findings that people in

Muslim nations do express support for democracy but generally reject prevalent Western attitudes toward divorce, abortion, gender equality, and gay rights. There would seem to be much more potential for human rights advocacy to focus on shared values than these most divisive issues.

51. For an academic survey defending the claim that economic and social rights must not be separated from civil and political rights, see Jack Donnelly, *Universal Human Rights in Theory and Practice* (Ithaca, N.Y.: Cornell University Press, 1989).

52. Ben Russell, "Blair Comes Under Fire Over Graphic Dossier on Saddam's Brutality," *The Independent* (UK), December 3, 2002 ("Amnesty International . . . spokesman said: 'We are concerned about . . . political opportunism'"). As war approached, AI protested that while President Bush "prepares his country for war, [he] has maintained his support for killing at home"—by allowing a scheduled execution of a convicted murderer in Indiana to go forward. Amnesty International, Press Release, March 18, 2003. Human Rights Watch (which, in contrast to Amesty, had supported the NATO war against Serbia in 1999) followed up with a sizable document, purporting to demonstrate that the war in Iraq could not be justified as a humanitarian intervention and was therefore contrary to international law (Human Rights Watch, "War in Iraq: Not a Humanitarian Intervention," *World Report*, 2004).

53. Amnesty International's position paper on Palestinian suicide bomber operations was not issued until July 2002—nearly two years after the onset of the bombing campaign (Amnesty International, "Without distinction—attacks on civilians by Palestinian armed groups," AI Index: MDE 02/03/2002). Human Rights Watch took even more time to weigh in with a full report (Human Rights Watch, "Erased in a Moment: Suicide Bombing Attacks Against Israeli Civilians," November 1, 2002, HRW Index 2807). Human Rights Watch issued twelve critical reports on Israeli occupation that year to balance this one report. Both organizations issued extended denunciations of Israel's efforts to construct a defensive barrier against infiltration by terrorists. Israel was told, in effect, to seek security by relying on human rights advocates to provide verbal admonitions against terror attacks. Meanwhile, both AI and Human Rights Watch championed international conferences to address the ostensible illegality of the Israeli crime of allowing Jews to settle in the old city of Jerusalem, already the subject of several resolutions of the General Assembly and the UN Human Rights Commission by the late 1990s. See David P. Forsythe, *Human Rights in International Relations* (Cambridge: Cambridge University Press, 2000), 169, for a brief account of AI's "bitterly" angry reaction, when an international conference, the first ever convened to address specific violations of Geneva Conventions, adjourned without issuing a condemnation of Israel's occupation policies. For some reason, neither Amnesty International nor Human Rights Watch urged the UN to address the subject of suicide bombing attacks, which have never, in fact, been clearly condemned in any UN resolution. Human Rights Watch took the trouble to notify all

participants in the Camp David peace talks, while the negotiations were in their last rounds, that a peace agreement must guarantee the right of all Palestinians to return to Israel and not only the proposed new Palestinian state. "Israel, Palestinian Leaders Should Guarantee Right of Return as Part of Comprehensive Refugee Solution," Press Release (New York, December 22, 2000). Amnesty International took the same position, released a few weeks later. "The Right to Return: The Case of the Palestinians," March 30, 2001, MDE 15/013/2001.

54. For broad surveys of actual experience, with rationales for different approaches, see Martha Minow, *Between Vengeance and Forgiveness* (Boston: Beacon Press, 1998); and A. James McAdams, *Transitional Justice and the Rule of Law in New Democracies* (Notre Dame, Ind.: University of Notre Dame Press, 1997).

55. The preamble to the ICC Statute includes a provision "[r]ecalling that it is the duty of every State to exercise its criminal jurisdiction over those responsible for international crimes"—with no qualification of this "duty" (par. 6).

56. Kant offers this motto at the end of the first appendix to his essay on "Perpetual Peace," where he describes the saying as "true, albeit somewhat boastful" and defends it as "a sound principle of right that cuts across the sinuous paths of deceit and power." Immanuel Kant, *Perpetual Peace and Other Essays*, trans. Ted Humphrey (Indianapolis: Hackett Publishing Co., 1983), 133.

Chapter 5: Trade Rights and Sovereignty

1. See, e.g., John Jackson, "The WTO Constitution and Proposed Reforms: Seven 'Mantras' Revisited," *Journal of International Economic Law* 4 (March 2001): 67, insisting that concerns about "national sovereignty" are a mere "mantra," which is "used to avoid thinking certain issues through." He identifies the relevant issue as, "How do you want to allocate power? What decisions do you want made in Geneva, Washington, Sacramento, California or a neighborhood in Berkeley? By viewing it as a decision about how to allocate power, we can disaggregate the question of sovereignty and make people think about how to correctly design that allocation." By viewing it this way, we can also abstract from the fact that our national Constitution already establishes certain "allocations" and does not permit them to be reallocated by treaty. We can further abstract from the political question of whether U.S. law will claim equal loyalty or respect if it is made in pursuance of our historic Constitution or by whatever arrangement happens to appeal to thinkers who favor disaggregating issues in different ways. And, finally, we can abstract from the awkward fact that people disagree on what policy is best and don't readily submit to those they dislike just because some trade experts have decided these are good policies.

2. Initially published in 1568 as *La Réponse de Maistre Jean Bodin Avocat en la cour au paradoxe de Monsieur de Malestroict*; then republished in 1578 as *Discours de Jean Bodin sur le rehausement et diminution des monnoyes*, enlarged with extensive

extracts from *Six Livres de la République* (bk. 6, ch. 3, on the same subject). An English translation of the expanded edition, by Henry Tudor and R. W. Dyson, has recently appeared as *Response to the Paradoxes of Malestroit* (Bristol, England: Thoemmes Press, 1997), with an extended introduction indicating the importance of the work in the history of economic theory.

3. Adam Smith, *Wealth of Nations*, eds. R. H. Campbell and W. B. Todd. (Oxford: Clarendon Press, 1976), bk. 5, ch. 1, p. 707.

4. Ibid., bk. 4, ch. 9, p. 687.

5. Articles of Confederation, art. 6, par. 3: "No State shall lay any imposts or duties which may interfere with any stipulations in treaties . . . already proposed by Congress to the courts of France and Spain."

6. "Report on Manufactures," in Hamilton, *Writings*, 667–69: "If the system of perfect liberty to industry and commerce were the prevailing system of nations . . . each country would have the full benefits of its peculiar advantages to compensate for its deficiencies or disadvantages. . . . But the . . . general policy of Nations . . . has been regulated by an opposite spirit. . . . If Europe will not take from us the products of our soil, upon terms consistent with our interest, the natural remedy is to contract as fast as possible our wants of her." Hamilton urged government assistance, through protective tariffs and other devices, to reassure investors regarding "any project which is new, and for that reason alone, if, for no other, precarious." But the argument as he posed it was for the development of industry in the United States and should therefore be aimed at "sagacious capitalists both citizens and foreigners" (671). On similar grounds, Adam Smith defended the policy of bestowing trade monopolies "for a certain number of years" on companies establishing outposts in "distant and barbarous countries" and needing "recompense" for "hazarding a dangerous and expensive experiment, of which the publick is afterwards to reap the benefit." Adam Smith, *Wealth of Nations*, bk. 5, ch. 1, 754.

7. Keith Whittington, *Constitutional Construction* (Cambridge: Harvard University Press, 1999), 100–106, tracing this understanding to the political settlement following South Carolina's threat to "nullify" the protective tariff measure adopted in 1828.

8. John Quincy Adams, "Instructions to Mr. Anderson, Minister to Colombia," May 27, 1823, reprinted in *The American Diplomatic Code*, ed. Jonathan Elliot (Washington: J. Elliot, Jr., 1835), 652–53. Adams defined the "most liberal of principles" as "placing the foreigner, in regard to all objects of navigation and commerce, upon a footing of equal favor with the native citizen, and to that end, of abolishing all discriminating duties and charges whatsoever." But he warned that "while two maritime and commercial nations should bind themselves to it as a compact operative only between them, a third Power might avail itself of its own restrictive and discriminating regulations, to secure advantages to its own People, at the expense of both the parties to the treaty." Accordingly, "the fairness" of the "liberal principle . . . depends upon its being admitted universally."

9. Ibid., 653.

10. The idea that trade could be protected amid conflict was not so visionary for someone (like Adams) who was familiar with eighteenth-century practice. European states often allowed trade to continue during wartime—even with opposing belligerents. Britain even allowed insurance companies to offer coverage to enemy vessels, and to compensate enemy owners for damage inflicted by the Royal Navy. The Dutch commentator Cornelius van Bynkershoek noted in 1737 that "the interests of the mercantile class and the mutual needs of peoples have almost annulled the laws of war relating to commerce." Stephen C. Neff, *Friends But No Allies: Economic Liberalism and the Law of Nations* (New York: Columbia University Press, 1990), 33–34.

11. The wording of the First Amendment, barring Congress from making any law "prohibiting the free exercise" of religion, allows no exceptions for international diplomacy. When the United States was provoked by a decision of the pope prohibiting Protestant worship in Rome in the 1840s, it withdrew diplomatic envoys to the Vatican, but it seems never to have considered the notion of retaliating by prohibiting Catholic worship in Washington.

12. U.S. Constitution, art. 1, sec. 9, par. 5: "No Tax or Duty shall be laid on Articles exported from any State"; art. 1, sec. 9, par. 6: "No Preference shall be given by any Regulation of Commerce or Revenue to the Ports of one State over those of another."

13. For a contemporary account, see J. Laurence Laughlin and H. Parker Willis, *Reciprocity* (New York: Baker & Taylor, 1903), which concludes that "there is nothing to be expected in a general and far reaching way from the policy" (435).

14. *Field v. Clark*, 143 U.S. 649 (1890), which upheld such reciprocal agreements as similar in principle to the arrangement in *The Brig Aurora*, 7 Cranch 382 (1813), in which the Supreme Court approved a statutory scheme allowing the president to lift trade sanctions on either France or Britain, when conditions specified in the statute were determined by the president to have come into effect. *J. W. Hampton & Co. v. United States*, 276 U.S. 394 (1928) approved a provision of the Tariff Act of 1922 which directed the president to increase tariff rates as necessary to "equalize . . . differences in costs of production in the United States and the principal competing country."

15. Moore, *Principles of American Diplomacy*, 160.

16. Harold James, *The End of Globalization: Lessons of the Great Depression* (Cambridge, Mass.: Harvard University Press, 2001), 132–38, offers a useful overview.

17. Conflict between tariff reduction efforts and other New Deal policies was obvious at the time to students of trade policy; see Henry J. Tasca, *The Reciprocal Trade Policy of the United States: A Study in Trade Philosophy* (Philadelphia: University of Pennsylvania Press, 1938), esp. 82–98.

18. Richard N. Gardner, *Sterling-Dollar Diplomacy* (Oxford: Clarendon Press, 1956), 371–78, notes that much criticism against the ITO in the United States focused on its seeming endorsement of restrictions on investment and its seeming

accommodation of currency controls and other restrictions on trade, apart from tariffs.

19. John H. Jackson, *The World Trade Organization: Constitution and Jurisprudence* (London: Royal Institute of International Affairs, 1998), 67, notes that the GATT council authorized retaliation in only one case (arising from a complaint of the Netherlands against the United States), and that the right to retaliate was not actually exercised in that case, though the offending policy (of the United States) was not changed.

20. Robert E. Hudec, *The GATT Legal System and World Trade Diplomacy*, 2nd ed. (Salem, N.H.: Butterworth, 1990), 55–56.

21. UN General Assembly, "Permanent Sovereignty over Natural Resources," Resolution No. 2158 (XXI), November 25, 1966, followed by UN General Assembly, "Permanent Sovereignty over Natural Resources," Resolution 3171 (XXVIII), December 17, 1973, reprinted in I.L.M. 13 (1974): 238.

22. See Declaration on the Establishment of a New International Economic Order (adopted by the General Assembly on May 1, 1974) and Resolution 3202, Programme of Action on the Establishment of a New International Economic Order, reprinted in I.L.M. 13 (1974): 715, 720.

23. Neff, "Third World Plans for a Social Democratic World Order," chap. 7 in *Friends But No Allies*, 178–96.

24. UN Committee on Economic, Social and Cultural Rights, General Comment 3 (1990), U.N. Doc. HRI/GEN/1/Rev. 1, reprinted (in part) in Henkin et al., *Human Rights*, 1151–55.

25. "Convention on the Elimination of All Forms of Discrimination Against Women," reprinted in I.L.M. 19 (1989): 33. Article 11(d) admonishes state parties to "ensure, on the basis of equality of men and women . . . the right to equal remuneration . . . in respect of work of equal value. . . ." On European regulations implementing this concept, see Rhoads, *Incomparable Worth*, 130–47.

26. *Defrenne v. Sabena*, Case 80/70, 1971 E.C.R. 445, invoked ILO Convention No. 111 on Sex Discrimination in Employment to impose new obligations on the Belgian state airline, which subsequently helped trigger extensive regulations in this area by the European Commission.

27. "ILO Declaration on Fundamental Principles and Rights at Work," adopted at the 86th session of the International Labour Conference, June 1998, in Geneva.

28. As early as 1992, the European Parliament urged that European tariff rates should protect member states against "environmental dumping": Res. A3-0329.92. A report adopted by the European Parliament in 1996 called for new international controls "requiring international firms to conduct trade in an environmentally friendly manner." "European Parliament Adopts Report on Trade and Environ-ment," *Europe Environment*, no. 478, May 31, 1996.

29. Marc Pallemaerts, "International Environmental Law from Stockholm to Rio: Back to the Future?" in *The Greening of International Law*, ed. Phillippe Sands (New York: New Press, 1994), shows the greater concessions to "development" demanded by developing countries in 1992, as compared with twenty years before.

30. To put the level of risk in perspective, it is worth noting the calculation of British health officials on the eve of the Montreal conference, that even if the worst of "the postulated ozone depletion did occur, it would result in increased exposure [to UV-B radiation] equivalent to a person moving from northern to southern England" (since such radiation is more intense, the closer one moves to the equator). The chief American negotiator for the Montreal Protocol subsequently reported this claim, without disputing its validity, but insisted on "the distinction between a voluntary move made with no knowledge of radiation consequences and the involuntary subjection of entire populations to known increases." Richard Benedick, *Ozone Diplomacy: New Directions in Safeguarding the Planet* (Cambridge, Mass.: Harvard University Press, 1991), 38. A study by the World Bank estimated the cost of eliminating ozone-depleting substances in China alone would reach $1.4 billion by 2010. Ian Rowlands, *The Politics of Global Atmosphere Change* (Manchester, UK: Manchester University Press, 1995), 184. By the end of 1998, the Multilateral Fund, organized by parties to the Montreal Protocol to assist developing countries to comply, had authorized only $20 million for China (and $220 million for all countries eligible). Ironically, the main chemical compounds used to replace CFCs in the 1980s, hydrochlorofluorides, were subsequently suspected of contributing to global warming, and environmental advocates urged bans on these chemicals as well, without countenancing a return to CFCs.

31. The cartel character is apparent from the fact that both Israel and Monaco were excluded from participation, though neither lacks the wealth or sophistication to handle recycling.

32. Jonathan Adler, "The Precautionary Principle's Challenge to Progress," in *Global Warming and Other Eco-Myths*, ed. Ronald Bailey (Roseville, Calif.: Prima Publishing, 2002), 265–91.

33. Gregory Conko and C. S. Prakash, "The Attack on Plant Biotechnology," in ibid., 171–217.

34. Calculated from figures in the World Bank's *World Development Report, 2000/2001* (New York: Oxford University Press, 2001), 292–93. To put the comparison less abstractly: On a per-capita basis, China's electric power consumption in 1998 was a mere 6 percent of per-capita electric use in the United States. World Bank, *World Development Indicators* (New York: Oxford University Press, 2001), 302–4. In the same year, the United States had one passenger car for every two people, while China had one for every 250 people. *The World Today*, ed. Barry Turner (New York: St. Martin's Press, 2000), 187.

35. The argument is well-developed, with useful illustrations, in Thomas Schelling, *Costs and Benefits of Greenhouse Gas Reduction* (Washington, D.C.: AEI Press, 1999).

36. Hudec, *GATT Legal System*, 52–53. Even the procedure for referring disputes to expert panels was a subsequent improvisation rather than a formal provision in the original agreement of 1947.

37. Appellate Body, "United States, Standards on Reformulated Gasoline," WT/DS2/AB/R (May 20, 1996). As John Jackson comments: "[T]here has been some dispute about whether [the WTO] was a 'separate regime,' sort of sealed off from normal concepts of international law, but the AB explicitly states that the WTO is part of international law, and it goes on to engage international law principles of treaty interpretation very deeply, referring to the 'Vienna Convention on the Law of Treaties.'" Jackson, *World Trade Organization*, 89. Jackson notes that even the Statute of the International Court of Justice stipulates that rulings of the court will only be binding on the immediate parties to its rulings (art. 59), whereas the Dispute Settlement Understanding that established the WTO's Appellate Body does not include such a restriction. He reports that diplomats attributed this omission to an oversight (87). But the AB seems to be making the most of it. For an extended account of dangers this may pose, see Claude Barfield, *Free Trade, Sovereignty, Democracy* (Washington, D.C.: AEI, 2001), 45–69.

38. F. W. Taussig, *The Tariff History of the United States*, 8th rev. ed. (New York: Capricorn Books, 1964), 364, commenting on the tariff law of 1909, whose animating principle could be extrapolated to this: "that the more disadvantageous it is for a country to carry on an industry, the more desperate should be the effort to cause the industry to be established" (365). He goes on to note, in paraphrase of Adam Smith's famous remark about the growing of grapes in Scottish hothouses, that "very good pineapples can be grown in Maine, if only a duty be imposed sufficient to equalize the cost of production between the growers in Maine and those in more favored climes" (364).

39. The original GATT agreement of 1947 authorized countries to exclude goods produced by prison labor, in conformity with a prewar international convention banning trade in products of prison labor. By the 1970s, GATT rounds had imposed restrictions on various kinds of subsidies to export industries, so a receiving state could impose countervailing tariffs to protest improper subsidies to production in another country.

40. World Trade Organization, Appellate Body, "United States-Import Prohibition of Certain Shrimp and Shrimp Products," WT/DS58/AB/R (November 6, 1998).

41. World Trade Organization, Appellate Body, United States-Import Prohibition of Certain Shrimp and Shrimp Products," WT/DS58/AB/RW (November 21, 2001).

42. Clyde Haberman, "Japanese Are Special Types, They Explain," *New York Times*, March 6, 1988.

43. In fact, the GATT is not literally a treaty. It is an "agreement" (which was what put the "A" in GATT). It has never been ratified by two-thirds of the Senate in the manner of a formal treaty. For nearly three decades, tariffs established in successive GATT rounds simply rested on congressional authorization for the president to set lower tariffs by agreement—an authority periodically renewed from the Reciprocal Trade Agreements Act of 1934. Since 1976, Congress has given itself a more direct role: The president is authorized to negotiate new trade agreements that Congress (by majority vote in both houses) votes upon, with the self-imposed condition that it must vote within a restricted time period and accept or reject the agreement as a whole. The procedure was adopted after Congress delayed in enacting changes to nontariff measures agreed to in the Tokyo Round (involving reduction of domestic subsidies to exporters). Other countries then balked at entering a new round of negotiations, if the United States would not follow through on past commitments. The origins and operation of this system (with instructive foreign comparisons) are described in John H. Jackson, Jean-Victor Louis, and Mitsuo Matsushita, *Implementing the Tokyo Round: National Constitutions and International Trade Rules* (Ann Arbor: University of Michigan Press, 1984), 145–55. From the standpoint of other nations, however, trade agreements remain international agreements, regardless of the procedure by which the United States ratifies them. And the general scheme here is not at all exceptional. Kevin C. Kennedy, "Conditional Approval of Treaties by the U.S. Senate," *Loyola International and Comparative Law Journal* 19 (1996): 89, reports that of 12,000 international agreements entered by the United States between 1776 and 1986, only 10 percent were formal treaties ratified by the Senate. Loch K. Johnson, *The Making of International Agreements* (New York: New York University Press, 1984), 12–14, reports that of all agreements signed by the United States between 1946 and 1972, over 86 percent were cast as "congressional-executive agreements" and only 6 percent as formal treaties (with barely more than 7 percent resting on the sole authority of the president).

44. Robert O'Brien et al., *Contesting Global Governance,* 72, 83. (The official is not named, and the claim about labor organizations is the phrasing of the authors.)

45. Ibid., 84, citing ICTFU, *International Workers Rights and Trade: The Need for Dialogue* (Brussels, 1996).

46. Maastricht Guidelines and associated commentary published in *Human Rights Quarterly* 20 (1998): 691–730, quoted passage on 725.

47. "Integration of ILO Core Rights Labor Standards into the WTO," *Columbia Journal of Transnational Law* 39 (2001): 555; Robert Howse, "The WTO and Protection of Workers' Rights," *Journal of Small and Emerging Business Law*, 3 (1999): 131, relying on exemptions in art. 20 for measures "(a) necessary to protect public

morals; (b) necessary to protect human, animal or plant life or health; . . . (g) relating to the conservation of exhaustible natural resources . . ."; Steve Charnovitz, "The Moral Exception in Trade Policy," *Virginia Journal of International Law* 38 (1989): 689.

48. In a press release issued September 16, 2002, Friends of the Earth-Europe called on the European Commission to impose special duties on U.S. goods which were produced with energy-intensive production methods, arguing that such tariffs would be a legal and proper penalty for U.S. failure to ratify the Kyoto Protocol: "The US rejection of the Kyoto Protocol is unfair and puts European business at a disadvantage. With Bush's increasing rejection of international agreements that are essential to protect our environment, Europe should have every right to penalise US goods for the pollution they cause." The statement can be found at http://www.foeeurope.org/press/AW_16_09_02_GMOsynergy.htm.

49. See Alec Stone Sweet and Thomas L. Brunell, "Constructing a Supranational Constitution: Dispute Resolution and Governance in the European Community," *American Political Science Review* 92 (March 1998): 63

50. Notably, Ernst-Ulrich Petermann, *The GATT/WTO Dispute Settlement System* (London: Kluver International, 1997). Petermann, a "Legal Advisor to the WTO," sketches a broad vision of a world constitution in which the WTO plays a central role: "[T]hrough the traumatic experiences of World Wars I and II . . . governments finally learned to accept the need for worldwide constitutional rules (such as the prohibition of the use of force and collective security arrangements in the UN Charter) and their collective enforcement through international organisations (such as the UN and the Security Council). Not only within states but also among states do the limitation of government failures and the supply of 'public goods' depend on agreed procedures and institutions for rule-making, rule-application and rule-enforcement. . . ." (25–26). In a similar spirit, but with more precision: Joost Pauwelyn, "The Role of Public International Law in the WTO," *American Journal of International Law* 95 (2001): 535.

51. It has been argued that this procedure, by which Congress binds itself to approve and implement an agreement negotiated by the president, by simple majority vote, is already a departure from the scheme envisioned in the Constitution, by which treaties require two-thirds majority support in the Senate. For the most elaborate version of the argument, see Bruce Ackerman and David Golove, "Is NAFTA Constitutional?" *Harvard Law Review* 108, (1995): 801. But the scheme has been defended as consistent with authority granted to Congress in the Constitution "to regulate commerce with foreign nations" (art. 1, sec. 8, par. 3) and not, therefore, a precedent for a general refashioning of the treaty-power into an ordinary legislative process. John C. Yoo, "Laws as Treaties? The Constitutionality of Congressional-Executive Agreements," *Michigan Law Review* 99 (February 2001): 757.

52. Arguments for regarding AB rulings as legally binding are reviewed in Ronald Brand, "Direct Effect of International Economic Law in the United States and the European Union," *Northwestern Journal of International Law and Business* 17 (1997):

550–96; the contrary arguments are asserted in Judith Hippler Bello, "The WTO Dispute Settlement Understanding: Less is More," *American Journal of International Law* 90 (1996): 416–17.

53. There was not only a jump in the number of disputes pursued to panels, but a dramatic increase in the complexity and detail of the resulting "decisions." Where panels produced 86 pages of "findings" each year, during the last decade of the GATT, under the WTO, reports from panels exceeded 6,000 per year by 2000. Gregory Shaffer, *Defending Interests, Public-Private Partnership in WTO Litigation* (Washington, D.C.: Brookings Institution, 2001), 47–48.

54. See, for example, the position of Ernst-Ulrich Petersmann, former legal adviser to the WTO, calling for "constitutionalizing international trade principles," by elevating "the rights of an individual to trade freely with foreigners [to the level of] a fundamental human right," cited in Thomas Cottier and Krista Schefer, "The Relationship between World Trade Organization Law, National and Regional Law," *Journal of International Economic Law* 1 (1998): 94.

55. Quoted in William Greider, "The Real Cancun," *The Nation*, September 22, 2003, 13.

56. For a political analysis of the ECJ's success in drawing new constituencies into its orbit—which then served to block government efforts to restrain the court—see Alec Stone Sweet and Thomas L. Brunnell, "Constructing a Supranational Constitution: Dispute Resolution and Governance in the European Community," *American Political Science Review* 92 (March 1998): 63.

57. Starting with *U.S. v. Lopez*, 514 U.S. 549 (1995). Continuing in *City of Boerne v. Flores*, 521 U.S. 507 (1997); *U.S. v. Morrison*, 529 U.S. 598 (2000).

58. See David Vogel, *Trading Up* (Cambridge, Mass.: Harvard University Press, 1998), for a review of recent experience.

59. For background on the political interests in the dispute over the Foreign Sales Corporation tax provision, see Shaffer, *Defending Interests*, 73–74.

60. Robert O. Keohane and Joseph S. Nye, "Introduction," in *Governance in a Globalizing World*, eds. Joseph Nye and John Donahue (Washington, D.C.: Brookings Institution, 2000), 31–32, noting that the World Bank has been "relatively successful in co-opting NGOs," but acknowledging that they have made the bank "more beholden" to NGOs. The "green agenda" that has taken hold in the bank was the target of James M. Sheehan, *Global Greens, Inside the International Environmental Establishment* (Washington, D.C.: Capital Research Center, 1998), 143–58.

61. *WTO Dispute Settlement Review Commission Act*, S 16, 104th Cong., was referred to the Finance Committee; the counterpart, HR 3314 (sponsored by Representative Ralph Regula) was referred to the House Ways and Means Committee, Subcommittee on Trade. Neither bill came to a floor vote.

62. Lloyd Gruber, *Ruling the World: Power Politics and the Rise of Supranational Institutions*, ch. 6 (Princeton, N.J.: Princeton University Press, 2002), 166–67,

on NAFTA negotiations as a source of leverage in simultaneous U.S. negotiations over the Uruguay Round (that culminated in the founding of the WTO).

63. The problem was noticed under the earlier United States–Canada agreement from which NAFTA was later constructed: James Chen, "Appointments with Disaster: The Unconstitutionality of Binational Arbitral Review under the U.S.-Canada Free Trade Agreement," *Washington & Lee Law Review* 49 (1992): 1455. The arguments were noted in *Coalition for Competitive Trade v. Clinton*, 128 F.3d 761 (D.C. Cir. 1997), but jurisdictional issues prevented a decision on the merits.

64. The NAFTA side accords do not require the three participating nations to maintain the same labor or environmental standards. They require only that the participating nations enforce their own national standards. Or, to be precise, they require that they not engage in nonenforcement for the sake of securing some competitive advantage against another nation in NAFTA. The accords do not even prohibit national legislatures from adopting changes in national laws that would weaken or reduce the previous level of protections for labor and the environment. The accords simply prohibit the exercise of administrative discretion in the enforcement of existing national laws for improper purposes (that is, to secure a competitive advantage in trade). Each accord establishes a separate trilateral commission to hear complaints about improper enforcement policies. If the commission fails in its efforts to secure a voluntary settlement, a dispute may be referred to an arbitration panel. If the panel finds that the accused nation has enforced its labor (or environmental) laws improperly, the complaining nation may impose compensatory tariffs—but the proceeds from this tariff must be returned to the accused nation to help finance improved enforcement of its own laws (regarding labor or environmental protection) in the future. In their first decade of operation, the side accords do not seem to have had any measurable effect on American regulatory policy toward either labor standards or environmental protection.

Chapter 6: American Aims in a Diverse World

1. In this, as in so much else, the Declaration follows Locke. Locke acknowledges that "if the unlawful acts done by the magistrate be maintained (by the power he has got), and the remedy which is due by law, be by the same power obstructed," those so injured "have a right to defend themselves and to recover by force what by unlawful force is taken from them." Even in such cases, however, "the right to do so" is not likely to be exercised "if it reach no further than some private men's cases" because it is "impossible for one, or a few oppressed men to disturb the government, where the body of the people do not think themselves concerned in it. . . ." (Locke, *Second Treatise*, par. 208). Popular revolution will ensue only when "a long train of abuses, prevarications and

artifices, all tending the same way, make the design [to impose a general tyranny] visible to the people and they cannot but feel what they lie under and see whither they are going" (par. 225). The issue is neither justice to each individual nor rebellion against actual, established tyranny, but a political judgment regarding dangerous tendencies.

2. Gordon Wood, *Creation of the American Republic* (Chapel Hill, N.C.: University of North Carolina Press, 1998), 271–72.

3. *Federalist* 23, p. 121.

4. The precise holding is in *Larkin v. Grendel's Den*, 459 U.S. 116 (1982), which struck down a Massachusetts law that purported to give schools and churches the right to veto liquor license applications for any establishment operating within 500 feet of a school or church. The Supreme Court allowed the arrangement for schools but not for churches, on the ground that the mechanism would, in effect, delegate regulatory authority to churches.

5. G. Lundestad, *"Empire" by Integration* (New York: Oxford University Press, 1998), 149, concludes that while the United States encouraged European participation in new international structures after the Second World War, American policy consistently held that the United States "would not give up any real sovereignty to anyone under any circumstances."

6. Article V, after setting out procedures for amending the Constitution, stipulates that "no State, without its Consent, shall be deprived of its equal Suffrage in the Senate."

7. See Jack Rakove, "Europe's Floundering Fathers," *Foreign Policy* (September/ October 2003): 28, emphasizing this difference between the EU constitutional treaty and the U.S. Constitution—that the latter was ratified by specially elected bodies, which allowed it to be conceived as an act of the people, while the EU treaty would simply be another treaty among the member states.

8. James Madison, for example, reflecting on "the abuses" of the republican regime in France in the 1790s, warned against "politicians" who "caricature the scene as to cast an odium on all Republican government" but also criticized those who "infer from the vices and usurpations charged on the French government, the propriety of a blind and unqualified reliance on the infallibility of our own [government]." He argued instead for studying "the true causes of the abuses in France" in order "to maintain the character of Republican government in general and the principles of [our] own in particular." He advocated, in other words, support for properly conducted republican government in the United States— whatever might happen in Europe. "Political Reflections," originally published in *Aurora General Advertiser*, February 23, 1799, collected in Madison, *Writings*, 599–607, quoted passage on 607.

9. In 1937, Winston Churchill received a special briefing from the Dutch prime minister, who explained Dutch preparations to "confront an invader with

impassable water obstacles." In his postwar memoir, Churchill recalls this episode with the dismissive remark, "[A]ll this was nonsense." Winston Churchill, *Their Finest Hour*, vol. 2 of *The Second World War* (Boston: Houghton Mifflin, 1949), 34. The Dutch, in fact, relied on their neutrality to prevent a German attack and made no effort to coordinate defense efforts with potential allies until after their own defenses had been overrun.

10. Shortly after the al Qaeda bombing that killed over two hundred people in Madrid in March 2004, for example, Romano Prodi, chairman of the European Commission, insisted that the terror attack had "shown us how the American approach has not been sufficient to deal with the situation. . . . Europe's response must be more wide-ranging than the American reaction." He then emphasized that improvements in security would only come "when we have resolved the conflict between the Israelis and Palestinians." Whether the "conflict between the Israelis and Palestinians" could be resolved to the satisfaction of terrorists—at least while a Jewish state or even a Jewish presence remained in the Middle East—was not something Prodi made any effort to clarify. There seemed no limit to the concessions European statesmen were prepared to demand from others to enhance their own security. George Parker, "US Anti-Terror Strategy of Force 'Is Not Sufficient'" (reporting on interview with Prodi), *Financial Times* (London), March 16, 2004.

11. Winston Churchill, *The Hinge of Fate*, vol. 4 of *The Second World War* (Boston: Houghton-Mifflin, 1950), 219 (reflecting on Roosevelt's suggestion that India should immediately be granted independence, even in the midst of the war).

12. When France regained title to the Louisiana territory, President Jefferson instructed the U.S. minister to France on the implications: "The impetuosity of [France's] temper, the energy and restlessness of her character, placed in a point of eternal friction with us, and our character, which though quiet and loving peace and the pursuit of wealth, is high-minded, despising wealth in competition with insult or injury, enterprising and energetic as any nation on earth, these circumstances render it impossible that France and the U.S. can continue long friends when they meet in so irritable a position. . . . The day that France takes possession of New Orleans fixes the sentence. . . . From that moment we must marry ourselves to the British fleet and nation. We must turn all our attention to maritime force, for which our resources place us on very high grounds: and having formed and cemented together a power which may render reinforcement of her settlements here impossible to France, make the first cannon which shall be fired in Europe the signal for tearing up any settlement she may have made and for holding the two continents of America in sequestration for the common purposes of the united British and American nations." Letter to Robert R. Livingston, April 18, 1802, in Jefferson, *Writings*, 1104.

13. Gruber, *Ruling the World*, 166–67.

14. See, e.g., M. J. Peterson, "International Fisheries Management" in Peter M. Haas, Robert O. Keohane and Marc Levy, *Institutions for the Earth* (Cambridge, Mass.: MIT Press, 1993), 249–308, describing failure of global agreements on conservation in this area and the greater success achieved by unilateral promulgation of conservation zones by concerned nations, such as Canada and the United States.

Index

About the Author

Jeremy A. Rabkin is a professor in the Department of Government at Cornell University, where he teaches courses on international law and American constitutional history. He received his BA from Cornell and his PhD from Harvard University (in political science).

His scholarly work has appeared in journals of law and political theory; his topical essays have appeared in *The National Interest*, *The Weekly Standard*, *National Review*, and other magazines and opinion journals. Rabkin has testified on international law questions before both houses of Congress, and has lectured on sovereignty and international law in Canberra, Beijing, London, Brussels, Jerusalem, and at many forums in the United States.

Nelson W. Polsby
Heller Professor of Political Science
Institute of Government Studies
University of California, Berkeley

George L. Priest
John M. Olin Professor of Law and
Economics
Yale Law School

Jeremy Rabkin
Professor of Government
Cornell University

Murray L. Weidenbaum
Mallinckrodt Distinguished
University Professor
Washington University

Richard J. Zeckhauser
Frank Plumpton Ramsey Professor
of Political Economy
Kennedy School of Government
Harvard University

Research Staff

Gautam Adhikari
Visiting Fellow

Joseph Antos
Wilson H. Taylor Scholar in Health
Care and Retirement Policy

Leon Aron
Resident Scholar

Claude E. Barfield
Resident Scholar; Director, Science
and Technology Policy Studies

Roger Bate
Visiting Fellow

Walter Berns
Resident Scholar

Douglas J. Besharov
Joseph J. and Violet Jacobs
Scholar in Social Welfare Studies

Karlyn H. Bowman
Resident Fellow

John E. Calfee
Resident Scholar

Charles W. Calomiris
Arthur F. Burns Scholar in
Economics

Liz Cheney
Visiting Fellow

Lynne V. Cheney
Senior Fellow

Thomas Donnelly
Resident Fellow

Nicholas Eberstadt
Henry Wendt Scholar in Political
Economy

Eric M. Engen
Resident Scholar

Mark Falcoff
Resident Scholar

J. Michael Finger
Resident Scholar

Gerald R. Ford
Distinguished Fellow

David Frum
Resident Fellow

Reuel Marc Gerecht
Resident Fellow

Newt Gingrich
Senior Fellow

James K. Glassman
Resident Fellow

Robert A. Goldwin
Resident Scholar

Michael S. Greve
John G. Searle Scholar

Robert W. Hahn
Resident Scholar; Director,
AEI-Brookings Joint Center
for Regulatory Studies

Kevin A. Hassett
Resident Scholar; Director,
Economic Policy Studies

Steven F. Hayward
F. K. Weyerhaeuser Fellow

Robert B. Helms
Resident Scholar; Director,
Health Policy Studies

Frederick M. Hess
Resident Scholar; Director,
Education Policy Studies

R. Glenn Hubbard
Visiting Scholar

Leon R. Kass
Hertog Fellow

Jeane J. Kirkpatrick
Senior Fellow

Marvin H. Kosters
Resident Scholar

Irving Kristol
Senior Fellow

Randall S. Kroszner
Visiting Scholar

Desmond Lachman
Resident Fellow

Michael A. Ledeen
Freedom Scholar

James R. Lilley
Senior Fellow

Lawrence B. Lindsey
Visiting Scholar

John R. Lott Jr.
Resident Scholar

John H. Makin
Resident Scholar; Director,
Fiscal Policy Studies

Allan H. Meltzer
Visiting Scholar

Joshua Muravchik
Resident Scholar

Charles Murray
W. H. Brady Scholar

Michael Novak
George Frederick Jewett Scholar
in Religion, Philosophy, and Public
Policy; Director, Social and Political
Studies

Norman J. Ornstein
Resident Scholar

Richard Perle
Resident Fellow

Sarath Rajapatirana
Visiting Scholar

Michael Rubin
Resident Scholar

Sally Satel
Resident Scholar

William Schneider
Resident Fellow

Daniel Shaviro
Visiting Scholar

Joel Schwartz
Visiting Scholar

J. Gregory Sidak
Resident Scholar

Radek Sikorski
Resident Fellow; Executive
Director, New Atlantic Initiative

Christina Hoff Sommers
Resident Scholar

Fred Thompson
Visiting Fellow

Peter J. Wallison
Resident Fellow

Scott Wallsten
Resident Scholar

Ben J. Wattenberg
Senior Fellow

John Yoo
Visiting Fellow

Karl Zinsmeister
J. B. Fuqua Fellow; Editor,
The American Enterprise